JANI CONFIDENTIAL

JANI CONFIDENTIAL

A MEMOIR

JANI ALLAN

First published by Jacana Media (Pty) Ltd in 2015

10 Orange Street
Sunnyside
Auckland Park 2092
South Africa
+2711 628 3200
www.jacana.co.za

ISBN 978-1-4314-2021-6

Edited by Alison Lowry

Cover design by Thomas Houghton-Dixon

Every effort has been made to locate the copyright holder of the front cover photograph. Any omission will be acknowledged in future impressions.

Back cover image © Ave Maria Blithe

The extract from *Noseweek* on page 232 is reproduced with kind permission.

All content derived from the *Sunday Times* is used with kind permission of the *Sunday Times*.

Set in Sabon 11/16pt

Printed and bound by Creda Communications

Job no. 002409

Also available as an e-book
d-PDF ISBN 978-1-4314-2207-4
ePUB ISBN 978-1-4314-2208-1
mobi file ISBN 978-1-4314-2209-8

See a complete list of Jacana titles at www.jacana.co.za

For my American daughters,
Molly, Breeze and China

Thanks to Gareth for persuading me to start writing again, Bruce for convincing me I had a story that had to be told, Bridget for making that phone call from the Frankfurt Book Fair and Alison for being an extraordinarily splendid editor.

1

MY MOTHER, MYSELF

MY MOON IS IN CAPRICORN. Astrologers will tell you that this signifies a plate-glass cold maternal figure, distant and given to withholding praise and affection.

So it was with Janet Sophia.

She scooped me up when I was a runt with cabbage ears. I could fit in a shoe box. She named me Isobel Janet. She didn't tell me I was adopted until I was eighteen. She was short-fused and I had annoyed her about something or other. 'I didn't want you. I really wanted a little boy!'

I ran out of the house and sat in the stable for hours.

But I am my mother. More importantly, I am her creation. Then – and still now – the long, thin beam of her spirit flashes over me and I am found wanting.

'After all the money I spent on making you a consort fit for a prince, you are a waitress in New Jersey. New JERSEY?'

John Murray Allan was born in Peterhead, Scotland. He came to South Africa for the climate. He met Janet Sophia – or Molly, as she was called – at a funeral.

Before she met Jack Allan, my mother was married to a drunk who beat her. Once he broke all the fingers in her right hand. She would sit at a bus-stop through the night rather than go home or turn to a neighbour. Hers was a troubled life.

But when she met Jack Allan happiness struck her like a Highveld shower.

He was the chief sub-editor at *The Star* newspaper. A slight man with a small moustache who loved to have piano sing-alongs while enjoying a wee dram or two.

He died when I was eighteen months old. I have no recollection of him, save that he gave me a book of dog breeds. I scribbled over the Airedale terrier. He must have been an evolved soul to have chosen me.

My mother went to work at De Beers and left me in the capable hands of my Zulu nanny, Dennis. I have pictures of Dennis pushing me on a swing. He is a gentle, pock-marked giant.

In addition to adopting me, my mother fostered three other children. One of them, a teenage boy of about sixteen, took me into the garage when she was at work and did inappropriate sexual things to me.

I screamed, but there was no one to hear me.

When he let me go, I burrowed into my mother's cupboard, sobbing into her expensive coats. I hid there until she came home. I never told her what happened. I feared that it was my fault.

Memory is a lasso, with which we capture the wild ponies of the past and attempt to tame their chaos. Sometimes we have to let a pony go because it is threatening our sanity. That was one such pony. I blanked it out of my mind until I started thinking about my childhood to write this.

My mother disapproved of the foster children's mother. She would come to visit bearing OK Bazaars bags of sweets on which they would gorge themselves until they all suffered bilious attacks.

When the foster children departed I was the cynosure of my mother's attention. I remember once putting my tiny hand through the mangle of the old washing machine. She let me sit on her lap and listen to Alfred Cortot playing Chopin's preludes in an attempt to drown out my screams.

There was always music in the house. Opera and piano recitals. I remember the sound of the needle poised on the records making the noise of hushed applause before the music started.

When I was four my mother asked me if I would like to learn to play the piano. I replied that I would teach myself. She immediately set about finding me a teacher.

My first piano teacher was a glamorous young girl called Letitia van Onselen. Mrs van Onselen was a blowsy redhead, who told me, 'Her name is really "Laetitia". Lae. It is the Latin word for "wisdom".'

The Van Onselens lived in a red-brick house in Linden with manicured hydrangea bushes on the stoep. There was never any sign of père Van Onselen. I would wait in the ante-room on the tapestry couch until Letitia opened the doors and released the preceding victim.

Then commenced the instruction. Intricate torture – of learning scales, arpeggios and one hour of Hanon finger exercises every day. Playing the piano and practising the piano are two different things.

Straight after school, three days a week, my mother would drive me to Linden and wait in the car reading her antique silver hallmark book or her *McCall's* magazines. She was vaultingly ambitious for me.

Her ambitions were realised. For some reason, still unbeknown to me, it turned out that I was a child prodigy. Every piano competition I entered I won. After each win I was given a Noddy book.

When I was ten I played with the Johannesburg Symphony Orchestra. I still have the tiny blue dress I wore. For that achievement I was given two Noddy books and a large flat box of chocolates bound with blue silk ribbon with a photograph of ballerinas on the top.

Letitia taught me piano. Her friend Jenny Barlow taught me ballet. Then there were elocution lessons, art lessons, and Scottish dancing lessons. My mother deserved multiple medals for her dedication to my cultivation.

I remember my first experience of public rejection as though it were yesterday.

I am at Franklin D Roosevelt Primary School. It is a freezing Highveld winter's morning. My mother makes me wear a pair of blue corduroy pants instead of the regulation brown skirt.

A knot of little girls giggle and point.

'What's wrong with you? Bluey! Bluey!' they chant.

Hot tears course down my cheeks.

More discrimination is to come. Since my mother home-schooled me from the age of three, I am far in advance of my classmates. I am sitting next to a girl called Yolanda (who presses too hard with her

HB pencil) when Mrs Bosman calls me to the front.

'You're going to go straight to Standard One,' she tells me kindly. Then she hugs me. As she squashes me to her massive bosom a little nervous dove flutters in my stomach. I am gutted at the good news.

Later, I am moved to Blairgowrie Primary School. My mother designs the school uniforms: Murray of Atholl tartan kilt and a cut-away jacket. I have a picture of myself, a clipping from *The Star*. I am aged seven, proudly modelling the uniform. My mother is also proud. She had researched the precise tartan that was appropriate to Blairgowrie in Scotland. She also got her way by insisting that the jacket be cut-away, not the regular blazer.

My hair is in a ponytail. I am wearing hand-made crocheted socks. I hate the socks because they slide down under my little heels. I wish I had cheap nylon socks like the other kids.

More than anything I wish I were more like the other kids. I wish my mother didn't have antique furniture. I wish we had ordinary furniture – the kind my mother refers to as 'shop furniture'.

Decades later I encounter the same kind of snobbery. Alan Clark, one of Mrs Thatcher's cabinet ministers, says contemptuously of the Conservative MP Michael Heseltine: 'The trouble with Michael is that he had to buy his own furniture.'

My mother, the virgin matriarch, is an unapologetic snob.

✲

I wanted a pony. My bedroom was plastered with pictures of horses. There was a caveat. If I got a pony, I would have to take care of it.

Prince was thirteen hands high and slightly coffin-headed. I thought he was beautiful. When I put my ear next to his and I heard the glug-glug of him swallowing water I thought I would die of happiness.

I would muck out the stables before practising the piano, which was before going to school. On rainy days I would take his bridle apart, clean every piece of tack and reassemble it.

Some nights before a gymkhana, my friend Sandra and I would sit up all night playing Monopoly. Then at five in the morning we would groom the ponies and set off. Puppence, a mutt with a permanent smile on her face, would sit on the pommel of the saddle when she grew tired of running beside us.

My mother would be at the gymkhana grounds with peanut-butter sandwiches and thermos flasks of orangeade.

When my mother refused to buy me a fly-sheet, I cut up a candlewick bedspread and sewed a blanket on my doll's sewing machine. It was probably the first and last time I was motivated to sew.

I wrote prayers of thanks for those days on little pieces of paper and each night kneeled in thanks. I pleaded for God to make me a good little girl.

One day when we are driving to town we come across a man with a donkey and its foal. He is taking them to the abattoir. My mother pays him for both. We tie the jenny's legs together and manoeuvre her onto the back seat of the BMW. The tiny brown foal sits on my lap.

Daisy Mae and Bambino are the first of many donkeys my mother will rescue. Actually, she was always rescuing things.

I was another rescue.

*

When I was five my mother remarried.

She had met an English widower, Walter Eric Monteith Fry, at a funeral. (Funerals were evidently fruitful grounds for meeting people in those days.)

I cried bitterly.

'I thought that when I grew up you would marry *me*,' I protested.

I believe my mother married not for love but rather because she wanted to be able to stay home and take care of me.

My beloved nanny Dennis and I both cried. He didn't factor into the merger at all.

I have a picture of myself as the flower girl at my mother's wedding. She is a severe and elegant woman, towering over me. My face is upturned like a flower at the foot of a cross.

We moved to Ferndale to a thatched-roof home called Littlestones.

Daddy Fry had grown children, Margaret and Geoff. They hated their new stepmother and in return she disliked them. Geoff would turn up with a gang of motorbikers on Sunday afternoons, not so much to visit, but to torment.

I was considered a spoilt brat. After Daddy Fry turned the garden hosepipe on me one day I never trusted him. Until the day he died we lived in the same house but had an empty, minor-key relationship, scarcely talking. Mostly we avoided each other the way a stream flows around a discarded wheelbarrow.

My mother, as it turned out, with her relentless disciplining and her refusal – or inability – to adore me the way I wanted to be adored, was teaching me the lessons I would need in order to be able to survive.

When I fell off my pony, she made me get up and ride. 'Cease this detestable boo-hooing!' she said.

Once when we were riding to hounds, my pony Blue Boy – Prince had been joined by Blue Boy, Quantas and a lovely bay mare called Can Can – pulled like a train.

'Keep that pony under control! Will you keep that pony under control?'

Blue Boy promptly stopped dead in front of a jump and the field galloped over me.

Exasperated, my mother eventually asked Ernest Hayward, a local horseman of note, to take me – and Blue Boy – under his wing. For a while Blue Boy was stabled with Ernest. Now Ernest took over the bullying. 'Ride that pony! He's on the wrong leg. He's on the wrong *leg*!'

When we went to a show in Kelvin, Ernest offered to walk the jumps with me.

I tripped over the boundary rope. I was mortified.

'First fall of the day!' said Ernest heartlessly.

Some days my mother would ride with me. She was magnificent on a horse and quite fearless. Once, Can Can shied violently at something in the bush. My mother was unseated and her foot caught in the stirrup-iron. She was dragged for a hundred yards before Can Can stopped.

'Unfortunate,' was all she said as she swung herself up into the saddle.

Letitia felt that I needed expert tuition and I was passed on to her piano teacher, Grace Brockwell. Grace was a tiny hamster-like spinster who taught in rooms in Eloff Street.

Straight from school I would catch the 74 bus on Barry Hertzog Avenue to Loveday Street. From there it was a short walk to Fattis and Monis, where I sat at the counter and ate lunch: a hotdog and a cup of coffee. There was change from twenty cents.

I always prayed before I went into the building in Eloff Street. There was an ancient, juddering lift with heavy concertina cage doors.

I waited in the Stygian gloom of a cramped entrance hall until it was time for my lesson.

Miss Brockwell's room was next door to Professor Epstein's. Professor Epstein was a celebrated concert pianist who only taught the *crème de la crème*. Occasionally I caught a glimpse of him – an emaciated Beethoven-looking character.

While Grace Brockwell was gently guiding me through Mendelssohn, Professor Epstein was not as tolerant with his own students. I could hear him shout through the thin wall.

'No! No! No! ON the beat. Then *pianissimo*,' he hissed.

Mid-town Johannesburg was quite safe for a little girl of eleven. The greatest threat, according to my mother, was from the low-lifers who would hang out in the Loveday Street Milk Bar. According to my mother, tattooed bus drivers were low-life.

The other peril was falling asleep on the bus on the way home. I remember one time waking up only when the driver had reached the terminus in Fontainebleau. He came upon me curled up in the back seat when he was checking the bus for lost property.

*

My mother was exacting about table manners. Once when I handed her a cup of tea, some of which was spilled in the saucer, she flung it at me. Table manners loomed large on her agenda. 'Show me a man's table manners and I'll show you who he is.'

But her devotion to my education and cultivation was *sans pareil*.

She sewed my ballet costumes. One was a can-can costume, black-and-white gingham. The lining with its tiers of ruched tulle was a miracle. No Moulin Rouge dancer could have had a costume stitched with such care. I fancy love flashed like scissor blades as my mother cut the satin cloth.

There was a moonbeam costume too, diaphanous and spangled with stars.

But horse-riding was my obsession.

At the age of ten, when I debuted with the Johannesburg Symphony Orchestra, Stephen Mulholland, who was a young reporter with *The Star* newspaper, came to interview me. My mother told him that I read Chaucer before I went to sleep. (It was true.)

When he asked me what I wanted to be when I grew up, I told him that I wanted to be a jockey. My mother was narked.

'He probably thought you meant a disc jockey,' she said superciliously.

When I contracted rheumatic fever, I was in bed for weeks. Our GP Dr Perlman would come and see me every other day and listen to my heartbeat. Say 'Aaaaah.'

'Aaaaah,' I would echo dutifully, although I never could really see the point.

One Friday night I heard on BBC radio that 'four mop-topped boys from Liverpool who call themselves the Beatles are set to take America by storm'.

Daddy Fry and my mother had rows. Usually, they were about money. Once she threw a heavy pot of her Estée Lauder face cream at his head. Then she yanked me out of bed and told me we were leaving. The routine was fairly predictable. We would walk up Hendrik Verwoerd Drive and Daddy Fry would follow us in the car and beseech her to calm down.

Her nerves were the blue rim flickering dangerously on a gas ring.

At the same time that she opened her antiques shop she took me house hunting.

One of the first places we went to view was Liliesleaf Farm in Rivonia. I recall a ramshackle property set well back from the road and a dead rat floating in a brown swimming pool. Someone had made a fire in the sitting room. On the wall was spray-painted 'Fuck the Whites. Viva ANC'.

My mother put her hands over my eyes.

'Not this one,' she told the realtor firmly.

I graduated from Miss Brockwell to Professor Epstein. I still feel his clammy, ancient tree-toad fingers guiding mine as they fly over the keyboard. I still smell the musty music books, the dusty venetian blinds and I see the faded, embroidered silk shawl on the Bechstein grand piano.

*

High school presents a fresh hell. I wear a blazer to conceal my lack of breasts. My legs are like twigs stripped of their bark.

The boys call them Wednesday legs. 'When's dey gonna break?'

My classical music training is also an embarrassment. When it is announced at morning assembly that I have been selected to play at the Young Artists' Concerto Festival I am embarrassed.

I start having pre-recital nerves. I resent the three hours I have to spend at the piano each day.

I start furtively listening to LM radio on my little transistor radio under my pillow.

My interest in fashion amuses my mother. She admits that she finds the Beatles' 'Ob-la-di-Ob-la-da' quite catchy. She sews a splendid Sergeant Pepper military coat for me. It has buttons like doorknobs and a red lining.

On Friday nights, parents take turns ferrying a bunch of us to the Lemon Squeezer where we listen to The Staccatos playing 'Cry for Me'. I wear a silver tent dress and false eyelashes like the spines of tiny animals. My thermometer-thin legs are encased in white lace tights and on my feet are dolly-rockers.

A butterfly of sorts is emerging into a safe, white-bread world.

2

LIVING IN A WHITE-BREAD WORLD

MY MOTHER'S AMBITIONS FOR ME were the blood that coursed through her veins.

I was to be a concert pianist.

'Like Gina Bachauer,' she said. Gina Bachauer was an Athenian pianist with a vast bosom. She happened to be born in the same year as my mother.

At age eleven I jointly win the Trinity Cup of South Africa. I tie with Greta Bagel, a 21-year-old pianist. My mother's ambition haemorrhages. I should have won the Cup outright, she says. Afterwards I go to my room and sob noisily, hoping that she will come and reassure me.

What is the sound of one hand clapping? is a traditional Zen koan – a question posed by a Zen master to a student. It is said that all koans must be answered from within; each koan has many answers. Perhaps my relationship with my mother is a koan.

She doesn't come to comfort me.

*

Jacob Epstein was becoming too frail to teach and so I was accepted as a pupil by Professor Adolph Hallis. Piano lessons took place in his home in Gleneagles Road in Greenside, a short, tree-lined walk from the high school.

Middle-class white South African Greenside in the '70s was low face-brick walls, manicured driveways, rosebushes and probably a Penguin pool in the back yard.

Professor Hallis was an exacting teacher. (His other star pupil was Marian Friedman.)

'Even if there is no piano, you can practise!' he said. 'Practise on the table! You know what they say?'

I didn't know what they said.

'If you don't practise for one day, you will know it. If you don't practise for two days, I will know it. If you don't practise for three days, your public will know it.'

Theory lessons were at Dr Klaus van Oosteen's in the part of Blairgowrie where the Schachat Cullum houses formed a houndstooth pattern on the newly sub-divided land.

I struggled to score Dvořák's New World symphony while Dr van Oosteen puffed away at a cigar the size of a bazooka.

From time to time ash would drop onto my musical notes. Dr van Oosteen swept it onto the floor without missing a beat.

*

I cut my waist-length chestnut plait when I was in Standard Seven.

Perhaps it was a subconscious attempt to sever the umbilical cord.

My mother took me to a hairdresser in Randburg where you had to lean forward into the sink. A chap called Hendrik cut my hair. He wore a pink jacket. There were whispers that he was queer. Hendrik was the first gay man I met.

I had been poring over *Petticoat* magazine. Of course I wanted to look like Twiggy.

'You look as though your hair has been painted on your head,' said Daddy Fry when I got home.

I was crushed.

*

Mine was not a political world, but memories flap like torn curtains.

Dr Hendrik Verwoerd was assassinated in Parliament.

'The same week *Time* magazine called him Africa's ablest leader,' my mother tut-tutted as we listened to the radio broadcast which told us that thousands went to his funeral.

We lived in the middle- to upper-middle class, white suburb of Bryanston. You knew it was almost suppertime when black servants dressed in white livery with maroon sashes were sitting on the grassy pavements outside the houses they worked in, chatting and laughing together.

After my beloved nanny Dennis departed for Natal, we had a series of 'house boys'. They lived in the servants' quarters and slept on beds that were raised up on paint-tins to avoid the ground-hugging *tokoloshe*.

My mother summoned them by ringing a bell outside the kitchen door. They had their own tin cups and ate doorstops of bread with apricot jam for lunch. At supper time, they made stew from 'boys' meat' and ate it with stiff *putu* and *morogo*.

Edworks, Phineas, Day Off, July … a rolodex of unsuitable employees. Either they were Malawian ('wonderful workers but illegal'), or they smoked dagga, or scoured a silver teapot with a Brillo Pad, which exasperated my mother.

The one I remember most was Ananias. He was a charming Venda man with a gap between his front teeth through which you could herd sheep. When he became inebriated – most weekends – he would get into fights. He would come into the kitchen on Monday morning holding his head in his hands.

'Hau! Nonnie! I take the puza and I am suffar-ring.'

My mother would give him aspirin and tell him to lie down and come back when he felt better.

Once Ananias went missing for two days. When he finally staggered home, his face looked like a gobbet of meat. One of his eyes had been gouged out. Blood leaked over the grey leather seat of the Cortina station wagon as my mother drove him to Baragwanath hospital.

Our life could have been Downton Abbey South-African style. We didn't have the wealth or the pedigree, but there was certainly an upstairs and a below stairs and they were mutually dependent. No one was in any doubt where the lines stopped.

*

Finally my mother could take my mewling about wanting to be a model no more.

She enrolled me with the Stella Robertson and Stella Grove Modelling Agency.

The agency was opposite Anstey's Department Store in Jeppe Street in downtown Joburg.

Every Monday night the class of aspirants would gather to be lectured by both the Stellas.

'Always, always, wear a girdle, girls. Even when I was at my thinnest – I think my hips measured 32 – I still wore a girdle,' said one of the Stellas. 'Now here's the diet I want you to follow. You can never be thin enough or rich enough.'

The first Stella handed out roneoed copies of the Mayo Clinic Diet.

We took turns in strutting down the catwalk.

'You're not the prettiest girl, but you're the best walker,' said the other Stella.

*

Quinney's Antiques opened in Randburg in my final year at school. The name came from a play about an English couple called Quinney who had an antiques shop by the same name.

To find stock for the shop my mother and I would go to estate sales and auctions. I learned the difference between Sheraton and Chippendale.

'Chippendale was fashionable in the third quarter of the 18th century and named after the English cabinetmaker Thomas Chippendale. It was the first style of furniture in England named after a cabinetmaker rather than a monarch. It became the most famous name in the history of English furniture at a time when such craftsmanship was at its zenith,' I would read from one of my mother's antiques books as we drove. 'Many of the Rococo designs were French in origin, but Chippendale modified some of them for the less flamboyant English market; among these are his French chairs, based on Louis XV designs.'

'Now Sheraton. Read what it says about Sheraton,' she said.

'Sheraton-influenced furniture dates from about 1790–1820. It's named for the London furniture designer and teacher Thomas Sheraton (1751–1806), who trained as a cabinetmaker. A neoclassic style, it falls within the Federal period in the U.S. The Sheraton style tends to be simpler, almost severe, and favors "a fiercely rectilinear silhouette".'

Many were the times we would load the station wagon up with antiques that were supposedly destined for the shop but would end up in our house. One such was a marvellous Sheraton walnut three-panelled mirror.

My mother had *horreur de vacui* – horror of empty spaces.

Persian carpets were layered upon each other. There were regiments of antique silver cruet sets, silver chafing dishes, silver food cover domes on chiffoniers, chaises-longues, antique sewing boxes, Georgian tables, library stairs, antique four-poster beds, water bowls and pitchers, Victorian lamps and copper bed-warmers. It was a madwoman's knitting basket.

It was my home. These are the things I grew up with. This is the patina of life that I remember.

Censorship, pass laws and job reservation. District Six. The Sharpeville massacre. The jailing of Nelson Mandela. These things mostly passed me by. They did not form part of my world view. This was not my landscape.

The whites of my eyes stretched wide when I learned of them.

3

ME AND MY AVATAR

A POET ONCE WROTE that adopted children are self-invented because they have to be.

Like many adopted children, I felt that there was a question mark at the beginning of my life. (Come to think of it, perhaps that is why I have no interest in learning Spanish. How can you trust a language that starts a sentence with an inverted question mark?)

When you don't know your ancestry it is like missing the opening scenes of a movie. Or finding that the first pages of the novel you are reading have been torn out.

Who are you? Where do you position yourself?

For me the missing pages – the abyss beyond which there be dragons – had to be filled.

To say I was as shallow as the enamel on a tin tray would be to overestimate my apparent superficiality. But perhaps not. Or of course it could be. I could just be finding an excuse for my finessed lunacy.

My taste was becoming expensive. Modelling jobs enabled me to pop in to Stuttafords in Sandton City and spend hundreds of rands on a jar of Estée Lauder Re-Nutriv cream. In those days you could have bought a small second-hand car for roughly the same amount of money. I would slice open the cellophane and ease the box open. Then I would hold the heavy gold jar aloft, like a bishop about to crown a queen.

When I stroked the dense, silky cream on my face I felt as though I were writing my signature.

I shopped at designer boutiques in Rosebank. There was a white Courrèges coat, a rainbow-hued Vivienne Westwood gossamer gown suspended by straps thin as a fingernail-paring, and a pair of spectator pumps.

When one of the dogs chewed the heel of the pump (who on earth even wears spectator pumps in South Africa?), my mother laughed merrily.

'Vain. You're becoming too vain. In any case, in that white suit and the pumps you look like a lady bowler.'

Being adopted is a powerful sculptor of human identity. My sense of non-belonging reverberated through the taut violin-string of my being.

I was especially unable to relate to men. I would wait until a man liked me and then I would withdraw. For me sex was something you withheld. Even if things were good, I would make sure something went wrong.

I was making sure that the other person knew what it felt like to be the one who didn't belong. It was impossible for me to believe that anyone could love me for myself.

In my books, to love was to lose.

There was Marc Roussos, a Greek stockbroker. Marc's father was a large fromage at Rothmans. Marc would take me to Norman's in downtown Johannesburg every Sunday night for prawns. We would go to the Three Ships at the Carlton Hotel and eat Lobster Thermidor. The maître d' would make crêpes Suzette tableside. I took these things as perfectly natural.

Now that I am in the September of my life, I would consider it a lesser miracle if a man were to offer to buy me a cappuccino.

But then and now are two different creatures.

Marc bought me a diamond ring from Michaelis in Athens. It was a Titanic affair, encrusted with diamonds – the ring, I mean. When the diamond ring didn't reassure me, one Easter Marc resorted to buying me dozens of chocolate bunnies of varying sizes.

What lies beyond what I say? Perhaps it's just too painful. Or meaningless. I am not sure which at this stage.

The world is unfair, unjust and unknowable.

And so, to an extent, was I. Probably to myself and certainly to others.

*

I have a sketch the cartoonist Teddy Winder did of Jack Allan, the Scot who adopted me. It pictures Jack as the chief sub-editor of *The Star* looking at a newspaper headline which reads 'MAN KILLS A THOUSAND WOMEN, ROBS BANK' and the caption: 'We will use this. If we have space.'

It was a comment on the stringent way in which Jack Allan evaluated the newsworthiness of stories.

The late Henry Edward (Teddy) Winder had worked for the SAAN group for 60 years. His ability to do humorous sketches was remarkable. For some 35 years he illustrated the weekly column 'The Passing Show' written by Joel Mervis, the former editor of the *Sunday Times*.

When I was invited to supper by Teddy's son, Frank, at their home in Parkview, I am sure I was disinterested and curt. I showed more interest in a rather attractive black cat that was curled up on the sofa than I did in either père Winder, Mrs Winder – or Frank.

I had agreed to accompany Frank to a dance the following week. He turned up for our date in a kilt – quite apropos, given his military and Scottish background – and I refused to go out with him. My mother observed a look on my face that was looking for somewhere to go.

'He looks like a young fogey,' I finally shrugged.

The truth was something else. Frank was an intelligent, attractive young man. Better I reject him before he rejects me.

Desperately insecure, I was always expecting people to cheat and lie. Possibly I put the energy out in the ether and they responded.

While I was dating Doug Gordon, he was writing a weekly column about the adventures of Grondo John in the Thursday *Daily Mail*. I was made mention of, but not to the extent that his editor Kate Lee Marshall was. Kate was Gypsy Lee Kate. I was as jealous of her as Mona Lisa's sister.

In 1975 an Israeli consulate security guard named David Protter took over the building in Fox Street, Johannesburg, and held its occupants hostage while police and army units massed outside. Protter killed the consulate's chief security officer and then sprayed the street with bullets, wounding 34 people. He gave himself up after a siege lasting 21 hours. Doug and his photographer friend Renier Botha were reporting on the siege. I fretted. The news was taking Doug away from my side.

He gave me a necklace with the word 'Superbyrd' inscribed in silver. It did nothing to reassure me.

I was that most annoying of girls, the one who wants you to say that she is the first person you have ever loved. No, make that the *only* person you have ever loved. I was a tiresome, bottomless pit of neediness.

And yet once the tantalising and challenging options were boiled down to that one big, boring, bulimic word 'relationship', I had to move on lest I be found wanting in some way.

*

Our identities are always in flux. My avatar, the painted modelly-type, was part of me, but it wasn't the totality of me.

Often she wasn't who I was at all. But I clung to the clothes and the make-up, hoping that they would tell the world that I wasn't just a waif who had been given away like a puppy. Of course avatars or alter egos can be more like oneself than one realises. I bonded with my model avatar because I saw her as an extension of myself.

This is me, I said to myself. *I am wearing expensive clothes and driving a sports car. I am desirable. Aren't I?*

The void I felt in my life was expressed when I would drive aimlessly along the highways late at night. Criss-crossing was soothing. The internal void found external expression.

I would listen to the Slave Chorus from Verdi's *Nabucco*.

Or if I was in a really soppy mood, Gordon Lightfoot singing, 'If I could read your mind, love ...' I did want a hero, but not the part where the heartaches come.

4

LOOKING FOR MOTHER

MY MOTHER GAVE ME EVERYTHING I wanted. But she hadn't given me the gift of life. My response to this was shameful and unoriginal. Whenever there was a row or a disagreement my default response was 'You're not my real mother.'

The soul chooses the womb into which it must be born in order to learn the lessons of life.

How apt then that I was the illegitimate, unwanted baby of a wild, pretty girl who gave me away.

My existential angst was surely established in my mother's womb.

At the time when I was born, an unwanted pregnancy was a scandal. My young mother must have drowned in waves of shame. Treason, as someone once said, is a matter of dates. Who would dare to say Brad and Angelina's children are 'illegitimate'?

'She was a pretty girl and well dressed,' said my adoptive mother. 'That's all I know about her. She wanted you back, but by then the adoption papers had gone through.'

A yippity-yap terrier of curiosity was aroused in me. I contacted some or other child welfare association, which advised me kindly that 'the records are closed'.

They helpfully suggested that perhaps I needed to talk things through with someone.

So I became an outpatient of Dr David Norris at Tara.

Dr Norris was a short, stout chain smoker. I would sit in the waiting room with the other outpatients, pretentiously reading Bergson, Camus or Herman Hesse, while they would strum air guitars and have lively conversations with themselves.

All patients are said to fall in love with their psychiatrists and I did fall a little in love with Dr Norris.

'You're not looking for your mother as much as looking for your roots, your heritage,' he told me.

He was right. But I couldn't look at my hands without wondering if my father had the same bony fingers. I wondered if I had siblings and whether they were tall. I couldn't even fill in the form in the doctor's offices that asked 'Do you or any of your family suffer from mental illness?'

'It's very dangerous to go on an expedition to excavate your birth mother,' said Dr Norris. 'She may have her own life and not want you to be part of it. She may disillusion you.'

He matter-of-factly metaphorically piled up the perils like poker chips.

My mother, meantime, had other hashes to settle.

The neighbours in Bryanston were complaining about the honking of the donkeys. Beyond the tennis court and the swimming pool were the stables. The donkeys (by now there were five) would see her coming with their feed buckets and start a chorus of brays that would set the neighbours' dogs off.

When I told her that I had been to see Dr Norris she looked at me in disbelief.

'Get over yourself!' The syllables fell like needles. 'We have a *real* problem. I am going to have to move the donkeys to Tumbleweed.'

Tumbleweed was the name my mother had given to a huge plot of land she'd bought because of her love for aloes, rocks and thorn-trees.

It was halfway to Pretoria.

Edworks Ndlovu was entrusted with overseeing the land, a task to which he was spectacularly unsuited since he was perennially stoned. Every weekend I had to drive with my mother to check on the donkeys. Invariably, Edworks would have left the gate open and the donkeys would be found wandering on the tar road. Or he would have forgotten to water and feed them. Once he proudly showed us a litter of puppies he'd strangled. He thought that he would save us from having to look after them.

As far as I was concerned the only redeeming factor about Tumbleweed was that, according to Professor Revil Mason, the South African-born archaeologist, it was the site of a 15th-century Sotho kraal.

People are oftentimes biological reflections of their environment. My mother was never more content than when she was sitting on the hilltop at Tumbleweed overlooking the Pilanesberg. I would look at her and see her as part of the iconography of the landscape.

5

WITS UNIVERSITY

THERE WERE TWO PUPILS at Greenside High School who wrote the Trinity College music final exam – Ronnie Gehr and me. Ronnie was a small, talented violinist with hair like badly bound broccoli.

Both of us were ridiculed for our classical music studies.

My best friend at high school was Helen Handle. She was tubby and afflicted with pimples that covered her face like risotto. The boys called us Wednesday and Handle with Care.

Sometimes I was called Neuter Allan. Neuter because in Latin class we learned that nouns can be masculine, feminine or neuter. I was as asexual as it was possible to be.

My mother instilled in me from an early age that sex was the inevitable result of a man getting the better of you. It was also something only loose women did.

'If you have to sit on a man's lap, put a telephone directory on his legs before you sit,' she said.

When Hilary Graham, an up-and-coming young painter, who looked like a Botticelli-faced Hell's Angel, came to teach art, some girls openly flirted with him. I secretly envied them.

I would catch myself staring at him as he read aloud the 5th-century epic poem *Beowulf* as we drew.

I was enchanted with *Beowulf*. The main character is a hero who travels great distances to prove his strength at impossible odds against supernatural demons and beasts. It's an elaborate history of characters and their lineages as well as their interactions with each other, debts owed and repaid, and deeds of great valour. The warriors follow a manifesto of rules on heroism called *comitatus*, which is the basis for all their words, deeds and actions.

The poem may have been brought to England by people of Geatish origins. Some believe *Beowulf* was first composed in the 7th century in East Anglia, since the Sutton Hoo ship burial indicates connections with Scandinavia.

I didn't care about its origin. It spoke to me. When Mr Graham read 'Beowulf bears no weapon because this would be an unfair advantage' (over Grendel the troll), I fell in love. Not with Mr Graham, but with the bravery and chivalry of the young warrior.

On Mondays I had to go straight from school to modelling classes. I changed from my school uniform into civilian clothing and put make-up on my face in the cloakroom.

Once, all Mary Quanted-up, I bumped into Mr Graham as he was coming out of the staffroom. He didn't recognise me. My make-up then (as it is now) was a carapace, a shield behind which I could hide.

Without make-up I felt as vulnerable as a baby bird surprised in its nest.

Radical and subversive events and trends hallmarked the decade. In Africa the 1960s was a period of political change. Thirty-two countries gained independence from their European colonial rulers. The '60s was a seismic time, but the complex inter-related cultural and political trends across the globe scarcely impacted on white, middle-class lives in South Africa.

Some say that the era was akin to a Jungian cycle: the individual breaks free of the social constraints of the culture by deviating from the norm.

Perhaps my coming of age was a microcosm of global zeitgeist.

I was finding liberation in different ways. For one, I rebelled against the three-hour-a-day piano practice.

It was decided that I would go to Wits University to study for a Bachelor of Music. My mother was dubious about the place.

'Isn't that a hotbed of radicalism?' she said. 'Well, I suppose it's slightly better than the University of Cape Town. That's Moscow on the Hill.'

At the last minute I changed my mind about doing Music. I enrolled for a degree in Fine Arts instead.

I yearned to be a hippie and wear tie-dyed clothing and hand-tooled leather sandals.

I still helped my mother in Quinneys. I would study my History of Art notes while perched on a chair behind the counter. One-eyed Ananias was now a shop assistant.

But I was slipping away from my mother like a knotless thread.

Her response to this reality was to collect more strays. Dogs, cats, birds and donkeys.

When she joined the Cycad Society of South Africa, I would drive her on expeditions to legally dig up a specimen of the protected plant which, though it is a minor, threatened and endangered component of the plant kingdom today, was extremely common during the Jurassic Age.

There would be three or four dogs in the front of the Ranchero. The schipperke was the most annoying. He would race up and down behind the headrests emitting piercing beeps. My mother would ignore him as she sliced oranges on the dashboard.

I hated myself for hating these expeditions. I disliked the granola countryside. I wasn't interested in whether a cycad was male or female or how prehistoric it was. I hated the woodcut harsh African light.

Once we drove all the way to Barberton. The Lowveld town was founded during the frisson of the gold rush in 1880 when treasure hunters scuffed their boots on its hills in search of glints of gold.

'These Makhonjwa mountains around Barberton are amongst the oldest in the world. They date back three and a half billion years,' said my mother.

'Who cares?' I muttered under my breath.

'What? What did you say?'

'Nothing.'

I navigated to the site where it was legal to dig, but we hadn't factored in a local rugby match, the fans of which filled the hotel.

When night's clapper-board came down, my mother had a suggestion. 'Let's go to the local police station,' she said. 'We'll explain that we need somewhere to stay.'

We spent the night in a dank, moth-filled police cell. I grumbled without ceasing as I tried to settle down in the upper bunk under my black maxi coat, but my mother held up the cycad she'd dug up like a child holding an adopted puppy.

'What a beautiful Cycadophyta. I'm not sure whether this is from the Cycadaceae or the Stangeriaceae family. Of course it could even be from the Zamiaceae … I'll look it up when we get home.'

I ignored her.

'This is fun!' she chided me. 'Where's your sense of adventure?'

The guilt I felt at not sharing her joy brands me still. It's a tattoo that won't fade.

*

I graduated from the catwalk and was told that I would be a 'lovely' model. My enthusiasm was at a rolling boil. Becoming a model would be my redemption for being the girl all the boys laughed at.

The first advertisement I answered was the usual 'unique opportunities in the glamorous world of fashion' one. I agonised about what I would wear. Then I painted my face, toiled into town on the 74 bus and found the address: a sleazy joint above a curry restaurant in Pritchard Street.

I wondered if I had wandered onto the wrong set. Where was the white ducoed office with purple velvet drapes? Where was the chandelier, the montage of famous models on chaise-longues, or at least on the walls?

The air had the smell of curry on its breath.

A small trapdoor of doubt swung open in my stomach.

'Howzit! You must be … er … from whatsits Stella …'

The man with the camera who appeared from a back office looked as though he should carry a government health warning.

He gave me a let's-lick-the-sauce-off-this-spoon look and shoved some forms at me.

'Fill these in,' he said.

Then he told me to lie on the floor.

'To re*lax* you. *Jeez!*' His tone insinuated that only a novice would imagine that this was not a perfectly normal request.

He then proceeded to attempt to hypnotise me: 'You're feeling sleeeepy. When you hear me click this shutter you will feel beautiful and turned on ...'

I giggled nervously, feeling foolish lying on the floor listening to this lunatic chant.

Then the photographer abruptly changed tack.

'Let's start off with some underwear shots,' he leered.

'But that's not the sort of thing you see in *Vogue*,' I protested.

'Have you seen how undressed *Vogue* is becoming these days?'

Inexperienced as I was in the ways of the world, even *I* was starting to suspect that the situation was as fishy as a trout in milk.

I grabbed my brand-new model bag and fled.

The next Sunday I read a long and sordid story in a newspaper about some fake photographer who enticed young would-be models up to his 'studio' to seduce them. One of his methods was to hypnotise them.

The episode shook me. A tiny presage of future shocks.

But people kept insisting that I would be 'a lovely model', so I went back to the agency and let them find jobs for me.

The glamorous jobs, though, were rare as unicorn droppings. Instead there I was, the 'lovely model', opening fridge doors, simpering at lawnmowers and trying to look alluring in portable showers.

I did land a job for pack shots of Arwa stockings, despite or because of my Wednesday legs. I was contracted to fly all over the country for Arwa. Hans Tiervelde, the then owner of Arwa stockings, his publicist and me and another model would set off at 4 am in the private jet.

It was money for jam.

After a few trips I packed it in, though, because I couldn't get up that early.

*

Wits University in the '70s shines like a diamond in the dust-bunnies of my memory.

There were drawing, painting and design classes. Social Anthropology, English and History of Art. I loved going into the violin-case dark auditorium and watching the slide shows presented by Professor Elizabeth Rankin. They were visual capsules of civilisation. With her little flashlight she would point at what we should be paying attention to.

'*Contrapposto*. This is a term in the visual arts to describe a human figure standing with most of its weight on one foot so that its shoulders and arms twist off-axis from the hips and legs.'

'For the first time in Western art the human body is used to express a psychological disposition.'

'The Kritios Boy you see here suggested a calm and relaxed state of mind, an evenness of temperament that is part of the ideal of man represented in Classical Greek sculpture.'

'Now let's look at Michelangelo's David ...'

I didn't study History of Art. I consumed it. I loved the quiet, monumental frescoes of Giotto in the Arena Chapel in Padua. I marvelled at the egg, painted in exquisite perfection and suspended above the Virgin Mary, in Piero della Francesca's Montefeltro Altarpiece. I was fascinated by Piero's interest in the theoretical study of perspective and the contemplative approach to his paintings.

I loved the quiet blond tones of the Northern Tuscan artists.

Decades later my head is still filled with dates. Giotto di Bondone, 1266–1337. Italian painter and architect from Florence who broke from the stylised representation of the human being in medieval times.

The Salon des Refusés, French for 'exhibition of rejects'. Generally this was an exhibition of works rejected by the jury of the official Paris Salon, but the term is most famously used to refer to the Salon des Refusés of 1863.

The Luncheon on the Grass, the greatest work of Edouard Manet. Decades later details of this particular painting will be useful. But not in circumstances I could even imagine back then.

*

Gedinka Bak was the prettiest girl on campus. She was crowned Rag Queen. Construction workers would whistle at us. Well, they would whistle at her.

Gedinka and I would go to Pop's Café in Braamfontein, which was next door to Campus Bookshop. We would sit and drink milkshakes and watch rainbows dancing off the Oppenheimer springbok fountain across the road. Wilson, the short-order chef, would scold us if we ate sandwiches brought from home.

'This place you buy the food. You don't bring your own food.'

Sometimes we would go to Mangles in Braamfontein, a tiny health food restaurant, so-called because of an old-fashioned mangle in its window.

For R2.50 we could get bowls of Greek yoghurt heavy with honey and studded with nuts.

Opposite Campus Bookshop on the other side of the road was a Shell service station. On top of the building next to it was a revolving restaurant. Or so it was said. I never went there and I never saw it turn.

During my first year at university I was overwhelmed by the self-assurance of the other students. Most of them had wealthy parents. Well, I assumed they must be monied because, for example, Richard Mendelssohn's mother, or so we were given to believe, promised to give him an Alfa Romeo 1750 if he cut his hair. In lectures I usually sat next to Linda Moross and Susan Rhodes-Harrison. Both were the daughters of well-known Westcliff architects. The names of my fellow students should give you the Polaroid: Lazarus, Tabor, Katz, Cohen.

The girl I was closest to was Carol White, a Françoise Hardy look-alike. We always wore black with death-pallor pale lipstick. Heads turned when we went to the cafeteria together to share a plate of chips.

In those days painting equipment was relatively inexpensive. Fat tubes of Titanium White, Cobalt and Prussian Blue, Cadmium Lake, singing yellows, siennas, ochres, fistfuls of sable hair brushes, watercolour paper as heavy as a shroud, moth-nose-soft 4B pencils.

I would go through a bottle of turpentine a day, splashing it onto my canvas and wiping it away so a luminous ghost of a shape would be left. Mostly we painted on hardboard which we whitewashed and sanded ourselves. The first mark on a canvas was akin to the first footprint in virgin snow.

The Fine Arts students were assigned cubicles in a hangar. Heather Martienssen was professor of the faculty.

My design teacher was Cecily Sash. I was terrified of her. She had been lecturing in art at Wits since 1955. Although she had studied in London, she came from Delmas, a small town in the Transvaal.

She was constantly re-inventing her painting style, but to me she personified the stage in which her work bristled with fundamental elements: dry, arid, spiky-thorned and attenuated. She thought I had a good sense of design but said my execution was deplorable.

I used to paint late at night on a makeshift table in my bedroom with a single, naked light bulb above. Painting music was T. Rex, the Beatles and Pink Floyd.

Judith Mason was another memorable teacher. I loved the haunted, sinister yet whimsical nature of her paintings and drawings. Moths with human-like features, crucifixes and strange crouching creatures, part landscape, part beast.

Once she admired a painting of a pomegranate I had done and offered to swap it for one of hers. I was too shy to accept such generosity.

Then there was Robert Hodgkins who, as young child in London, used to hide in the Tate Gallery on the Embankment. Robert used to tell us that painting was 'a bit like surfing' in that a good deal of time is spent bobbing about, waiting for the right wave to come along. For Hodgkins art was an 'auto-intoxication that allows one to live through marriages, divorces, deaths and unhappy love affairs, and come up smiling all the time'. He had a child-like playful energy, but his critiques were always thoughtful.

I adored the careless way he dressed. I was to see the same *déshabillé* dressing in Richard Ingrams, editor of *Private Eye*, many years later.

Robert liked my painting and we became chums, of a kind. He would explain that there are paintings that stem from memory and from a sombre look at the human condition.

'Paintings can be one-night stands or lifetime love-affairs – you never know until you get cracking,' he said. 'There are paintings about the construction and confusion of contemporary urban life, but there are also paintings about the pleasures of being alive, pleasures that crowd in upon the pessimism everywhere and refuse to be ignored.'

A painting of my life at Wits would be such a painting.

Pleasures crowded in my life every day. There were parties at communes in Parktown, Melville or Houghton. 'Tassies', the red wine that stained your lips black, would flow and the air would be filled with the smell of pot and joss sticks. Indian kurtas and Afghan sheepskin waistcoats were the preferred code of dress.

Sometimes we would go and listen to the Otis Waygood Blues band. Rob and Alan Zipper, Ivor Rubenstein and Leigh Sagar were from Bulawayo. They had come to South Africa in 1969 on a playing holiday and were soon signed by Clive Calder and Ralph Simon. Their blues-jazz fusion made them one of the top live bands in country.

At these parties in the '70s there were many discussions about politics and student activism and the crowds were very mixed. Everyone seemed to be tuned in to what was going on in the country and I began to realise just how naïve I was and what a sheltered life I had led. The name Steve Biko was one that was frequently heard. In 1972 the Black Consciousness leader had been expelled from the University of Natal because of his political activities. The following year he was banned by the apartheid regime.

'Being banned meaning that he was not allowed to speak to more than one person at a time,' a girl called Judy explained to me. 'Hectic!'

I vaguely recall a slight, blonde girl named Helen Zille, talking to a gathering in the open-air auditorium outside the canteen about the draconian measures taken against those who took a stand against apartheid. I had gone along mainly because the object of my biggest crush at the time would be there. He was a denim-clad boy with nine-inch hips. His nickname was Zapper. He rode a Harley Davidson. Helen Zille, along with newspaper editor Donald Woods, would expose the truly horrific circumstances of Biko's death half a dozen years later.

Robert and Jan Neethling were working on an exhibition called 'Pretty Boy Floyd'. They had produced some 60 experimental silkscreens of the gangster and they hung them on washing lines in the gallery. I invited them to my 21st birthday party.

The party was to be held at a farmhouse nearby in Witkoppen. Some friends tried to burn fire breaks so that we could put candles in paper bags on either side of the driveway. A fierce wind blew up and flames from the fire engulfed part of the house. The venue of the party was hastily moved to Eaton Avenue.

I was 21. I was wearing a fabulous chamois dress and about to get engaged to a civil engineering student called Roddy McGillivray. The soundtrack of my life was Carole King's *Tapestry*. The scent of jasmine blossoms was heavy in the air and the pink bougainvillea covering half of the house was in full bloom.

My life was as joyous at least as Renoir's painting of *Dance at Bougival*.

6

THE TEACHING YEARS

IN THE EARLY '70s I was living at home with my mother. I wrote film reviews for some unimportant music paper and classical music critiques for *The Citizen* newspaper, which was then owned by Louis Luyt, the fertiliser king.

I was modelling and reading. Never novels. Apart from Scott Fitzgerald and Raymond Chandler. My mother was as eccentric as ever. She had taken up Bauernmalerei. She made a wooden cross and painted it. Peonies on the front. On the back she wrote 'Live your life according to the Bible'.

My days at Wits were memory-cluttered happiness. Painting in the hangar with T. Rex blaring. The gorgeous smell of acrylic when you prepared a masonite board for your next painting. Skiving off on a Friday afternoon in 1973 and driving to Maseru in Lesotho to see Des and Dawn Lindberg's production of *Godspell* there because it was banned in South Africa. When Des and Dawn brought the show to South Africa some months later to open at the Wits University Great Hall, it was immediately banned, ostensibly on the grounds of 'blasphemy'. This banning was widely and immediately recognised as a political smoke-screen for the real issue of racial mixing, a direct challenge to the apartheid laws of the government of the day. The Lindbergs challenged the banning in the Supreme Court, and won their case. As a result *Godspell* toured South Africa for two years, and succeeded in opening doors to all races on both sides of the footlights wherever it played. It was a theatrical triumph, and a political and legal breakthrough.

I was wearing wide denims, platform espadrilles, Venetian beads from Totem Meneghelli Gallery and armfuls of silver bangles.

The languid afternoons of lying on the library lawn discussing Jean-Auguste Dominique Ingres and Paul Klee and how he took a line for a walk ... then pootling along with Tony Starkey in his little maroon Volkswagen and him so stoned that he would bump every traffic cone over whenever there were roadworks.

*

I got a first for painting and design and a local gallery owner, Trevor Coleman, offered to give me a one-woman exhibition.

Jasmine blossoms and a tiny taste of recognition were a heady combination. Michael de Morgan, a British newscaster, opened the exhibition and the art critic Richard Cheales said I was talented but too hasty and flashy. Probably he was referring to the portrait I had done of Bruce Millar, the actor who played Jesus Christ in *Godspell*. I used a lot of chocolate wrapping paper for a collage-like effect.

I was pretty, I was plump and the world was optimistic. When I was interviewed by the *Sunday Times* they said I was talented and exotic.

One day an elderly British gentleman came into the gallery and declared himself impressed with my work.

'You should be at the Redfern Gallery,' he said.

He told me he had an organisation that sponsored young artists from all over the world. He was going to write me a cheque to buy the whole collection and fly me to London. Months went by and I didn't hear from him. Then came a letter from Pentonville Prison in London. He regretted to tell me that he had got involved in a small incident of fraud.

*

I loved being a student. I loved Wits.

How could I leave?

In order to prolong my stay I enrolled for a post-graduate high school teaching diploma. I didn't really want to teach.

I took over Judith Mason's Thursday lecturing gig at Greenoaks in Rissik Street and although I enjoyed the showmanship I came to realise that prep for a one-hour lecture could be twelve hours. Greenoaks was a sort of finishing school and commercial college run by Mildred and Joe Bloom. In addition to office skills the girls who attended it were taught a little culture. That was where I came in. Once a week I would lecture them on the History of Art. Occasionally I would make a little oxbow into popular culture. I lectured on the artistic references of the *Rocky Horror Picture Show*.

The girls seemed to enjoy my lectures. Decades later I met up with some of them on Twitter. They have become captains of industry and I am a waitress.

Our beginnings, as TS Eliot said, never know our ends.

Still, a one-hour lecture once a week wasn't a proper job.

'Why don't you apply for a teaching job at Bryanston High School?' suggested my mother.

And so, one morning at 7:30 sharp, I presented myself at the headmaster's office. I dressed to convince him that I wasn't teacher material. Red platform boots, skin-tight pants and a military jacket. It was the '70s, for God's sake.

Mr Viviers looked me up and down and told me I was employed.

I was to teach English and Art.

During my teaching practicals one of my lecturers suggested that I was in the wrong profession. She thought acting might be more appropriate. I resented that. It wasn't my fault that one of the kids had taken the African mask I had brought for the lesson and was hamming it up with me.

English was just up my street. We read the syllabus and then some. I got the kids reading *One Flew Over the Cuckoo's Nest* and *All the President's Men*.

Art was more of a challenge. In addition to teaching, I had to control 30 kids with 30 water pots and 30 drawing boards.

Of course I made mistakes. I was less than a decade older than the older pupils. One kid actually drove to school. Steven Ellis. It was rumoured that he had been in Matric for several years.

I started off as all young teachers do. I was idealistic in the extreme. I had a suggestion box in my classroom. The kids would write suggestions like 'Your car needs mag wheels and GT stripes'.

I loved the lesson preparing and in fact I still have a book of lesson plans. The kids made me laugh but they also infuriated me. Once in class I asked each pupil to tell me their names.

One small boy replied, 'Lachlan McLahan.' I thought he was being a smart alec. I may or may not have made him stay for detention and sand desks with one-inch squares of sandpaper …

In art class I had the desks arranged in a horse-shoe shape. I did my own little cabaret of sorts. If any former pupils of mine are reading this and may have been wounded by my sarkiness, I apologise.

I may have been creatively up to the task, but in terms of organisational skills, I was lacking. I would lose sets of exercise books. I would write outrageous comments on work such as 'If so and so would sit down and give her sex-appeal a rest she would do well.'

In mitigation, I repeat: I was a handful of years older than the kids.

One memorable night I took the school combi and ferried some kids to the Johannesburg Art Gallery in Joubert Park. Even then it was the largest gallery in South Africa. It was housed in a beautiful 1911 building designed by Edward Lutyens, who later went on to design many buildings in New Delhi. I allowed the kids to dress in civilian clothes and we went to Hillbrow afterwards for shawarmas. Then we drove home to Bryanston singing at the tops of our voices to songs from *Saturday Night Fever*.

*

On Friday nights, everyone went either to the Balalaika Hotel in Sandown or the Sleepy Hollow, but mostly it was the Balalaika.

Founded shortly after World War II, in 1949, originally as a tea garden with a couple of rondavels in the countryside about 15 kilometres to the north of Johannesburg, it used to be an 'outspan stop' on the old wagon road between Johannesburg and Pretoria. Travellers would park their wagons and let their oxen graze.

There are two versions of why the hotel was named the Balalaika: the first is that it was named after the Eastern European musical instrument, and the second is that it was named after a 1939 movie called *Balalaika*, a love story set in a small café in Paris. The theme song was romantic.

> At the Balalaika
> Where there is magic in the sparkling wine
> And mellow music in the candles' shine
> I have a rendezvous!
> At the Balalaika
> Who knows what ecstasy tonight may bring ...

There was never any ecstasy. Just a lot of Blue Nun liebfraumilch.

7

I Become a Columnist, and My Gordon Story

Each degree of the Zodiac is represented by a symbol.

The Sabian symbol for the Sun today as I write this is Pisces 3: A PETRIFIED FOREST, AND ETERNAL RECORD OF A LIFE LIVED LONG AGO. This symbol shows the ability, or the need, to be respectful of the gifts that come out of the past. The 'petrified forest' shows remnants of past civilisations; of what went before. You may need to retrieve, sort through, or go over records from the past. History always has something amazing to teach us.

It seems that this degree speaks to story-telling.

When we tell a story we exercise a kind of control over our lives. There will be spaces in our stories and on some level we hope that the spaces and silences will be intuited by someone else.

Someone once said we are the stories we tell. We all construct personal narratives and we spend our lives working and reworking them. Our memories may be unreliable. We fabricate, embellish and embroider. We cross-stitch and unpick.

We weave a tapestry self and it is through this tapestry self that we construct a unified whole out of the many strands, skeins, ribbons and cloths that contribute to our sense of self.

DNA can be sequenced. Brains can be scanned. Batteries of personality tests can be run.

But you won't find the essence of someone in any of them. It's the stories they tell that will provide that interpretatve layer.

If you really want to know who I am, let me tell you a story. The windows of my memory are not casually framing pictures of a roseate hue. I just happened, for a while, to be at the top of a layer cake with icing decorated with stars.

The story I am going to tell you contributed immeasurably to my sense of self. It is my Gordon story.

*

Gordon Schachat will tell you the story. My shrink will tell you the story.

Gordon said he saw me walking down the steps at the Great Hall at Wits University and decided then and there to marry me.

That day my avatar was wearing a chocolate suede midi-skirt buttoned up the front and a pair of matching chocolate suede thigh boots. I was 21.

Gordon took to hanging around the canteen when he knew I would be around. He was handsome and tanned. He looked like a short Kris Kristofferson. He had a way of talking quietly so that I would have to lean in towards him.

He would drive up to the hangar where we painted in a series of flashy cars. My fellow students drove ancient puddle-jumpers or, in Gregory Kerr's case, Vespas.

When I asked him why he was so tanned Gordon told me he was a builder.

The fine arts students explained. He's Gordon Schachat.

'Schachat Cullum the *builders*,' they explained when I looked blank. 'Haven't you heard of Norscot?'

I had. It was about three blocks away from Eaton Avenue.

The sale of Ernst Eriksen's Norscot estate in Witkoppen was a splendid social event in 1982. It was described as the largest house sale in the southern hemisphere. Some 3 000 items were offered for sale. Those seen bidding included Marino Chiavelli, Gary Player and Barbara Barnard.

The catalogue was impressive: Anton van Wouw bronzes, the

maquette for John Tweed's statue of Cecil Rhodes, a rare Peter Wenning still life. Early 19th century views of Table Bay. Two Frans Oerders.

My mother was rather keen on a beautiful antique (1812) carved cradle which had been filled with flowers as a floral arrangement at the 1953 Rand Club Coronation Ball.

The original Norscot farm, which had stretched as far as today's Fourways Crossing, was split up and most of it was purchased from the Erikson family by Schachat Cullum.

I was embarrassed by Gordon's attention at first. I was so much taller than him for a start. But his eyes read me like an autocue. He was smart and confident.

Gordon knew the longitude and latitude of my insecurities and vanities. Weeks would go by and I wouldn't hear from him. Then he would send me cuttings of modelling photographs of me, just for a lark, to let me know he hadn't forgotten me.

Once he turned up at the hangar with his Rolls Royce full of flowers. On another occasion, at a whim, we drove to Durban in his Mercedes 450SL with the top down.

When we checked into the Oyster Box we didn't make love. Instead we watched *Butley*, one of my favourite movies, which is based on a play by Simon Gray.

The play is about the trials of a pair of gay intellectuals at a London university, and it makes frequent references to TS Eliot. Some of the lines were to become 'our' language, Gordon's and mine:

'Lust is no excuse for thoughtlessness.'

'You didn't ask me this before.'

'I didn't ask you now, either.'

'I know, but I got tired of waiting.'

We would watch and re-watch the scene where Butley (played by Alan Bates) is questioning Joey about his new boyfriend.

'What does he do, Reg's dad?'

'He owns a shop.'

'What kind of a shop? Just a shop? Just a shop like Harrod's, for example? What does he sell?'

Joey [after a pause]: 'Meat, I think …'

'In that case he either owns a meat museum or, if it was for sale, he is what's called a *butcher!*'

We would fall about laughing. Perhaps it was really good pot.

Poor Roddy, my current boyfriend and almost fiancé, was eclipsed by Gordon's flash.

I was as careless as a man looking for honey who overlooks the precipice.

Gordon would fetch me in the convertible – he always wore a newsboy cap and would have one in the glove box for me – and we would go and look at Schachat Cullum show houses. The Schachat brothers, Louis and Hymie, were from Robertson in the Cape. From becoming building contractors, they segued into buying vast tracts of land and then, by dint of clever marketing, were in the very profitable business of selling lifestyles, rather than mere houses.

Buying a Schachat Cullum house meant that you were probably professional, probably white, and this was your first time as a home-buyer. Gordon and I drove around in the convertible with the Police or Talking Heads blaring from the speakers. He took me to the Zoo Lake Restaurant and taught me to eat strawberries with fresh black pepper.

He was on good terms with the Greek café owners in Illovo. He seemed to be able to speak Portuguese to the greengrocers and Zulu to the petrol pump attendants. He had gone to school at Kearsney College.

When he allowed me to drive his car home one night I began to think he liked me. Or perhaps he was just very stoned. At Hyde Park Corner, just as I started driving along William Nicol highway, it started raining. By the time I got home to Bryanston I was soaked. I was also unable to figure out how to put the soft top back up.

I left my mother's house to move in with Gordon. I wanted to belong and what better club to belong to than a Jewish one. Even back then I had Jew envy.

We stayed at the Rosebank Hotel until we were able to move into the home Gordon had bought for us at 33 Kallenbach Drive, Linksfield. The Rosebank was a herky-jerky kind of place but we found it amusing.

I had been with Gordon for a few weeks when I started writing my classical music reviews for *The Citizen*. I would go to the City Hall for a concert, leave as the applause ended and rush to *The Citizen*'s offices in Doornfontein around midnight to type up my review on an old-fashioned typewriter. It was an exercise in solitude, but not, in those days, in danger.

After a few months of writing music critiques and emboldened by Gordon, I had the temerity to ask the then editor of *The Citizen*, Johnny Johnson, if he would let me write a column for the paper.

'Only special people can write columns,' he said. 'You're not … special enough. You're a … Barbie doll.'

A week later, again shored up by Gordon's belief in me, I went to the *Sunday Times* to apply for a job. Madeleine van Biljon, the doyenne of columnists, was resigning and her column was up for grabs. I wore a black-and-white dotted shirt-dress for the interview and Estée Lauder Berry Basket lipstick. I was fearless. Gordon was my soft place to fall.

Tertius Myburgh, the editor, cast a glance over my music critiques, which I had carefully pasted in a hard-covered book.

'So you have no previous journalistic experience?' he said.

'No, but no one's perfect,' I replied.

'Well, anyone who can write about "muscular bowing" must know something,' he shrugged.

Within a week Leslie Sellers had designed the logo for my debut column. It had three byline pictures and it was called 'Just Jani'.

'We have to drop the T from Janet otherwise it won't fit,' explained Leslie. So Jani I became.

My first column appeared in March 1980. It was a profile of Bill Haley who was about to perform in Johannesburg. Adele Lucas Promotions had organised an escort of Hell's Angels for him from the airport.

'I thought you were dead,' I said to Bill Haley.

'I thought I was dead too,' he responded.

*

I keep thinking about what happened and what I would have done differently. Pretty much everything, I suppose.

Graham Greene's observation that fame is a powerful aphrodisiac is only partly true. Fame can make some men powerfully attractive to women, but it works exactly the opposite way for women: on the whole fame is the most unattractive quality a woman can possess.

As my column and yes, my 'fame' – limited as it was in South Africa – grew, so did my anxieties. By then I was writing my regular column (three or four pieces) as well as a radio column and an art review. I had to come up with someone interesting to interview every week. I was also doing a nightly pop news spot on the David Gresham Show on Springbok Radio.

It is said that there are two phenomena common to successful people which are perhaps complementary: a sense of isolation (particularly in childhood) and a supra-ordinate belief system which affords them a definite place in the scheme of things. I certainly had the sense of isolation. And I was driven. Gordon had to live through my weekly angst about the column. It was like re-inventing the wheel every week. My validity as a partner hinged – or so I thought – on my success as a columnist.

I couldn't have got it more wrong.

The column was the all-consuming Moloch. When it had been put to bed, there was nothing left of me.

An adopted only child is not good at sharing. I couldn't share a bed with Gordon, preferring to go to the spare room. I was excruciatingly shy about my body (my mother's daughter) and was unable to blend the three kinds of love Eros, Agape and Amor in our relationship.

I disliked sex. I remember reading that in India the god of love is a large, vigorous youth with a bow and a quiver of arrows. The names of the arrows are 'Death-bringing Agony' and 'Open up'.

I didn't have the courage for that kind of physiological and psychological surrender.

8

'Just Jani' – The Early Days

Writing a book starts out as an adventure, then it becomes a mistress and, finally, a tyrant. The same might be said for writing a column. The shock and reality of having to come up with an interview subject and a couple of other sparkling pieces each week make me want to go to bed and stay there like Stalin did when he heard that the German army had invaded his country after all, despite his instructions that it should not.

Instead, Gordon would drop me off at the SAAN building in downtown Johannesburg, I would go through a casual security check and then walk up the stairs and into the newsroom on the first floor.

Even though it was 8:30 in the morning and the air reeked of stale cigarette smoke and last Sunday's gossip, there was always a sense of excitement in the newsroom. Each journalist was assigned a space on communal desks. The news reporters had a bigger laager than the Lifestyle department. We had the apron in front of the corner office. Sue Fox did fashion, Marc Dobson did features, Gwen Gill was the consumer journalist, and Leslie Sellers did a food column.

The VDTs (video display terminals) were lined up in the passageways. They were grubby in the extreme. Sometimes you would extricate a piece of something from between the 'P' and the 'O' keys. There were ziggurats of newspapers everywhere. Research was done by poring over old yellowing copies of the *Sunday Times* that were affixed to a desk. Failing that you went upstairs to the library. You would ask, for example, for a file on some famous person you'd be planning to interview and be rewarded with a cardboard folder which contained all the stories that had been written on that.

To answer the telephone and say expectantly 'Jani Allan Sunday Times' at first gave me a small frisson of excitement. (Later, when adversity was to cover me like mould, the same words would be said in cadences of defeat and admission.)

Before long all the PRs in town – and further afield – were putting me on their lists to attend garden parties, movie premieres, to go down gold mines or up in hot air balloons. It was all rather extraordinary. *I* was the one who was being sought out. It was *my* presence required at the latest play, cabaret or private game reserve. In reality I knew it was never me. It was Jani Allan, the person who could give them publicity in a Sunday newspaper column. But it was better to be the one they sought after, the soughtee, than the soughter.

My column's tag line was 'Sparkling as Ever'.

*

One of the features of the 'Just Jani' column was called 'Quirks'. It was the local equivalent of *Private Eye*'s 'Colemanballs'. The idea was simple: people listening to the radio or watching TV who caught a verbal slip by the presenter would write them on a postcard and send them in to me. The published 'Quirks' were rewarded with R5. I would get hundreds of these slips a week, some of which made me laugh out loud:

As you've heard, World War III starts with the help of Rock Hudson. Dorianne Berry, SATV.

We hope you're feeling better and that your painful legs will soon disappear. Esme Euvrard, 'Hospitaal Tyd'.

This word can be found in the Oxtail ... er ... Oxford English Dictionary. Radio 702 announcer.

And here's Navratilova ultimately winning the game so far. Trevor Quirk, SATV.

*

On Monday morning we would have a staff meeting. Len Ashton was the editor of the Lifestyle section. He was quite the most charming and instructive man a fledgling columnist could hope to have. He nurtured and guided me, and made many suggestions.

Within weeks of joining the *Sunday Times* I was sent to Corfu to interview Roger Moore on the set of the latest James Bond movie *For Your Eyes Only*. The movie was the twelfth spy film in the Bond series and the fifth to star Roger Moore as the fictional MI6 agent.

I thought I would burst with joy. Girl reporter on international assignment!

Corfu is the Ionian island that is emblematic of Greek history and mythology. Poseidon, God of the Sea, is said to have fallen in love with the nymph Korkyra, abducted her, and brought her to the island. In marital bliss, he named the island Korkyra.

The island's history is laden with battles and conquests. The legacy of these struggles is visible in the form of castles punctuating strategic locations across the island. Two of these castles enclose its capital, which is the only city in Greece to be surrounded in such a way. As a result, Corfu's capital was officially declared a *kastropolis* – castle city – by the Greek government.

I read all these things in a guidebook and I was raring to go. Things began to go slightly pear-shaped when I missed the connecting flight from Athens to Corfu, unaware that Corfu City is still called Kerkyra …

I waited anxiously in the deserted air terminal for the daybreak flight. An old man who was mopping the floor half-heartedly looked at me in a way that made me believe I wasn't the first foreigner to make the error.

I would never find out, however, because the only Greek that I remembered from my days with Marc Roussos was the sentence '*Parakalo thoz mou ena paketo* Marlboro' (Please give me a packet of Marlboro).

When I finally arrived in Corfu I was dismayed to discover that I had not been booked into the Corfu Chandris, where the stars were. I had been assigned to a bungalow in a bed and breakfast. The bungalow was not within walking distance of the Chandris. I was forced to ask an old man on a Vespa to give me a ride to the night-shooting set on the cricket pitch in the middle of the old town.

Night after night I would join the onlookers who gathered to watch Roger Moore doing his facial expressions. I counted at least three: bemused, faintly surprised, slightly annoyed.

During the day I called Len Ashton.

'How are things on your first assignment?'

'There's a lizard in the bloody bidet!' I complained. 'And I can't get Roger Moore to talk to me.'

'Hush. There, there,' he said. 'So you'll write a piece about the local colour.'

That night, armed with a single rose, I accosted Mr Moore. Literally.

'I'm Jani Allan of the Sunday Times and I would like an interview with you,' I babbled.

'Hop in the car. Now. When are you going to give the schwartzes a vote?'

With the interview in the bag, I was able to relax slightly. I spent time with Luisa Moore, who told me: 'Roger, 'e no remember when we meet. 'E remember when we mate.'

I also interviewed Topol, Julian Glover and Carole Bouquet, who was Roger's leading lady. None of them knew that I was being driven to the Corfu Chandris every day on the back of a scooter.

If it sounds like I was a spoiled brat, you would be right. I was.

✳

Prestige is especially dangerous to the ambitious. I was ambitious in the extreme.

If you want to make ambitious people waste their time on errands, the way to do it is to bait the hook with prestige. That's the recipe for getting people to give talks, write forewords, serve on committees, be department heads, and so on. And so I came to judge beauty competitions, compère dog fashion shows and give talks.

Someone once said it might be a good rule simply to avoid any prestigious task. If the job didn't suck, they wouldn't have had to make it prestigious.

9

HOOKING THE RICH FISH – AND THE HELDERBERG GOES DOWN

PART OF THE FUN of being a columnist on the *Sunday Times* was getting invited to impossibly glamorous events that ordinary mortals only get to read about in the glossy mags.

A few years after I started writing 'Just Jani', the column morphed into 'Jani Allan's Week'. I would attend six or seven functions in a week and write about who was there and what they were wearing and saying.

Occasionally a week would be taken up by one event. One such event was the annual Marlin Fishing World Cup in Mauritius.

Where the boys were, that scorching December of 1986, was at La Pirogue. Twenty-five teams from 14 countries had a week to angle for the biggest fish in the sea.

SUNDAY NIGHT
The gathering of the clans is happening at the Centre de Pêche. The synonym for marlin is macho. We're officially here for the drawing of the boats but it's more like a display of biceps and bank balances.

There's a lot of drinking of the old hooligan soup and even more guffawing at dirty jokes. There are also plenty of gold Rolexes in evidence.

Marlin fishing is only for the big fish.

Counting all the costs involved, the estimated worldwide figure to land just one (fish) is R60 000. Money is a measure of wealth, and we invent money as we invent the Fahrenheit scale of temperature or the avoirdupois measure of weight ... By contrast with money, true wealth is the sum of energy, technical intelligence, and raw materials.

But I didn't think about those philosophical things then.

I was jotting everything down in my spiral-bound notebook:

There's an Austrian diamond dealer, an Australian golf shoe manufacturer, a Japanese property developer ... well, I assume he is a property developer because he keeps making triangular shapes with his hands. Perhaps I misunderstand him. Perhaps he is merely manufacturing a new kind of Rubik's cube. Or praying.

There's a Swiss director who makes all the Marlboro ads. 'Zese peeble are crazy. Zey are spending up to $25 million dollars for ze shooding of one commercial.'

Andrew Slome, the button-cute blond tournament organiser and GM of La Pirogue, welcomes the international visitors. Then Sir Gaëtan 'King Creole' Duval, deputy prime minister of Mauritius, pads across the sand to say his own words of welcome. He's wearing a Marlin Fishing T-shirt and is evidently on top of the world, if somewhat under the weather. A couple of his aides hold colourful umbrellas aloft to shield him from the steamy drizzle. Their faces are stern as spanners and they look slightly disapproving of the roistering revellers.

Loudest and largest of the Hemingway-esque mob is a vast walrus of a man whose name is CJ. He's something else. His Stetson could cast a shadow across a caddy and he has a belt buckle the size of a tombstone.

CJ ('You can call me Chip') is 'rootin' for all 'yew South Africans'. He's going to be spending money in South Africa and drinking in our bars. He is from New Mexico and he races mules, ranches cattle and rides rodeo. He just loves to come marlin fishing and he's jest going to get drunk and stay drunk.

Klaus Grogor (of the House of Sports Cars in Rosebank) is a member of a South African team aptly named The Marlin Marauders. He confides to me that 'Zumtimes zis waiding and waiding drifes him mad, but it's egziting when you haff a strike.'

The most sought-after boat, *Nitor*, belongs to South African Denis

Stephens. It's called the honeymoon boat for reasons I don't really wish to know. It's got a deep-freeze and radar. As luck would have it, for the first three days' fishing, Austrian Hans Cik, who drew it last year, will have it again.

With some difficulty, Barbara Ickinger, brunette beauty and PR for Sun International, manages to herd a by-now thoroughly unruly mob onto a bus.

'We have to be up at 4 am tomorrow,' she pleads.

Back at La Pirogue, even the sensual sega dancers are forgotten as the old, middle-aged and young men of the sea swap fishing stories and compare superstitions. Everyone agrees: no smoked marlin, boiled eggs or bananas on board.

How do you recognise a marlin fisherman? By the size of his Rolex and his girth.

How do you recognise a landlubber journalist? By the silver dot behind his right earlobe. The silver discs, which work by some osmotic process, are said to prevent seasickness. There is a lot of frenetic bartering. 'I'll swop six Dramamine (anti-seasickness pills) for a Scopoderm' (the silver sliver).

TUESDAY

I decide to cast my lot in with the Japanese contingent which comprises a Japanese woman, thin as the husk of an insect, and the Japanese gentleman with his triangles.

Our skipper is a blond, blue-eyed Mauritian, Bernard le Court de Billot, who doesn't smile and doesn't speak. He is a CLOSE friend of Princess Stephanie of Monaco and clearly has known better things and is dwelling on them.

At precisely 07:00, the daring men in their fishing machines put to sea. It's an impressive sight. With their outriggers resembling giant antennae, the fleet looks like a lot of sinister creatures from the imagination of Steven Spielberg.

By 07:10 the thrill is starting to pall. There is nothing as far as the eye can see but the Quink blue sea. Sometimes the Quink turns to blue black. At other times its Penguin black. Hour after hour we trawl.

The sun, plugged in like God's own arc lamp, scorches down relentlessly.

The Mikado and his wife do not speak.

At one stage he paints a stripe of Shushine down his nose and under each eye. Ancient technique of the Kabuki dancer perhaps.

I sit in the prow. I am turning into the colour of a terracotta figurine from the Middle Minoan period. I am mesmerised by the monotony. Nipponese could be having a lot of fun, but it's hard to tell. Their expressions are inscrutable.

Time passes slowly as a cloud. I lie on the deck. I bruise as I roll this way and that, according to the heave of the ocean. I suppose the damage to my skin will be irreparable.

Photographer Mike McCann clambers up beside me, ungainly as a gouty hippo.

'Bloody waste of petrol, if you ask me,' he mutters.

ZOINGGGGG!

A strike!

The Mikado leaps for his rod. He yaps commands while his wife frantically pulls and pulls and winds and winds. She lands a bonito. The bait for the big one.

We finally nose our way back to the tiny jetty at 6 pm. I feel as though I have been at sea for three weeks.

CJ's face is about as joyful as a round of meat. It tells me all I need to know. He caught nuttin'.

Others have been luckier. I watch in horrified fascination as Hans Cik's catch of the day is borne away on a metallic stretcher to the weighing scales. The marlin weighs 90 kilos.

The single topic among the landlubbing media is who threw up? I am gazed at with considerable curiosity when I admit that I wasn't nauseous at all. Well, not until I saw the poor bloody marlin hanging by its tail.

Robert Powell is at the quayside. He and his wife Babs are in Mauritius for the first time. Not that I would have recognised the star of *Jesus of Nazareth* or *Shaka Zulu*. He's wearing specs and sporting a perm. But he did kindly agree to act like Fynn and pose beside the marlin caught by Boksburg large fromage Chris Basson.

I am lolling about on the deck about to bite into a lemon cream biscuit when Peter yells, 'Strike!'

The marlin, dancing on its tail, looks noble and magnificent. The crew exhorts Harvey the Australian as though they are seconding a boxer. They pour water down his throat. They soap his seat so that he can easily slide back and forth. 'Give him hell, Harv. Give him hell.'

Have I just witnessed a man having a R60 000 thrill?

'You bet,' says Harvey. 'This is one of the most exciting moments of my life.'

By the time we return to shore, the marlin has changed colour. The gleaming creature of opalescent viridian, cerulean and Prussian blue has transmogrified into a dull, defeated charcoal.

Only the blood on the deck is the original colour.

✳

The next year I am invited again to cover the tournament in Mauritius.

The press gang arrives in Mauritius at 10:30 on Friday night. At 6:30 am on Saturday morning Tertius Myburgh is on the phone.

'Get your skinny backside to Sir Ramgoolam airport. A plane has gone down.'

Flight 295 (a Boeing 747 named *Helderberg*) was a commercial flight that suffered a catastrophic in-flight fire in the cargo area and crashed into the Indian Ocean east of Mauritius on 28 November 1987, killing everyone on board.

Sunday Times colleague Geoff Allen and I negotiate the potholed roads and squawking chicken in a cab that is festooned with joss-sticks and beaded buddhas.

There is nothing going on at the airport.

We nose around and ask questions but no one seems to know anything about a plane having gone down in the ocean. By sunset, however, the world's press has converged on the island. Thousands of journos and photographers have flown in, carrying no luggage. Barbara Ickinger has to supply toothbrushes and toothpaste to most of them. A surprise arrival at the island is Pik Botha, South Africa's minister of Foreign Affairs.

What relevance can the *Helderberg* crash have for him, we wonder.

The media circus rages for weeks. Myburgh puts in ICO reporting, following the guidelines of the Information Commissioner for protection of names and data that could attract media attention. Heaven forbid we should hang anyone out to dry. Much to the amusement of my fellow journos, we comply with his instructions.

'Lois Lane is on the flight deck! Lois Lane is on the flight deck!'

For the first time I witness how the press can take breath-taking liberties with the facts. The old maxim 'Don't let the facts stand in the way of a good story' is in play. One French journo files an interview he has had with a local fisherman. The fisherman, he claims, showed him a little dress he had found in the ocean. The dress, he avers, must have belonged to one of the passengers of the *Helderberg*. Given that a pirogue can go no further than 10 miles off shore and that the *Helderberg* plummeted into the sea some 134 miles north of Mauritius, this story, like so many that are mentioned in dispatches and filed, seems marginally far-fetched.

'Dateline. Mauritius.'

The official inquiry, headed by Judge Cecil Margo, would report that it was unable to determine the cause of the fire that caused the plane to blow up. A number of conspiracy theories would also be advanced in the following years, but at the time the press and public opinion suspected that terrorism had brought down the *Helderberg*. South African Airways was perceived as representing the South African apartheid government and the airline was government-owned.

Dr David Klatzow, a forensic scientist, put forward a theory that the fire was likely to have involved substances that would not normally be carried on a passenger aircraft and that the fire was not likely to have been a wood, cardboard, or plastic fire.

South Africa was under an arms embargo at the time and so the government therefore had to buy arms clandestinely. Klatzow's theory postulated that the South African government had authorised placing a rocket system in the cargo hold, and that vibration caused unstable ammonium perchlorate to ignite.

When we return to South Africa, as a joke Geoff pushes me into Jan Smuts terminal in a wheelchair.

10

IN WHICH I MEET EUGÈNE TERRE'BLANCHE

IN THE MODERN WORLD there is what Saul Bellow called a 'house cleaning of belief'. We have stripped the world of mystery. I have always on some cellular level known that there is more to the stories we live and make up about our lives. We choose the myths or the scripts for our lives based on what we need for our soul's growth in this incarnation.

Before I tell you this part of my story, best you cleanse the doors of your perception. House cleaning time.

Yes, I am wry and sassy, but also not so much. In my heart I am still searching. For the experience of life, not so much as the meaning. Who knew that one's carefully constructed Lego life could be so easily reduced to pieces? There is a point of wisdom beyond the conflicts of illusions and truths by which lives can be put together again.

I am at that point.

*

News conferences at the *Sunday Times* in Johannesburg took place on Tuesday mornings. The various editors and columnists traipsed down 'mahogany row', as we called it, and crowded into Tertius Myburgh's wood-panelled office. The males, boiled-egg freshly shaven and hung over, the women's hair freshly Carmen-curlered and their faces Kenitexed.

In my case it was Estée Lauder Berry Basket on lips, Lancôme mascara (always Lancôme) – tonnes of it so that my eyelashes were extra long, and very spiky – and some or other smoky eyeshadow. My hair, done by Ilana at Oggi in Norwood, owed a lot to Farrah Fawcett (whose didn't?).

On that Tuesday morning I was probably wearing one of my 'looks'. Either a black jumpsuit (it *was* the '80s) or khaki pants, a khaki shirt and a leather necklace from Italy. Earrings like hubcaps, also from Italy, would have completed the look. There was a shop in Rosebank that used to call me when they got something in that they thought I would like. Like maybe a coat with attitude. Jayzuz. How that makes me squirm, now that I buy my clothes from the consignment shop around the corner.

At the weekly news conference one by one we were required to come up with what we were planning for the week, who we thought was newsworthy – and contactable. Lesson number one of being a journo is that no one is interested that you 'might' be able to get the story. Or you 'tried' to get the story. You get the story. *C'est tout.*

The room was filled with cigarette smoke. There were thoughtful silences – a short silence followed by a long silence, except they are so close together you can't tell the difference.

I was doodling on my spiral-bound notebook. Always the same doodle. Triangulated squares. Exquisite in their symmetry and repetition. My yearning for order and containment in my life expressed in a doodle.

Then 'Why don't we send Jani to have tea with Eugène Terre'blanche?' Tertius suggested.

Jimmy Souillier, the chief of photography, laughed snidely. There were giggles. Some were nervous, others malicious.

I shrugged. Sure. The three words I lived for in those days were 'Nice story, Jani'. I needed especially to hear them from Tertius Myburgh. To that end I would parachute out of airplanes, deep-sea dive, go down a mine … do all of the things that terrified me.

Eugène Terre'Blanche. The name sounded vaguely familiar, but I didn't have time to research him. I had a trip to Italy on my mind that was coming up. I would have to wing it.

I reassured myself by remembering Len Ashton's advice: always remember to write your impression of your subject. Don't allow yourself to be coloured by other people's experiences of them.

That advice, as it turned out, would be a poisoned chalice.

I made a few phone calls from my cubbyhole office in the Diamond Building in Diagonal Street in downtown Johannesburg. It was not the most difficult interview to set up and I would take my own photographs.

The date was Monday, 25 January 1988.

It was the day I would cross a Rubicon of sorts.

The Rubicon is a shallow river in north-eastern Italy just south of Ravenna. It is about 80 km long, running from the Apennine Mountains to the Adriatic Sea through the southern Emilia-Romagna region. The idiom 'crossing the Rubicon' means to pass a point of no return. It refers to Julius Caesar's armies' crossing of the river in 49 BC. The crossing was considered an act of insurrection. It is where he uttered the famous phrase '*Alea iacta est*'. The die is cast.

In truth, when I sallied forth to interview Terre'Blanche I didn't know that there was a die and that it was cast. I was just going to do my weekly interview.

It was the last Monday in Aquarius. Ronald Reagan was president of the United States. In America people were listening to 'Need you tonight' by INXS. In the UK 'I think we're alone now' by Tiffany was in the Top 5. *The Unbearable Lightness of Being*, directed by Philip Kaufman, was one of the most viewed movies to be released that year. Robert Ludlum's *The Icarus Agenda* was the book everyone was reading.

Perhaps the universe had an Icarus agenda for me too.

*

The road to Pretoria from Johannesburg is like most roads in South Africa: boring, straight, hypnotic. The black-top cuts through the countryside like a dull knife.

The interview is at 3 pm.

I am driving a Times Media Limited pool car which spends its weekends who knows where. It is grubby-fingermarked, overflowing ashtrayed, and forensically challengingly stained on the back seats. The odd beer bottle rolls around on the floor. I am a working journalist and this is my mode of transportation to interviews.

On the seat next to me is an expensive leather doctor's bag I bought on a trip to Italy. Beside it is a navy canvas photographic bag, a cassette tape recorder and the files I pulled from the library half an hour ago.

Just south of Pretoria I see the Voortrekker Monument. The massive granite structure prominently located on a hilltop was raised to commemorate the Voortrekkers who left the Cape Colony between 1835 and 1854 and with their ox wagons trekked north to get away from the British. These days it is a national heritage site, but originally it had been erected in homage to these founders of the Boer nation. It purports to be a potent shrine, a reminder to Afrikaners that they belong to a nation of heroes.

Against the huge, bleached blue of the sky to me it looks like a pop-up toaster.

Outside the city lie the headquarters of the South African Defence Force, adjacent to a suburb called Valhalla. Twilight of the Gods.

Pretoria has been described as having one foot in the last century and the other in Wal-Mart. How fitting a place for the offices of the Afrikaner Weerstandsbeweging, the so-called Afrikaner Resistance Movement, and its leader Eugène Terre'Blanche.

Before I get out of the car, I skim the press cuttings. I learn that Terre'Blanche is a 'self-styled quasi Übersturmbandführer'. Writer Christopher Hope describes him as a dangerous man, a demagogue and a sentimental neo-fascist. He is also the most vituperative, insolent, arrogant and aggressive opposition speaker one could hope to hear. The description 'messianic' is also used in places.

The offices appear to be deserted. Somewhere in the inner sanctum is the sound of someone shouting. I follow the decibels to their source. A knot of AWB doppelgängers are staring at a television, transfixed. The air is heavy with veneration. They are watching their *hoofleier*, the so-called one man high-dread industry. One of them takes a comb out of his sock and pulls it through his hair thoughtfully without taking his eyes off the screen.

On the TV, Terre'Blanche is at full throttle.

'Didn't someone say,' he demands, 'that if men cannot agree on how to rule themselves someone else must rule them?'

His disciples roar their approval.

'That was Mr T's Blood River speech,' a safari-suited man with large pottery ears tells me. 'If you want to, you can order a copy.'

When I indicate that I am not there to buy but to look, he seems offended. I am shown into a spartan office where the main interior-decorating feature is an ox wagon wheel and three flagstaffs.

Eugène Terre'Blanche doesn't walk into a room. He occupies it. Things shrink. The roomscape insidiously rearranges itself so that he becomes the focal point.

He's more attractive than his pig-in-a-safari-suit telegenic image. He tourniquets my hand briefly and asks whether I mind if he speaks in Afrikaans. His manners are exaggeratedly proper. Like someone from the wrong side of the tracks asking if they can have a 'libation', instead of a drink.

He uses the formal 'U' a lot.

I am somewhat taken aback. Where is the crazed political threshing machine?

He'll have coffee without milk or sugar. 'As long as there are hungry children in my land I won't have sugar or milk and I don't eat pudding.' This is difficult to believe since he is built like a barn door.

He lights a cigarette with a hand that resembles a hessian bag filled with sand. Some of the sand seems to have leaked out and lodged itself under his fingernails. The soil on which his convictions took place.

This is his third interview today, his sixth since yesterday. He has spoken to the whole media spectrum from international political television teams to local women's magazines. Up at dawn, he drove from his farm in Ventersdorp to be in the office at eight.

Could it be that people have the wrong image of him?

'I know so,' he says. 'Whatever you write about me your editor will probably not even print.'

It is as if he is throwing down a gauntlet.

He's no longer surprised that the press caricatures him. 'The press realises the rapid growth of our movement so it creates monsters out of its leaders. We must be made to look totally unacceptable to the public ...'

It is far too tedious to reprise the entire interview here. Suffice it to say that most of the phrases became part of the vernacular of the day. Some journeymen – and indeed even barristers – found it useful to use the interview to prove that I instantly became infatuated with Terre'Blanche.

Perhaps the gift of phrase is the semantic equivalent of something mathematical. I know I have it. I have the ability to paint verbal pictures. How delicious to punish me for it. How delightful.

'It is a rich, earth brown voice. Sometimes it has the loamy texture of a newly ploughed mealie field. Sometimes it is a gravel rash. Sometimes the syllables fall like clods on a coffin ...'

Oscar Wilde said: 'The worst vice of the fanatic is his sincerity.'

Terre'Blanche acted sincere pretty well. Perhaps he should have settled for being the Richard Burton of Ventersdorp.

Maybe my fabulously clever phrase about being impaled on the flames of the man's blow-torch blue eyes was too subtly self-mocking for the scribblers of the days, but this semi-inspired comparison has, tiresomely and predictably, been attached to my name for the last 25 years. In the course of time, but not in that decade or even the one after, I learned to be grateful for any quotation of any kind, however distorted. Every repetition boosted my stock in trade.

I also wrote:

'He writes poetry on scraps of paper, the back of cigarette boxes. Every man must have his own land. It is from land that everything grows. Culture, poetry ... everything. "*Uit gggrond groei dinge.*" It sounds like the distant rumble of thunder. "I just want my land. Not the whole of South Africa. I want the land that my nation killed 22 000 British soldiers for, that 34 000 Boers were killed for. I can't give that land to the ANC."'

'He goes on. "Today is my birthday. All I want is a *volkstaat* ... a land for my people. Like the Basques and the Kurds and the Quebeçois.

All we want is the right to self-determination, to rule ourselves, to uphold our traditions."'

'And: "Mine is the loneliest life any man could live."

'He is growing maudlin. He touches the wing of a bronze bird that perches next to an overflowing ashtray. The eagle is the symbol of freedom; it is also the emblem of the AWB. "Flight! Superiority! Purity! Strength!" The adjectives slash into the silence of the room. I am escorted out of the inner sanctum and off the premises by a pair of his Aquilas – henchmen, or foot soldiers.'

*

How did I feel after that interview?

I was a tad triumphant. Many journalists had failed to get an interview with Terre'Blanche because his press officer was good at shielding him from those who showed antipathy towards the Leader. As I felt when the *Helderberg* fell out of the sky and I was in Mauritius, I knew that I had a good story. Terre'Blanche was an easy caricature. Everything he said would make for great copy. I had succeeded in penetrating the enemy camp.

I go straight back to the by-now deserted offices of the *Sunday Times*. Later, as I am typing away at the computer, Tertius Myburgh, or Smiling Death, as we called him because of his ability to fire people with a smile on his face, comes in and peers over my shoulder.

'Nice job, Jani,' he says.

With a sigh of relief I bite into a nectarine and put my feet up on my desk.

Another triumphette from Chez Allan.

*

How blissfully unaware I was that this interview was to be a watershed.

In any other less mentally infantile country, a journalist would be applauded for getting the interview. Whether it was with Hitler, Saddam Hussein, Castro or Pol Pot. In South Africa they took a different view.

Interviewing someone was seen as promoting that person. Whereas in London, for example, readers might express their disapproval by writing a strong letter to *The Times*, in South Africa displeasure was demonstrated in a more extreme fashion.

What normal society would care? I was soon to learn just how much.

For one thing, after my interview with Eugène Terre'Blanche my apartment was bombed.

I was also accused of having an affair with him.

11
A TRIP TO ST LUCIA

WHEN TERTIUS MYBURGH leaned over my shoulder to read what I was writing, I looked up at him anxiously.

'Do you think this is too cheeky?' I asked. '"*I am impaled on his blow-torch blue eyes*"?'

'No,' said Smiling Death. 'Vintage Allan. Pictures?'

I handed him the transparencies of the photographs I had taken in Terre'Blanche's office.

Tertius held them up to the light. 'Mmm. A marriage made in heaven. Or hell.'

I was left pondering what he meant by this remark. Pondering, too, whether the rumours about him having an affair with the woman from Accounts could be true.

Perhaps I idolised him too much.

Before becoming the editor of the largest-circulation national newspaper in Africa, Tertius was a correspondent on *Farmer's Weekly*. Prior to that he had eked out a living playing the piano in a seedy joint in London. At least that's what I heard.

*

My story on Terre'Blanche, the one that Tertius deemed 'quite superb', is heavily puffed on the front page of the *Sunday Times*.

On Tuesday the telephone rings incessantly with congratulatory phone calls. During the week letters pour in lauding me for a 'chilling insight' into the man.

Some reporters, however, seem to be a tad resentful. The interview, the first Terre'Blanche has granted to an English journalist, is something of a minor journalistic coup. The trouble with success, they say, is finding someone who will be happy for you. The mining mentality prevails in Johannesburg.

My flat-mate, Linda, who is enjoying a rapprochement with Martin Kahnowitz, informs me that 'the kibbutz' – her description of his Glenhazel circle of friends – are displeased with me 'for giving the neo-Nazi publicity'.

Meanwhile the *Sunday Times* has launched its annual search for Miss South Africa. As is traditional, I am sent to interview the out-going goddess, who will recite the standard script (*A friend sent the pic of me to the newspaper I didn't expect to win what a wonderful year it's been I have met so many incredible people and made such good friends I hope I have been a good ambassador for SA*), and I fly down to Cape Town to talk to Wilma van der Bijl. We meet on the terrace of the President Hotel in Sea Point. She is wearing a pleated white skirt which grazes her sculptured ankles, an oversized green shirt and a scarf tied à la Flo Capp. She looks like a million. A million other girls. She could have come straight from work at the local bakery.

The transformation comes when she smiles. She has dimples you could stand umbrellas in. While sipping a Diet Coke, she tells me that she reads philosophical books 'like Og Mandino's *The Greatest Salesman in the World*. Her favourite flowers are babies' broth [*sic*]. Having an optimistic outlook seems to come as naturally as singing in the bath to beauty contestant competitors'.

Back in Johannesburg in the newsroom, Sandy, the secretary, informs me that Terre'Blanche called to thank me for the story. He will call again tomorrow to speak to me personally.

Later that evening my friend Bert arrives unannounced at the flat, bearing a hundred yellow roses for me and a Venus flytrap for Linda. For some reason she fails to be amused.

'Vile Kraut!' she snaps. She refuses to join us for supper at PD's. We manage to get a table outside and have a most convivial evening until Bert starts telling me that he 'laafs' me.

I put a finger on his lips. I have known him since he first landscaped Gordon's garden.

'Familiarity breeds content, not passion,' I tell him gently.

*

I suppose, like a foreign currency, life in the mining town that is Joburg is spent with reckless abandon. Creaking ox wagon reality is drowned out by the spirit of Concorde. (Well, it was then.) In a society where there are low emotional expectations, it is logical that there is a high monetary one.

South Africa in the '80s was like Berlin before the war. People tried to blot out the reality of what was happening in the country with the same desperation.

It was Gatsby with the style of the Charleston. The carelessness with which people treated each other was the same. People who outlived their usefulness were treated with electric indifference – as I would come to find out.

I often wondered how long my social currency would last. Manicured insecurity was on the loose.

*

Terre'Blanche does indeed call to thank me for what he describes as 'the first fair interview' anyone has written about him. He asks whether I would be interested in attending a training session of the AWB Aquilas.

For years these training camps have been the source of rumour and speculation. How powerful is the AWB? Could they derail the democratisation process?

'Are the Kennedys gun shy?' I joke feebly.

'*Skuus*? Pardon?' Then, 'I hope you will permit me to gift you with horticultural evidence of my movement's gratitude for your unbiased report.'

It is difficult not to giggle at the elaborate formality of his manner.

'My movement' sounds like a bowel movement.

Later that day an arrangement of proteas arrives in the newsroom. It is signed 'We are eternally grateful to you for your fair report on our leader. From your friends in the AWB.'

Jung said because plants are the 'thoughts of God' and the animals are 'priests of God' they are still metaphorically in the Garden of Eden.

Proteas? I am rather inclined to think they were booted out along with Adam and Eve.

For the benefit of the newsroom, Tertius reads the card aloud.

'Friends. Hnh. Now you have *friends* in the AWB.'

I shrug.

'It was you who sent me to get the interview, Mr Myburgh,' I point out.

*

Adele Lucas's office calls to invite me to the latest bash. (It's always a 'bash' or a 'junket' when Adele is doing the PR.)

It was she who had landed the job of selling Bill Haley (who I thought was dead) to South Africa when he'd toured the country in 1980, and she had organised a convoy of 300 Hell's Angels on Harley Davidsons to escort the ageing rocker to his downtown hotel. In lieu of payment, Adele granted the Angels free entrance to as many concerts as they wished. The creaky Colosseum in Johannesburg consequently shook, rattled and rolled. The theatre was demolished a few years afterwards. I don't think the events were connected.

But today Adele has other things on her mind. She has chartered a Dakota to St Lucia. The reason is an elaborately kept secret.

'Be at Jan Smuts Airport at 2:30 on Friday,' she bawls. 'Bring Linda if you like. She's always good fun.'

There is a protracted delay at Jan Smuts (some misunderstanding with the charter company), which Di Valentine, Adele's sidekick, takes care of by prudently organising caravans of free drinks trolleys to pacify the press corps.

Two hours later we finally board an aircraft that is straight out of

Casablanca – there is literally an uphill trudge to the front seats.

The Dakota heaves itself into the sunset with the ease of a gouty hippo. When we land there is another delay because Di has to find porters who know how to open the hold where our luggage is stored.

Ostensibly, the junket is to mark the launch of a large property development, but once the press and celebrity group are situated in a local restaurant, Adele confesses that the whole project is still at the drawing board stage.

'In the meantime,' she booms enthusiastically, 'I've organised a film show.'

To Linda's delight, Stan Katz, the manager of Radio 702, lopes over and joins us at our table. She adores men with big noses and tells Stan as much. He pointedly ignores her come-on.

'Jeez, I knew this place was tough when I saw the menu tattooed on the waitress's arms,' he says. 'They've got bouncers throwing people *in*. Waiter! Bring us a bottle of wine. Not the old stuff. I can afford a new bottle.'

Stan doesn't converse. He recites one-liners.

The weekend is not an unqualified success. In Richards Bay it has rained soggily for two days. It is difficult to believe we are in the place the glossy brochure describes thus:

Some 60 million years ago the sea receded and what was formerly part of its bed emerge as the sandy, sun-drenched coastal terrace of KwaZulu. St Lucia, a combined estuary and lagoon system, is formed roughly in the shape of the letter H. The left limb of the H is False Bay, some 25 kilometres long, 3 kilometres wide and 2 metres deep. The cross bar is Hell's Gate: the right, Lake St Lucia is 40 kilometres long.

The reed-covered islets and banks abound with hippos, crocodiles, aquatic birds and fish – including big game fish and sharks. On the verge of the lake antelope like nyala, bushbuck, reedbuck, suni and steenbuck graze. Birdlife is prolific. Flamingoes, pelicans, goliath herons, Caspian terns and pink-throated longclaw.

Wrapped in plastic bin-liners, the grumbling 'celebrities' and press are herded about on a punishing schedule of motor launch trips and sodden riverbank barbeques. The abundant wildlife has gone AWOL.

The more recalcitrant dig themselves into the bar, growing more sozzled and belligerent as each hour passes. Linda disappears with efficient swiftness with a tubby, grey-haired gentleman.

I hang about the bar with Stan, who amuses me by calling up the DJ on duty at 702 in Johannesburg and demanding that he play requests for me.

At one stage he passes me a note.

'To whom it may concern. I have been marooned on this island now for what feels like 18 years without the company of a woman. I was wondering if I gave you sufficient coconuts whether you'd marry me – or even marry someone else and have a torrid affair. PS I know a good caterer.'

Adele sees him passing the note to me.

'Yum! A showbiz wedding!' she shrieks. 'Stan told he'd only come on this trip if either Jani or Kelly LeBrock came too.'

'What's thish about a showbiz wedding?' Linda has reappeared from who knows where. Her fishnet tights have developed holes through which a hammerhead shark could pass. Tubby looks pink-faced. 'She can't marry Stan! *I'm* going to marry Stan. Well, either Stan or Eugène Terre'Blanche.'

The evening before we are to fly back to civilisation the rain stops. Fresh crayfish sizzle on the grill and Champagne flows. The party goes on until rosy-fingered dawn pulls back the cape of night.

When the Dakota takes off for Johannesburg most of the passengers are unwell. Stan is pale green.

'Have a biscuit,' I suggest, pushing a tin of home-baked shortbread under his nose.

He lunges for a paper bag.

The next morning he dedicates a record to me on his early morning radio show.

'This is a wake-up call for Princess Cool. She's so cool she makes you sick to your stomach. Here's your song, Princess Cool.'

'You win again', by the Bee Gees.

A small item on page 11 of *The Citizen* catches my eye.

'Not far from St Lucia, three bus-loads of Inkatha supporters returning from a prayer meeting were ambushed in the Kwa-Shange Valley. Their bodies were unidentifiable as ANC supporters from the local village had smashed the corpses' faces with rocks.'

The feuding between the ANC and Inkatha is now said to be five times more bloody than the feuding in Northern Ireland. Pietermaritzburg and Ulster have identical paraphernalia of anarchy: no man's lands and no-go areas, arms caches, protection rackets, the zones of control, the godfather and the informers.

On the front page of the paper, however, is a large colour photograph.

The caption reads:

'Managing director and top jock of Radio 702, Stan Katz, enjoys a joke with Sunday Times columnist and socialite Jani Allan. The pair attended the opening of a luxurious resort in the tranquil beauty of St Lucia.'

12

VALENTINE'S DAY AND THE AWB TRAINING CAMP

MY OFFICE LOOKS LIKE A FLORIST SHOP.

'No one has the right to have so many admirers!' adjudicates news reporter Charmain Naidoo. She counts off on her fingers: 'Bloody diamonds. Bloody red sports car. Bloody Italian car.'

It's a very South African thing to define someone by what they have, what they wear, what they drive and where they live.

I try to heed the caveat of my yogiraj Mani Finger: 'Take your work seriously, but not yourself. If you take your possessions seriously, what will happen if you lose them?'

What will happen if you lose them?

I put my column to bed with my usual fervent prayer of thanks. The column is my tyrant-lover, my marriage (Gordon and my soft place to fall are long gone) and my family substitute. Bitching about it is empty ritual. It doesn't take much to get me to confess that deadlines for me are also lifelines.

When I leave the office at sunset, the Highveld heat hangs over the mining town like a bell jar. I take the roof off the Lancia Gordon gave me on Valentine's Day one year and drive home with Talking Heads blaring. The song-snatching wind blows through my hair. At times like this it is easy to believe I have hit three gold stars on the fruit machine of life. Do I deserve my good fortune? What gods are smiling on me – but, more worryingly, will they always do so?

There is no sign of Linda tonight but there is spoor.

The height of the crockery in the sink makes it impossible to wedge the kettle under the tap. I have to fill it by the spout. Every surface is cluttered with dishes on which the remains of cornflakes, egg, etc. have been spot-welded. The yawning bread-bin presents a choice between a cast-iron loaf and a green one. Upstairs I mountaineer over piles of wet towels. Clothing hangs from every ledge and door knob.

In the bathroom there is a yard-long clot of henna red hair in the plughole and bright orange rusty blades on the side of the bath.

Linda's spoor.

'Gone to the kibbutz for the weekend. Love you madly!' yodels a note on my door.

I go into Linda's room to switch off the lights of her theatrical make-up mirror. Her bed is an unmade heap of linen.

Still. Our *moments musicale*s are great fun. When I accompany Linda on the piano and she sings Cole Porter in her rather marvellous voice, which sounds like damp fur being stroked, I love having her around.

✳

The day after Valentine's Day this year in the early afternoon I receive a call from one of Terre'Blanche's henchmen. He reminds me of the leader's promise to allow me to attend one of the AWB training sessions.

Until now no press have been allowed to witness the AWB in action at the training camps. The newshounds, both local and international, have been on the track of the story for months.

It would be something of another journalistic coup. Or at least a coup-ette.

I weigh up the options: Fochville to see Terre'Blanche's Aquilas in action or seeing Stan.

Since the St Lucia trip Stan Katz has been escorting me. He has the physique of a muscular praying mantis and he looks very handsome in a dinner jacket. Usually, he arrives to fetch me in the chauffeured Radio 702 limo. Behind the smoked-glass windows there is a telephone, a television and a well-stocked drinks cabinet.

When the radio station calls him he feigns fury. 'Goddammit! I told you not to call on this line.'

At times like this I adore him. The DJ on duty will then dedicate a record 'for Stan and Jani, who are on their way to the De Beers Diamond Collection at the Market Theatre in Johannesburg ...' Or 'on their way to Meo Patacca ...' This would alert the paparazzi to be on duty when we emerged from the Caddy. Stan didn't get to be managing director and top jock at Radio 702 without knowing the value of publicity.

Stan was married to Dixie, a German woman who had hair the colour of bleached bones. He used to laugh and tell me that it was rumoured that Dixie's father had been an officer in the SS. That was his sense of humour.

Dixie's boutique in Rosebank did a brisk trade in jewelled denim.

In any other country Stan and Dixie would be the name of a cartoon strip. In South Africa, they were über-celebs.

When it became evident that even on Olympus there is marital trouble, several magazine editors were deeply annoyed. One magazine had already printed the cover of their next issue: 'Stan and Dixie Katz – South Africa's Perfect Couple'. When Stan and I started dating, within weeks the headlines changed: 'Stan and Jani – South Africa's Best Looking Couple'.

After he appeared in *Darling* magazine wearing only a small towel, Stan was voted South Africa's Sexiest Man of the Year.

Life and people are not as simple as tabloid journalism would have us believe, however.

In his early days of broadcasting the persona Stan adopted for his radio show was Happiness Stan, the Doctor of Love. In truth he was a tortured soul. Sometimes he would call me at four in the morning. 'You gotta get here. It could be too late.'

I would drive over to his condo, which was five minutes away from where I lived, where he would be waiting for me at the door. Woe clung to him like Gladwrap.

I would follow him into his bedroom.

'This isn't hair. This is a disease!' he would say, clenching his hair in his hands and peering at his reflection in the mirror. Then he would lie face-down on the bed, clamped to the pillow by two white-knuckled fists. He couldn't do the early morning show. Dixie was demanding alimony in telephone numbers. And so it went on. I would encourage him and talk him through his angst. Nestling on the pillow his head looked like a small, black Persian lamb.

Miraculously – it was always the same – the show went on.

When he put those cans on, the Doctor of Love was brilliant and sexy and funny.

*

Five fifteen. Time enough to dash to the camera shop in Sandton City to borrow a flash for the Nikon before I set off.

Fochville lies in the Vaal Triangle between Johannesburg and Carletonville. The streets are wide enough to do a U-turn in an ox wagon. There is a small hotel, a filling station and a straggle of face-brick, corrugated iron-roofed houses with porches on which ferns grow in bi-sected motorcar tyres.

I have been instructed to wait at the filling station. Before long a BMW materialises alongside my car. Its driver is a Teutonic-looking bloke wearing pebble specs. He informs me that he is the chief security officer of the AWB and that I am to follow him.

There is a distant rumble of thunder. Needles of lightning knit across the coal-black sky. I tail the BMW through the thunderstorm. At a sign that says Jagersfontein the BMW swoops off onto a sand road. We travel along washboard corrugations for some five miles until the corrugations give way to farm track.

The BMW parks. Some 50 men are silhouetted in front of a starkly lit hangar. They look like cardboard cut-outs.

I am led into the sitting room of a deserted-looking farm homestead.

Beneath a large portrait of Eugène Terre'Blanche sits the original. Tonight the one-man political veld fire is smouldering silently.

One has to fight the urge not to giggle.

The press officer of Aquila is an attorney who prefers not to be named. 'The AWB is becoming soft! Talking English to the English,' he says truculently. 'We are patriots. Plain and simple. Those who make out that the AWB are a lot of radicals and liken them to the ANC should take heed. We find the comparison eggstremely offensive. The vigilante force is born out of the *volk*'s love of the Leader and concern for his safety.'

'I conquered fear a long time ago,' puts in Terre'Blanche smugly.

Then the press officer launches into how the AWB was forced to form its own registered security unit because members of the AWB were barred from joining the police force, how only last year Terre'Blanche was stopped in a police road-block and warned that an attempt was to be made on his life. Etcetera etcetera.

When I ask him about the exact size of the AWB and its membership, he becomes vague.

Terre'Blanche indicates that I should join him on the horsehair sofa.

'Listen,' he whispers conspiratorially, 'I'm raising an army. There will be a revolution.'

He reaches into his hip pocket and takes a long pull from a half-jack of whiskey.

Outside a soft rain has started to fall.

The Stormtroopers have journeyed from as far afield as the Cape and Namibia to spend the day being coached by crack professionals in the techniques of unarmed combat and combat shooting. I am eager to see them put through their paces.

The crack professionals (one of them, UK-born Keith Conroy, claims to be ex-SAS) look Cassius-like but the platoon that lines up contains a number of physical specimens that have the muscle-tone of ill-knit haggises.

The members who volunteer their services range in age from 18 to 80. Apparently, to be awarded with the silver falcon badge of honour of the Aquila is comparable with a sixth dan black belt in Boer karate.

'The public think of us as violent, but we won't hurt anyone as long as they don't stand on our toes,' says one Aquila.

'Should an attempt be made on Terre'Blanche's life, the would-be assassin will be taken out,' adds Danny, a young man with a disarming grin.

The men wheel and turn in the bile-yellow searchlights, locking in combat-like human threshing machines.

Afterwards they sit around the fire. You could almost be forgiven for mistaking them for an ordinary bunch having a beer together.

When Danny starts singing a cappella, one by one the voices mass around his, like a bodyguard. They sing Afrikaans *volk* tunes mainly but even 'Exodus' gets an airing. When they come to the part about 'God gave this land to me' Terre'Blanche joins in. His voice thickens as though blood has been stirred into it.

Then Terre'Blanche launches into a tale of spurious origin about how Frederick the Great recruited his soldiers by combing the streets for young men with the bluest eyes. 'Just like you men have,' he says. It's almost a leer. Several Aquilas flush with delight. Before they leave, each in turn embraces the Leader warmly. Too warmly perhaps.

'Mine is the loneliest life that any man could live,' Terre'Blanche says self-pityingly. 'Come, muchachos! Let's lead the lady back to the city.'

When I get back to the flat there are twelve messages from Stan Katz.

'Princess Cool, where HAVE you been?'

How I am going to answer that and stay fashionable?

13

GOD IS IN THE DETAIL

SAXONWOLD, JOHANNESBURG is a long way from Fochville and not only geographically. Tonight I am attending a Cartier fashion show held in the garden of Stephen Mulholland's mansion.

Steve's come a long way since he interviewed me when I was ten, my mother was planning for me to be a concert pianist and he had rented our cottage in Ferndale for R30 a month.

He's now MD of Times Media Limited. TML: Toe Mulholland's Line. The story journalists love to tell is how he once hurled a typewriter out of the window of the old SAAN building.

Actually, my first typewriter was a gift from Steve. It was an old Smith. It was so old they stopped making typewriter ribbons for it.

Lorraine Mulholland, Steve's newest wife, is the PR for Cartier. After marrying Steve, she changed her name to Lolly. Lolly sounded more glamorous than Lorraine, she told me once.

The usual cast of kugels are preening. The heels of their rhinestone-encrusted Frassinellis, Maglis and Blahniks are sinking like little Venices into the lawn.

'Merely installing a few scrawny impala on a plot outside Potch doesn't count as a game farm,' says a svelte redhead, aggressively decanting an oyster into her mouth. 'I told him straight. Pity my ex ended up with the game farm in Botsies. He was about to suggest we go to the Kruger National Park.'

'Gross,' shudders Noelle Bolton. 'At least if he'd said Mala Mala …'

'I should have known by the gold Porsche,' says Oyster Decanter.

'*So* video shop owner. Don't look now! That dressmaker is making a beeline for us.'

Greta Abrahamson, who has recently been named Designer of the Year, descends on us.

'Noelle, darling! You look so much better when you're carrying a little weight. Nice ring! New? Looks like two carats. *Three*? Is it *really*? My jacket? Yes, it is nice, isn't it? It's the detail, darling. As Mies van der Rohe said, God is in the detail. As for you' – she pokes my lapel accusingly – 'I never know quite what you're supposed to be. Journalist? Celebrity? Let me make you something stunning. A mini. Slashed to here. Cut on the bias. It will cost you nothing. Well, a tiny mention in your column would be nice – '

A fanfare interrupts her soliloquy.

'Ladies and gentlemen! Just to remind you that the proceeds of tonight's function will go to African Self Help. Now – the Errol Arendz Collection!'

A pair of black models glide down the ramp on invisible castors.

'What do you think?' Adele Searll hisses urgently in my ear. 'The pink or the navy? Maybe I should have both. Just to be safe.'

Tony Factor sidles up. He has just had a face-lift. He started out selling false teeth in Petticoat Lane in London. These days he is the Discount King of South Africa. He discounts everything. Even coffins. Will face-lifts be next?

Tony blows his nose ostentatiously. 'Look!'

Adele glances at his opened palm briefly and shrieks.

'It's only an oyster!' Tony guffaws.

Johannesburg has never been a place for the fastidious or the oversensitive. It is hideous and detestable, luxury without order, sensual enjoyment without refinement, display without dignity.

Just as I arrive home at the flat the phone rings. She's taking the pink and the navy. Just to be safe.

In South Africa acquisitiveness is not so much a virus as a chronic disease of epidemic proportions. Money is what death was to Keats. A preoccupation.

Writing one interview a week is infinitely more difficult than filling whole pages, as I did for nine years (in addition to writing art reviews and radio columns).

My energy was fuelled by fear of failure. At least when I'd run out of think pieces on pencil sharpeners, anxiety attacks and the advantages of being Italian, I was able to fall back on the gung-ho option.

I did acrobatic flying, kendo, went sailing with the Springbok yachtsman John Martin in the naval racing yacht *Voortrekker* ... I even wrote off a car in a celebrity race at Kyalami in pursuit of good pictures if not memorable prose.

When my column changed to 'Jani Allan's Week', my brief was to write on the banquet of life in South Africa.

As someone once remarked, 'South Africa has always regarded culture as an embellishment to a utilitarian life or a distraction from it.'

Travel broadens the mind. Tourism narrows it. Suburbia is to be always drifting from one overseas tour to the next. Here and now are unpleasant realities.

So, Joel Grey-like, I observed the cabaret – and with equipollent bemusement the tonnage of nonsense written about me.

'For the past nine years there have been luncheons and brunches and fan mail. An anonymous admirer still sends her a bottle of Moët & Chandon every Monday ... she flies to Cape Town for a lunch date and Mauritius for the annual marlin fishing. There are overseas trips and safaris to Chobe ...'

I think it was at Chobe, where the floodplain spreads out like a nursery tablecloth patterned with hundreds of toy elephants, that I really saw the gaping chasm that exists between what women's magazines call 'the Real Me' and the brashly confident, relentlessly glamorous persona invented by the *Sunday Times* that was 'Just Jani'.

It was on the *Mosi oa Tunya*, the river boat, to be precise. I was drinking (or in columnspeak 'quaffing') Dom Pérignon and watching the Campari-pink sky turn ink blue.

'Aren't you Jani-Allan-of-the-Sunday-Times?'

The game ranger's question was innocuous. He wasn't to be blamed for thinking I had a quadruple-barrelled surname.

So I attended race meetings where trainers were glued to binoculars the size of ice-cream cones and the glitterati were glued to the nearest celebrity.

And since South Africa had no royalty or real celebrities, I invented them.

'More than three mentions in JA's column and you're a celebrity,' declared Barry Ronge, the film critic and media personality. 'People are grateful to be insulted by her. It's better than being ignored.'

Only in South Africa would an observation that Goldie Hawn had a tea stain on her dress be construed as an insult. But then in South Africa in the '80s, a sense of humour was usually detained, if not placed under house arrest.

Still, instead of writs, there were requests for my presence at the next ball. And the next. Often the collaboration proved more nerve-racking than an open display of hostility.

Only the rich don't have to sing for their lunch.

✳

Although being in close proximity to scantily clad women who have curves like scenic railways intimidates me, I force myself to do at least three gym classes a week.

Janis Dorfman's classes are an excruciating who's who in the Kugel Zoo. To these women aerobics is a religion and a way of life.

Infinitely preferably to the deafening Dolby stereo and whooping about 'going for the burn' are my kendo classes. Probably because it can't be practised as a form of entertainment or sexual display, kendo hasn't become popular in South Africa.

Before every class I am filled with apprehension. There is always a frisson of thrill at dressing up in the Prussian blue armour of the Samurai warrior. My hands tremble a little as I pull on my *kote* and take up the *shinai* – the sword made of bamboo strips.

I am entering a medieval world redolent of mystique and the majesty of ancient ceremony.

Kendo is about intense concentration, the summoning of all the physical and mental resources. It is only when these powers are summoned that it is possible to deliver the death blow to your opponent with complete absence of anger. The *kendoka* does not use his strength in spite of the violence of the attack. What matters most is the technique of dealing with the blow. Over and over we practise the ritual bowing, slashing, slicing, striking, cantering and lunging.

David Sacks, who has the kind of body that demands to be planed rather than stroked, tries to teach me the principles of the *suburi* – the blows. Each stroke must be accompanied by the blood-curdling *kiai* – the blow that kills. The *kiai* should be a harsh and terrifying utterance designed to paralyse the opponent for a fraction of a second. The true *kendoka*, it is said, is able to utter a *kiai* that can make a bird topple from a branch.

My feeble squeaks would hardly waken a sleeping budgerigar but I keep going.

Afterwards I sit in Janis's kitchen smoking. Rivers of sweat like the lesser tributaries of the Yangtze are coursing down my face. After a kendo class ikebana always seems like an attractive alternative.

Janis is bemoaning the fact that there are fewer people attending her Sunday morning gym classes these days. They're either going to pistol shooting classes or taking the Rottie to dog training.

14

THE PALACE, AND A TRIP TO VENTERSDORP

DURING THE MID-'80s The Palace on Oxford Road in Rosebank is Johannesburg's most fashionable restaurant. It's owned by three Greek brothers. The interior is a cross between a high-tech bathroom and a box of sugared almonds.

Every surface is mirrored or has a video screen. The tablecloths are pink and black. The stemware is Riedel crystal and the flatware is Sabattini silver.

The Palace cost millions to furnish. Within a month of its opening there were five Sabattini fish knives left. A wealthy Sandton socialite boasted that she had purloined an entire set of cutlery by slipping it piece by piece into her Louis Vuitton bucket bag.

'Darling, I thought these people were my friends!' Cedric wails to me.

'A foolish assumption in a mining camp,' observes his brother Tony. 'These people are basically hooligans with money.'

Cedric looks disapproving when I turn up with Linda.

She's equally pleased to see him.

'Yoo hoo. Hello, Vile Toad.'

When Linda goes to the loo to reapply her black lipstick he delivers his usual 'God instituted spiritual ugliness as a warning that certain women should not be trusted since they are closet lesbians/terrorists/harbour inner bitterness …' tirade.

I point out that Linda is enormous fun.

Cedric shrugs. 'We'll see. Anyway, a racehorse owner has sent over a bottle of Bollinger.'

'Nice change from Tony Factor,' I say wryly. 'His horse Imperial Silver won the Guineas in Durban and on my return flight Tony sent me a piece of Kit Kat wrapped in a napkin. Written on the napkin was "Hello my angle".'

Linda is back. 'Dyslexic asshole,' she sniffs. 'He's so mean he wouldn't give you a fright.'

She sniffs some more when Cedric embarrasses me by announcing that The Palace has named a salad for me. The menu describes it as 'a rich medley of palm-hearts, avocado and mozzarella'.

'How lovely ...' I mumble.

'Fuck. Spare me from your sycophantic fans. Shall I puke now or later?' says Linda.

*

2 MARCH 1988

To Ventersdorp, the *sacré-coeur* of the Afrikaner Resistance Movement. Hometown of the Leader, his brother Andries and their aged mother.

Terre'Blanche has invited me to go riding on his farm. My editor Tertius Myburgh affects to be greatly amused and instructs me not to stand him up.

Beyond the western city limits of Johannesburg the concrete highway is flanked by characterless housing estates. The country is flat and treeless. After the first ten miles, my shirt has been replaced by cling-film. The landscape appears to be bubbling. A hundred miles further the flashing fuel gauge is becoming compelling viewing. My prayers are brief, but evidently suitably fervent. A road sign materialises, indicating a major fourway crossing ahead. Beneath it a smaller, hand-painted poster advertises 'Fresh Petrol'.

The filling station appears to be abandoned, save for a parchment-coloured mongrel lying in the doorway of a corrugated-iron shack which bears the legend 'Werkshop'.

Barely discernible in the gloom is a dozing petrol attendant.

I parp my horn politely and repeatedly. Finally he emerges.

'You want Boss Eugène? Hehehe.' He is amused. 'Hehehe.'

When he understands I am serious, he directs me in landmarks rather than street names.

After filling up, I drive through sleepy streets where ugly tin-roofed houses squat in wire-net enclosures. Terre'Blanche's house is the grandest in the street. It is built in 'Spanish' style. In this instance Spanish means that the builder had a cavalier attitude to the spirit level and the plasterer was an irritable expressionist.

I pull up and four men emerge.

'My muchachos: Dave, Dawid and Dawie,' says Terre'Blanche, smiling. 'Let's go!'

He wrenches open the door of a pick-up truck, simultaneously liberating several dead beer cans. I am jammed between two sets of thighs. Terre'Blanche seldom drives. Probably he needs to have his hands free to do his limp-palmed Hitler wave. I question him about the origin of his preferred method of greeting the *volk*. He becomes irritable.

'It's an old Roman way of greeting. It means "I come in peace!" How can I help it if Hitler also used it?'

We travel on in silence.

'The day lay like a lizard in the palm of your hand,' Terre'Blanche booms apropos of nothing.

Uys Krige. I recognise the quotation.

Outside the town, the dun-coloured landscape gives way to rolling hills and copses of bluegums. It's a harsh, stopped landscape.

I have heard that Terre'Blanche prides himself on being a great horseman but I soon discover that his style is more spaghetti Western than the classical school of equestrianship I was trained in.

He tells me that he used to break in horses during his school holidays. He charged ten shillings for each horse. A yearling gave him a little trouble once. 'I managed to control him by smashing him here, wiv a rock.' He stabs the centre of his forehead with his index finger.

I gaze at him with horror. Not for the first time do I question why I would rise to any challenge Tertius sets me.

The horses aren't all that interested in being saddled this afternoon either. Terre'Blanche grows annoyed. Thankfully there aren't any rocks lying around.

I am to ride Storm, a sixteen-and-a-half-hand chestnut stallion.

A BBC cameraman apparently still dines out on telling the story of how Storm threw him (i.e. he fell off) and almost trampled him to death.

Terre'Blanche mounts his horse, thwacks its rump and sets off at a gallop towards the bluegum copse. Storm bucks enthusiastically and bolts after him. I manage to collect him and try and get him on the bit.

The quartet are galloping four abreast ahead of me. It is preposterous machismo on steroids. They jounce up and down on their poor mounts' backs and yank the reins in the most brutal fashion. By the time we dismount, the horses are sweated up and their sides are heaving almost as alarmingly as Terre'Blanche's. I suggest that the horses should be rubbed down, but the men sneer.

'We don't do it the English way!'

I flinch when I see how they yank their saddles from the horses' steaming backs as if they are ring-pulls on cans of beer.

The ploughed fields in the sun's setting rays look as though God has made furrows in apricot jam with a giant fork. Terre'Blanche decides that this is the perfect time to show off his sunflower crop. We have hardly lurched along for more than a hundred yards when the pick-up hits a boggy patch in the track. The higher Dave revs the engine, the deeper the axle sinks into the quagmire.

We all disembark.

Dave and Dawie attempt to push the truck, but without success.

'We will have to go and get the tractor,' says one of them. They stand back, wiping their leaking foreheads.

'Am I not a man?' growls Terre'Blanche. 'Let me to do it!'

He wedges a barn-door shoulder against the grille. Time stands still as he heaves and groans. The veins on his neck resemble rhubarb stalks, but still he ignores the Aquilas' entreaties to give up.

Imperceptibly at first, the groaning is now accompanied by a noise like tearing canvas. The tearing canvas crescendos into a trium-

Freshly adopted in a crocheted shawl, 1952.

With my mother in Lourenço Marques, 1954.

With my mother, 1955.

With my nanny Dennis, 1954.

My mother and me on her wedding day, 1957.

My first day at Roosevelt Primary School.

The home in Bryanston, Sandton, 1987.

The cover of the JSO recital.

Modelling shot, 1977.

Modelling shot – rocking the shirt-waister – 1978.

Modelling Zed card, 1976.

Graduation night at Wits with my mother, 1979.

The teaching years in Bryanston. An auburn me in the middle, 1979.

Gordon and me in Mauritius, 1981.

Arm-wrestling with Linda Shaw in Johannesburg, 1981.

St Lucia, Linda in fishnet tights.

Stan Katz and me in St Lucia.

At Chez Schachat in Linksfield Ridge, painting by Norman Catherine, face by Estée Lauder.

With Tretchikoff in Cape Town, 1983.

The opening of my one-woman exhibition with Michael de Morgan, newscaster.

Pieter-Dirk Uys as me.

With Barbara Ickinger and Seaton Bailey in Port Louis, Mauritius, 1986.

With Tony Factor and Linda Shaw at the Annual Yearling Sales, 1987. Every picture tells a story.

With PR Barbara Ickinger and TV's Martin Locke at the Wild Coast Sun, 1985.

At the Durban July, 1986.

*On the SA Naval Racing Yacht
Voortrekker, 1985.*

*Plaisance Airport, Mauritius, with journo Geoff Allen a few
hours after the Helderberg fell out of the sky, November 1987.*

Chobe with Bea Reed, 1988.

My birthday and the sitting room is like a florist shop, 1988.

With Stan Katz, both being at and having a ball.

With Len Ashton and Stan Katz in Swaziland, 1988.

With fellow journo Jeremy Brooks in Kensington Gardens – before I was axed from the Sunday Times.

Derek Watts comes to Epping Forest to interview me. I wear a cream suit for the occasion.

On Battersea Bridge with an umbrella. I have just arrived in London, 1990.

phant *basso profundo* fart. The pick-up oozes backwards, leaving Terre'Blanche free to fall flat on his face. Even the mud cannot conceal his triumph.

'Am I not a man? Let's eat!'

Working on the basic principle that the radiator of a pick-up truck, after driving not too many miles, becomes very hot, all one has to do, apparently, is season your meat, wrap it in aluminium foil and tuck it between the radiator and the bonnet. A medium-rare steak needs forty miles. If you want it well done, you'll have to drive sixty. Alternatively, you can simply leave the vehicle parked and rev the engine. Overheated engines are a recurring theme in Terre'Blanche's life.

Clearly, Terre'Blanche lives life in hyperbole, the inevitable result of failing to be able to differentiate between the merely awful and the deeply terrible. The emotional amperage he must expend over a 24-hour period is alarming.

While we are waiting for the meat to cook he starts telling us an anecdote about his sister who, it seems, has married a wealthy man. The story has no tragedy count whatsoever, at least not that I can see, but the mere telling of it causes his voice to crack like old ivory. He shakes his great head, causing his come-over-and-meet-me hairstyle to become unstuck. He reaches into his pocket and brings out a can of travel-size Fiesta hairspray.

'My little sister. Can you believe it? Married to a rich man. And I am a poor farmer.'

Pfft. Pfft. He sprays, strokes, sprays and strokes some more.

Then, sighing heavily, he replaces the cap. Why he is sighing is not entirely clear (regret for his galloping alopecia, perhaps?). I giggle inwardly. Suddenly he lurches to his feet and drains the last of a half-jack of White Horse Whisky.

'*Vamoos, muchachos!*'

The men fall into line.

'Left! Left! Left!' Terre'Blanche barks. 'March! March! March!'

I watch as the men goose-step through the mealie fields until it looks like they have reached the horizon and the toecaps of their boots are going to nick the Southern Cross.

Far away a sheep bleats. The night has become cold as a mortician's slab. I shiver. It's time to go. We get back in the pick-up and head for town, but Terre'Blanche insists that before I leave I come into the house for coffee. He won't take no. He lets us in through the kitchen door, warning us not to wake Mrs White Earth and Miss White Earth, and leads the way into the rumpus room. Evidently Mrs White Earth cannot bear her husband's large noisy friends trampling mud all over her house.

A pair of carved batwing doors guard the entrance to the sitting room. Above a Dralon couch is a painting depicting an ox wagon about to plummet down a ravine.

'My people. That's how my people fought for this land. Our land.'

Oh no. Not the 'my people' saga again.

I escape to the bathroom where, I discover, the loo rolls wear crocheted jackets.

When I return to the rumpus room Terre'Blanche is pedalling furiously on a small exercise bicycle. His face is brick red. He dismounts and demands more liquid refreshment. Dave reminds him of Mrs White Earth's rules and prohibition.

'I'm not even allowed cooking sherry?' His pout tells me that his annoyance might be about to develop into a full-blown tantrum.

It really *is* time to leave.

Like a one-man Fellini movie, Terre'Blanche is unedited and baroque, and close up the baroque bits look remarkably like self-indulgence. It wasn't so obvious the first time I met him.

I get into my car and slot Verdi's *Nabucco* into the tape-deck.

I have a three-hour journey back to my world.

15

THE LAST PICTURE SHOW

DELLA REESE MULTIPLIED SEVERAL TIMES in the mirrored reception of the Royal Swazi Sun is an impressive panorama. In an industry that spawns insincerity she's rare. The only thing she requested when Hazel Feldman, the publicist, drew up her contract to appear at Gigi's was that she wanted happy people.

Della is a virtuoso in charm for whom an audience was invented. While the maître d' busies himself with the ritual confiscation and allocation of cutlery, Della cries: 'Daddy [her pet name for her husband Franklin Lett], ain't they gonna serve us anything but forks here?'

'I haven't eaten anything for days. I've been so rushed off my feet with this promotion,' says publicist Stevie Godson. She gazes resentfully at the press, who are tucking into lobster.

Since her weekly gossip column in the *Mail* has been axed, Stevie has become the quintessential PR – i.e. a twittering piranha. The relationship between the PR and the journalist is traditionally characterised by deep insincerity. PeeAars resent having to woo boorish journalists who behave obnoxiously in five-star foreign holiday resorts by ordering oysters for morning tea … and so on.

Della's show is sparkling, a dash of Tabasco in the rabbit-stew of has-beens and never-weres that are the more usual bill of fare in entertainment in South Africa. Since performing in Southern Africa tends instantly to render entertainers personas non-starter in an anti-apartheid world, not many can be lured into the laager.

The next morning, alone with Della, our interview is developing nicely into a chat.

'We're here to express the God in us. You have to go through all sorts of lessons to get down to where the Christ is in you. It's down here.' She thumps the lower region of her Rubenesque tummy.

The clattering of bangles and the friction of leather pants herald the arrival of Stevie, who bossily interrupts our entente cordiale. Della is her 'product' and Stevie is possessive of the product. Some discreet eye-rolling goes on between Della and me. When she asks for my address to send me a pair of earrings which she insists were 'simply made for you, honeychile', Stevie's face arranges itself into the lemon-sucking expression.

On the flight home, Stevie and Hazel lecture me earnestly about how wrong it was of me to interview Terre'Blanche, how appalling the rabid right wing are, and how bigoted and violent the man is. Professor Pavlov, ringing bells and plates of dog biscuits. Terre'Blanche is politically as passion-rousing as cheap scent.

An analogy lurks somewhere in all this.

I try to explain to the pair that given half a chance I would have interviewed Hitler. What journalist worth their salt wouldn't?

This is the Last Picture Show of a South Africa that is in its sunset.

My job is to interview the players.

*

An Israeli who claims his name is Haggai Schochot turns up at the office bearing a mother-of-pearl bead necklace as a gift. When I tell him I am on deadline he threatens, McArthur-like: 'I will return.'

On Sunday, when I am in bed with flu, Linda bangs on my bedroom door.

'Do you know that one of your adoring fans is on the doorstep? How did he get this address? Do you have any idea how sick and tired I am of being Jani Allan's Friend?'

Spite pours through the keyhole.

When I knock on her bedroom door this morning to ask where the garage keys are, her mood is much improved.

'Yoo hoo. Come in!' she calls happily. 'I've got a Yid in my bed.'

I put my head round the door. Linda is wrapped about the Israeli like a damp rag around a pot-bellied stove.

*

My story and the pictures I took at the AWB training camp are deemed worthy of a two-page colour spread in the *Sunday Times*. Whether by tasteless design or appalling coincidence, the early editions carry my byline picture beneath the AWB swastika.

This time there are a dozen ugly letters in my mail. All are unsigned. One is addressed to Jani AWBlonde – the grace-note preceding a symphony of abuse? There are also phone calls along the same lines. One could have been construed as a death threat. 'This time you've gone too far. We'll make sure you never write anything again.' The voice was heavy guttural Afrikaans. Have the *volk* always found violence therapeutic?

Am I to take these signs of disapproval seriously? Personally, even?

Surely it is Tertius Myburgh who is responsible for the editorial content of the paper? Is Myburgh receiving his quota of abusive calls?

I am plunged into a mood of Hellenic despair.

To cheer me up, my stalwart and journalist friend Geoff Allen takes me to Denis Worrall's first Johannesburg outing as the leader of the new Independent Party. Worrall is the current hero of South African politics, fresh from a term of ambassadorship at the Court of St James.

As inventor of the notoriously silly tricameral parliament which advocates separate houses for whites, coloureds and Indians, he is the kind of man who when asked to identify his favourite colour is likely to answer 'plaid'.

Apart from the black television cameramen in expensive leather jackets, the audience is a white Westcliff one – South Africa's equivalent to the Hampstead Thinkers in London. Gucci loafers and Jaeger-Le-Coultre watches are much in evidence.

The City Hall stage set is spartan. A Cambridge-blue curtain bears the logo of the party – a circle containing a *trompe-l'oeil* door opened partially to let in a shaft of light. It is a pity that the door bears a close resemblance to a tombstone.

'What a swizz. Give me an AWB meeting any day,' says Geoff glumly. 'No scuffles. No bunting. Not even any heckling.'

'Closer to Grotowski's poor theatre than other more flamboyant gladiators in the political arena,' I giggle.

A theatrical touch is provided when the man whom the stylish blads call 'The New Vision' materialises in a shaft of light at the back of the hall and pauses briefly before striding purposefully down the nave. The music from *Chariots of Fire* billows. It's a long walk, but the one-time sole white member of Nigeria's national athletics team has the requisite stamina. As the music crescendos Worrall ascends the steps of the stage.

The opening speeches are mind-numbingly boring. David Gant, a portly gent with a face the colour of jugged hare, is co-founder of the Independent Party. He tells us that South Africa is like a restaurant that has fallen on hard times. What the Independent Party is offering is a New Menu and Fresh Management.

Fresh Management is fresh out of patience, it would seem. The response to a largely inaudible but unmistakably aggressive rant from one member of the audience is: 'Well, I think you must jolly well bugger off and go and be a mechanic in Australia.'

In front of me a tweedy gentleman with ginger Brillo-pad hair squirms with pleasure.

The next morning, Worrall, tennis-biscuit blond hair flopping enthusiastically, opens the door of the Rosebank townhouse to me in which he is 'stopping over'. Coincidentally, it is the same townhouse in which I once lived. He suggests my old bedroom as an interviewing location 'so as not to bother the drones downstairs'.

While the drones drone on downstairs, Denis drones on upstairs.

'Receptive. Ye-es. Appreciative. Ye-es. Attentive. Oh definitely yes. I'd give last night's audience seven out of ten. The Ront [he means the Witwatersrand] is quite frankly a critical, demanding place. Challenging. There is a very high level of concern. We've had a whole slew of meetings and of course there has been some good-natured heckling, which a speaker likes,' he lies. 'Politics is a very passionate thing.' Then, 'I say' – he leans forward – 'was this really your bedroom?'

*

Tertius Myburgh emerges from his office brandishing a proof of my page. He is pop-eyed with rage.

'He didn't much care for your description of his friend,' explains the chief sub.

'*A polished man, Worrall, one suspects, is the kind who might insist on monogrammed caviar…*'

In my opinion Denis Worrall was the archetypal South African crypto-liberal who gathered at the dinner tables of the wealthy. At these parties the dissenting tradition of liberals could be upheld in comfort and academic polemic flourishes. Marinating in moral superiority and a rather nice bottle of Armagnac picked up in a little village in France, they could spend a couple of rather enjoyable hours agreeing with each other about the appalling injustices of the apartheid regime. Then, tiring of politics, while the black maids cleared the table, they might stroll across the shaved lawn to inspect the pool and discuss the share market. When they found that the (black) gardener had snarled up the Kreepy Krauly again and the pool was looking less than crystal clear, they could curse under their breath in perfect understanding and harmony.

Distinctly illiberal curses, if the truth be told.

16

THE STRIJDOM SQUARE
SHOOTING AND THE DAY
OF THE VOW FESTIVITIES

THE JACARANDA BLOSSOMS were in bloom; lace curtains that prettied the view of the Union Buildings in Pretoria.

Barend Hendrik Strydom, young, tanned and only 23, calmly strolled into Strijdom Square on 15 November 1988 and opened fire.

He gunned down and killed seven black people and wounded fifteen more. In an earlier incident he had killed one woman and injured another in a trial run in preparation for the massacre. He was sentenced to death.

At the time of the shooting I was in seat 17A on the SAA *Waterbok*, flying back from an assignment in Durban. I had been to interview the Queen's jockey, Muis Roberts. I was oblivious to what had happened in Pretoria.

Jan Smuts airport was sleepy in that mid-afternoon way. A lone man pushing a mop half-heartedly. A pair of flight attendants gossiping in the loo.

I left the airport and headed straight to the Diamond Building in Diagonal Street. The metallic ugliness of the mining town was in sharp contrast to the lush, viridian hills of Shongweni I had just come from.

Three pm. My most un-favourite time of day. Pointless as a childhood afternoon. Gordon used to say that I was too big for South Africa. It was too small for me. I should be in New York or London, he said.

Failing that, I needed the pulse, the urgency of the newsroom.

In the cathedral-like foyer with its water fountain, the security guards were carrying on a loud conversation. They stopped when they saw me.

'Hello, Miss Jan,' they said. 'Where you come from?'

'Durban,' I said.

Pwoing! The lift doors opened and I stepped in. I was whisked up to a world that I had come to love. Unless you have experienced it, you will find it difficult to understand the adrenalin that surges through a newsroom when a story is breaking.

Ray Joseph, the news editor, is on the phone, pacing, yelling instructions.

'Bring me those pictures! Get me the picture! We need a picture. Yes! He claims that he is the leader of the White Wolves. Find out if that is a figment of his imagination! Marlene!' Marlene Burger is standing by. 'We need a colour piece. He claims he's a Christian. Says he prayed for days before committing the crime. God says he had to do it. That sort of thing.' Marlene nods.

'You! Jani!' Ray wheels around. 'Go to Pretoria. Get Terre'Blanche to talk to you. This guy says he was a member of the AWB. Go. Now!'

I still don't have a clue what's going on.

'I've got the important stuff to do,' I say. 'The glamorous stuff.'

Ray is not impressed.

'You go to Pretoria and find out what Terre'Blanche has to say or there will be no more overseas trips!' he yells.

As I leave the building the security guards look at me and shake their heads.

'Where you going now, Miss Jan?'

'Pretoria.'

∗

Terre'Blanche is in his office. After some consultation it is decided we should go to a local steakhouse because he is hungry. We cause a stir when we enter the restaurant. People crane their necks and point. I put my tape-recorder on the table and ask him what his feelings are about the Strijdom Square shootings. By now I have caught up somewhat.

'First we eat,' he says.

There are six of us. Five orders of T-bone steak and a house salad for me.

'The only decent thing the English gave us,' says Oom Willie as he places a dollop of mustard on the side of his plate, his pinkie raised like a fox-terrier's leg. Willie Groenewald used to be Hendrik Verwoerd's secretary.

The conversation meanders hither and yon: hunting, shooting, whether Rottweilers are better guard dogs than German shepherds, the precociousness of Terre'Blanche's adopted daughter Bea and the beauty of Terre'Blanche's sister, who is 'as blonde as a white rat'. (This description is met with deep admiration.)

Finally, I am permitted to switch on my tape-recorder. Terre'Blanche deplores the massacre, but when I ask him the questions Ray Joseph had quickly jotted down for me, his heart doesn't seem to be in the deploring. Instead he gives me a list of nation states seeking independence: the Basques, the Kurds, the Chechens, the Quebeçois … and, of course, his *volk*. When he says the word '*volk*' it sounds like thunder.

Then Terre'Blanche becomes irritated.

'I don't know why they are blaming me for this thing in Strijdom Square,' he says. 'If a Catholic kills someone, is the Pope to blame?'

After a second Irish coffee he becomes maudlin and begins what is to be an oft-repeated theme of his soliloquies: his loneliness.

'I want to be like Frederick the Great. Surrounded by my *bloues* (blue-eyed boys).' He gazes at the men sitting around him. His face is like a boxing glove deep in thought.

Driving back to Johannesburg, I wonder if the reports of homosexuality in the ranks of the AWB and drunken, naked 'battle manoeuvres' on beaches could possibly be true. Some even say 'Sister Agnes' (Magnus Malan, the minister of Defence) is involved. Surely not …

*

The next morning Myburgh instructs Marlene, who is Afrikaans speaking, to help me write the story. Terre'Blanche had conducted the interview in Afrikaans and, besides, it's a news story, not a personality interview. We are still working on the transcript of the tape late on Friday night when Marlene murmurs, 'Terre'Blanche is the only one who's got sense.'

My mouth falls open like a trap door. I look at her. 'I didn't know you had sympathy for the right wing?'

'In this office it's best to keep your politics to yourself,' she replies.

*

Herodotus said that the Scythians were hard to defeat because they had no cities or settled forts: 'They carry their houses with them and shoot with bows from horseback … their dwellings are on their wagons. How then can they fail to be invincible and inaccessible for others?'

To have a home is to become vulnerable. My work was my home. Terre'Blanche was my adventure in alienation. Interviewing him and befriending him, in a manner of sorts, was a kind of exodus from my safe, Sandown world where the shopping mall was my cathedral and Stuttafords one of the apsidal chapels. It was the exodus of expansion, an authorised journey. Authorised and authored in the true sense of the word by Tertius Myburgh.

*

Terre'Blanche's response to the Strijdom Square massacre is run on the front page under my byline. Rival papers who were unable to get hold of him for a comment claim that I had run to his aid to 'save' him. The report, which Marlene and I had filed together and which was published entirely without editorial comment, is construed as my justification for Strydom's barbaric killing spree.

Cartoons in all the blads reflect this view.

Tertius does nothing to defend me and correct the widely held and totally wrong interpretation of the story.

To sin by silence, when we should protest makes cowards out of men.

Is he a coward or something more sinister, I can't help wondering.

I am filled with shapeless trepidation. Events seem to have gained a momentum of their own. When I call out of the office, my answer phone at home clicks on. I'm convinced my phone line is being tapped. When Marlene calls me later, our conversation is punctuated with clicking noises. We resort to childish bravado.

'Whoever is listening – do you know they say Pik Botha is having an affair with Reeva Forman?'

On Monday evening, as I am driving down Oxford Road doing about 70, the rear left wheel of the Lancia starts wobbling furiously. I crunch the car into second gear and try to correct the steering. As the wheel works itself loose, the car broadsides across the road and I come to a spectacular halt by smashing into the retaining wall of one of the houses on Bompas Road.

Instinct tells me that this is no accident. Reason tells me not to become paranoid.

Later, when I call Geoff Allen to tell him what happened, he laughs heartlessly. 'Just because you're paranoid doesn't mean they're not out to get you!' he tells me.

He could be right. When I walked into the newsroom from the library earlier on, one of the reporters, known to be a militant ANC supporter, lunged at me, grabbing my throat with both hands.

At first I thought he was joking but his grip was alarmingly vice-like.

'You white bitch! Why are you writing stories about Terre'Blanche and his bastard friends?' he shouts.

Rob Hudson and Ray Joseph rushed out of their office and pulled him off me. There was some scuffling, a couple of chairs overturned.

Dear, sweet Victor Khupiso came into my office to comfort me. 'He's been drinking, that's all,' he said. 'He didn't mean to hurt you.'

I am shaken and confused. In this South African movie it is becoming increasingly more difficult to know who to cast as the good guys and who to cast as the baddies.

There are still parties, fashion shows, openings and restaurants, but my life has been fractured. Things are happening of which I had succeeded in being blissfully unaware. Every time Smiling Death sends me off to interview a politician now, it is as though I am seeing the country for the first time, from a low-flying plane with the mind's eye slung like a camera under the belly of the plane, recording more quickly than I can take it in.

✳

The Day of the Vow, 16 December, is a public holiday. In 1988 it is on a Friday.

Joe Sutton, the deputy editor, told me late last night that I am to attend the celebrations in Pretoria and also the re-enactment of the Great Trek. Logistically, I pointed out, it will be impossible to do both: the government and its more liberal Afrikaners have secured the Voortrekker Monument for the celebrations and the Conservatives and their re-enactment have been banished to Donkerhoek, some 50 kilometres away.

'How am I to attend both rallies and return to the office to write the story by Friday night?' I yelped.

'You'll manage,' he said. 'You always do.'

✳

Edouard Manet comes to mind. By noon the scene at Donkerhoek is a Voortrekker *Déjeuner sur l'Herbe*: women in coal-scuttle bonnets unpacking picnic baskets; flaxen-haired children taking curtain calls from behind their skirts. The noonday heat has the smell of *boerewors* on its breath. There are barrels of *sousboontjies*, potato salad and *koeksisters* oozing syrup. Couples court beneath the shade of the wagons and old men with faces like dried river-beds sit silently and smoke pipes.

Terre'Blanche has forsaken his beloved shiny wedding suit and has chosen, instead, to wear his workaday farmer's khaki.

One of his heavily armed Aquilas has been assigned the task of holding a frilly parasol beneath which Mrs White Earth shelters, perched on a fold-up camping chair. Mrs White Earth looks distracted. Perhaps she's hoping that the maid will remember to switch on the deep-freeze when she's finished hoovering.

Terre'Blanche tells the story of the Battle of Blood River. It's always a rattling good yarn. Number of men fielded: Zulus 20 000. Boers 470. Final score: Zulus 0. Boers 10 000 (approx and alleged). He exhorts the Afrikaners to embark on another trek, a spiritual trek that will reawaken Afrikaner nationalism.

Terre'Blanche's talent is to recreate the myths and legends of the chosen *volk* in language that is both savage and lyrical. In that voice, some say, is the power to make waves that could break bloody on the shores of history.

'Gross,' says Jane Dutton, a cub reporter who is devoted to me and who is accompanying me today. 'These people are gross.'

'You can acknowledge the soloist without liking the music,' I say.

Television cameras swarm over the rocks like geckos. Many of them are pointed at Jane and me. As we are trudging back to the car to set off for the Voortrekker Monument three television cameramen ask whether I will be attending the stone-laying ceremony at Paardekraal. When I tell them I know nothing about a stone-laying ceremony, they exchange glances.

'It's a photo opportunity you can't miss,' they say.

✻

At the Voortrekker Monument, 150 years after God had delivered the Boers from the spears of the Zulu *impis*, the State President is evidently expecting an infinitely more dangerous enemy: his fellow Afrikaners.

Casspirs and barbed-wire laager the sacred *temenos*. Despite state funding and SABC-TV publicity, the President's box-office is slow. Five thousand, I'd guess – counting the thousand-and-a-half policemen. A squad of geriatric drum-majorettes in pantaloons provide part of the entertainment.

The PA system crackles. It sounds like bacon frying. The President's speech is lacklustre. It starts out as a celebration of ethnic exclusivity and ends up as a plea for power sharing.

'A nation doesn't die from attack from the outside. It dies as a result of suicide.'

The bacon abruptly stops frying and his warnings are mouthed soundlessly.

I find the Day of the Vow celebrations deeply absurd. Big people's Voortrekkers – boy scouts – camping in the open and wearing reproduction historic clothes and pretending that things are the same as they were a century ago.

Perhaps 50 years ago the Afrikaners could look at the frieze of the Voortrekker Monument and allow their chests to grow tight. They could look at their tribesmen depicted with uplifted from-whence-cometh-my-help eyes. They could respond on a visceral level to the tale they had been told: the noble, helplessly outnumbered pioneers, the attacking barbarians. And the triumph – the savages slaughtered in such numbers that the river ran red with blood.

But today? The mystique of the laager has been eroded. The dream-webs that bound the Boers together lie in tatters. Policemen with German shepherds, guns and tear-gas canisters have to patrol the holy of holies. Nietzche's words have come to pass: *Dead are all the gods*.

Jane Dutton and I – loyal, sweet Jane – drive back to the newsroom, where I write the story and hand in the film. As Joe Sutton had requested.

Jane goes off to a gay club.

17

PAARDEKRAAL PART 1

THERE IS A MESSAGE on the answer phone about the ceremony at Paardekraal. A fax from London saying that if I can do the story and provide pictures, there will be a market for it over there. This news provides extra impetus. Myburgh, naturally, insists that I go.

Geoff's remark before I leave is puzzling.

'Be careful, Jani,' he says quietly. 'You're being used.'

It is just after Christmas, 27 December. When I arrive at the appointed time and rendezvous – outside the Krugersdorp town hall – there are two BMWs waiting. In one is Eugène Terre'Blanche and in the other three cameramen Jane and I had met at the Day of the Vow celebrations, the ones who had asked me whether I was going to Paardekraal.

Terre'Blanche suggests I ride with him. My sports car will not do well on the rough terrain up to the monument, he says. He tells the others to go on ahead – 'I'se just buying smokes.' Hearing him speak English strikes me as slightly odd; Terre'Blanche nearly always speaks only in Afrikaans.

When we get to the monument we find the gate is closed and Terre'Blanche gets out of the car to investigate.

'*Toegemaak met 'n stukkie draad*' (Closed with a piece of wire), he reports.

He begins to fiddle with the wire while I wait in the car. I grow uneasy. Somewhere between the café selling Russian sausages and chips where Terre'Blanche bought his smokes and here, a TV crew has gone missing. How can that be? It is less than a mile from Krugersdorp town hall to the monument. Where is the other BMW?

I get out of the car. While I busy myself with my camera and flash, Terre'Blanche wanders over to the memorial. His pudgy outstretched arms embrace the twilight. 'This,' he soliloquises 'is the holy Paardekraal.'

'And this could be Candid Camera,' I murmur to myself.

At exactly this moment eight police vehicles come bouncing over the tussocks and impale us on their headlights. Within seconds we are surrounded by more than a dozen heavily armed policemen with dogs straining on their leashes.

I am ignored but Terre'Blanche is ignominiously spread-eagled and body-searched. He is subjected to a machine-gun rattle of questions and his BMW is searched too.

The police claim to be investigating a shoot-out that has been reported.

'Am I on Candid Camera?' I keep asking hopefully.

'We're from Beeld,' volunteers one man, who is dressed in plain clothes, at which a policeman kicks him smartly on the shin.

Terre'Blanche tolerates the total onslaught with relatively good humour. He only loses his rag when a ninth police vehicle shows up.

'This time the government has humiliated me once too often!' he says. 'I am calling Minister Vlok. RIGHT NOW!'

Adriaan Vlok is the minister of Law and Order.

*

The next morning I report the events to my mother over a late breakfast.

She is bemused. 'Has anyone thought of patenting a sea-sickness remedy for a storm in a teacup?' she says. 'Come and look at the bougainvillea. It's quite glorious.'

A *Sunday Times* scooter messenger arrives at the townhouse I share with Linda soon after lunch. By the smiley faces and kisses drawn on the envelope I can tell it's from Rob Hudson, the deputy news editor.

By the URGENT stickers all over it, it would appear that something is on his mind.

I read the note.

'There's a story in the Transvaler which could lead to a follow up. Please come in immediately.'

Puzzled, I drive to the café to buy the *Transvaler*. The lead story, banner-headlined on the front page, reads 'DAMAGE TO MONUMENT'. I'm still puzzled. I assume the reference is to the Voortrekker Monument and that it has been vandalised by hooligans. Only then do I notice the last paragraph:

'The suspected vandal was Eugène Terre'Blanche and in his company was an English columnist.'

Beneath a picture of Terre'Blanche wearing a hat with flaps over the ears that makes him look like Amelia Earhart is a photograph of me.

'Write a story,' says deputy editor Richard McNeill when I get to the office, wiping a tear of laughter from his eye, 'but in a flip way. "The REAL story about ET and me".'

The whole thing was a non-event and, frankly, in my opinion is a non-story. But I can do flip. Flip is probably just what it needs.

*

I have just returned home when the intercom buzzes.

'Visitors!' Obadiah the gatekeeper shouts importantly.

I open the door.

My surprise visitors are the Terre'Blanches: Mr *and* Mrs *and* Miss White Earth!

Terre'Blanche is the worse for wear. I hastily invite them to come in. Terre'Blanche collapses heavily on the sofa while Martie perches primly on the edge. It is Martie who has insisted on the visit. Something has to be 'done about *die pers*' (the press), she tells me.

I explain to her that there is nothing that one can 'do about' the press. It's the silly season and they have been gifted with a story that has all the ingredients of a farce. A high-profile, right-wing Afrikaner politician and a high-profile, English, 'blonde' (mature mouse) liberal columnist. Allegations of clandestine gatherings. And now a smashed padlock and a shoot-out.

It is a case of 'Cry havoc and unleash the baying newshounds'. There is nothing to be done. The holiday will soon be over and the world will return to normal. The White Earths return to Ventersdorp.

✳

Every paper carries a version of the story. One reports that an eyewitness claims to have seen Terre'Blanche assaulting me outside the gates.

Tertius Myburgh calls from Sol Kerzner's mansion in the Cape, where he is holidaying.

'Be strong,' he says. 'I know I was the one who told you to go and cover this. We'll support you. These things are bound to happen to pretty girl journalists.'

He is both unctuous and patronising.

The police, who up to now have shown no interest in me, suddenly find it imperative to take a statement. They arrive at the *Sunday Times* newsroom on Saturday afternoon. Brian Pottinger, the political editor, looks worried. He's almost tempted to accompany me to the infamous 'Blue Hotel'. I am marched to a police car waiting downstairs and driven to John Vorster Square. I provide a rival Sunday paper – which just happens to be lurking – with a great photo opportunity.

A policeman laboriously takes my statement in loopy writing in an exercise book and then I am driven back to the *Sunday Times* offices, where I hang around the newsroom until midnight playing Scrabble with Marlene and Rob. We are waiting for the first editions of the Sunday papers. At about eleven Charmain comes into Rob's office, giggling.

'I just told Rapport that Jani and Terre'Blanche are having supper at the Longhorn Steakhouse in Bedfordview. They're sending a couple of reporters out there immediately.'

Rapport leads with the story. The headline reads 'JANI AND ME'. Pages 3, 6, 8, 11, 14 and 17 carry features. Gucci meets khaki, etc., etc.

On the *Sunday Star*'s front page is a huge picture of Terre'Blanche on his knees, praying. The caption reads 'Fallen Idol'.

Rob, Marlene and I hug and wish each other a Happy New Year, albeit half-heartedly.

Oxford Road is deserted as I go home, driving past Saxonwold where Stephen Mulholland is no doubt slumbering peacefully in his mansion, probably dreaming of his next take-over bid. And down in the Cape, Tertius Myburgh is probably dreaming of the day Pik Botha will favour him by appointing him ambassador to the Court of St James.

Outside the Palace, the last stragglers are shrieking goodnight to each other. Their thin sharp voices snag the night like rogue toenails laddering a nylon sheet.

At every traffic light there are posters.

'JANI AND THE RAMBOER HUNK'.

'JANI AND ME'.

'JANI AND ET'.

One loose cannon reads 'POLICE SEEKING JANI ALLAN'.

At every traffic light I leave the engine running, leap out of the car and rip them down. Poster after poster I tear at them. I ignore the angry shouts of the newspaper vendors.

I carry the heisted posters into the flat. Then I go to the bathroom and throw up.

18

PAARDEKRAAL PART 2

AFTER THE PAARDEKRAAL non-event there are floods of abusive letters.

There are demands, too, that Myburgh 'take action' against me. But equally there are hundreds of calls and letters from sympathetic strangers incensed at what they see as my 'crucifixion' by the Fourth Estate.

I maintain my asana: cross-legged on my swivel chair in front of my computer in the Diamond Building. Outside the media storm rages unabated. Reporters and journalists keep vigil on the sidewalk. Local and international television and press jam the switchboards of the *Sunday Times*.

Marlene and Rob field most of the calls.

'Bloody hell – you should make money out of this misery,' says Marlene. 'Pay me a percentage! That last caller was a paper that was offering £5 000 for an exclusive interview …'

But Myburgh forbids me to speak to the media. Instead I am to write an interview with myself: 'Face to Face with Jani Allan'.

Richard McNeill's advice to write a tongue-in-cheek story had been the wrong advice – it had merely fuelled speculation. Should I do what Myburgh is instructing me to do? Against my better instincts and in stubborn subconscious pursuit of those three little words – 'Nice job, Jani' – I turn to my computer.

In the meantime Terre'Blanche gives countless interviews, denying any personal relationship with me and claiming that he has been set up by the government. The latter assertion is met with ridicule.

I happen to think it is true. I was there.

Myburgh runs my interview with myself on the front page under the heading 'I TRACK THE BITCH DOWN TO HER LAIR'. Alongside is a splash: 'Secret Sins of the AWB'.

The widely held belief is that since what has become known as 'The Paardekraal Incident', the AWB as a political force and Terre'Blanche as its leader are over.

The last Afrikaner leader whose private lifestyle came under intense scrutiny was President Thomas Burgers. A liberal Cape church minister who was president of the old South African Republic in the 1870s, Burgers fell from grace when his love of dancing and music became public.

The Calvinist puritanical – and prurient – streak found in Afrikaners is practically an industry.

'Distraught Afrikaner' writes to me: 'Eugene is finished. Even if he doesn't lose his leadership, he can't whip up emotions any more. He brought tears to people's eyes because they believed he was morally pure, that he was the chosen one. I am in a state of collapse.'

Frankly, I am in a state of collapse myself, but I suspect the reasons for my state of collapse are rather different from those which are causing Distraught Afrikaner to be indisposed.

I want to escape from my life. I want to forget I ever heard the word 'Terre'Blanche' but the world, it seems, won't let me. One letter from a stranger, however, touches me deeply. This letter is not written to someone who, with some justification, is considered public property. It is directed past a confusion of so many frenzied people, through the dust of publicity, at a real person.

The person is unusually special. It is just possible that the events of the recent past have been somewhat stressful for Jani Allan. What happened at Paardekraal or anywhere else is of little real importance, not counting the political brouhaha. What is important, if Paardekraal is not, is that Jani Allan the person should be preserved intact. Woe lest so much talent rolled up in one human unit be permitted to be seared and wrested from the grasp of us who admire human beauty for its own sake.

What is my little letter going to achieve? I guess nothing. Perhaps if another one like it and ten more and a thousand more all implore you to do the same thing, then perhaps it will have served its real purpose. It simply asks you to hang on, to ride out the storm. Not for a moment do I believe this storm is capable of snuffing out the blazing torch that is the person behind Jani Allan, the columnist.

The letter is a lily in the mud. When I read it tears of gratitude spring to my eyes.

The most kindness I receive is from strangers.

I remain skewered beneath the spotlight. And Myburgh has abandoned his initial pretence of support.

'You're supposed to write not *make* news,' he snaps irritably one day. 'For God's sake, just write your column. Business as usual and all that. All this publicity is making you unemployable.'

I feel like I am driving a car with a frosted windscreen. I have scraped a hole that gives me a limited view, but I am forced to lean forward, peering through the hole, and crawl along in low gear. What I see gives me only enough information to stay on the road and avoid hitting something.

The battering by the press is relentless and unrelenting. The humiliation and ridicule are bloodless and cruel in the extreme.

The robot in my subconscious carries on with the interviews, types my columns, drives the car, and occasionally remembers to eat.

*

This 'non-incident' will form part of a documentary that the BBC's Channel 4 will make in the UK. In it I will be described as being seen 'in flagrante' with Eugène Terre'Blanche in the flat I share with Linda Shaw.

19

THE PAIN AND THE RIDICULE

I KNOW THAT THE BODY occasionally sends telegraphic flashes of pain to the brain, but my back is writing long, baroque letters. Ceaselessly writing long, baroque letters.

I seek solace with my yogiraj Mani Finger.

'My little lotus. Beautiful women fear they will lose their beauty. Smart people fear that their brain will rot. Clever people who are also beautiful have to worry about everything. All these events that are swirling around you are political and therefore meaningless. Only the politics of nature is important. Meditate on the wondrousness of nothingness. Nothingness of everything.'

Mani teaches me a breathing technique and a mantra to ease both my psychic and physical pain.

Ohm soria pohummmm. Ohm soria pohummm.

'Isn't yoga a little like homeopathy?' I ask. 'It's effective if there is nothing wrong with you. The only way I can keep going is by taking pills.'

'Little lotus, then you need them. You have unwittingly embarked on a dangerous, disease-filled journey into the insanitary city of human nature. Why bother to read the rubbish they are printing about you? Even reading the papers can be dangerous. The inks used on the unsterilised paper on which it is printed could be giving off toxic fumes which could be lodging in your nostrils!'

My laugh is a single syllable from the cave of bones that has become my body.

I drive home. On Empire Road there is a giant graffiti which announces 'JANI ALLAN LIKES BOEREWORS'. The leather-tongued cruelty of the bourgeoisie.

To paraphrase Pablo Neruda:

'There's no forgetting, there's no winter
That will wipe your name ... from the lips of the people.'

*

When I turn up at the Sandton Sun to interview Ursula Andress, John Badenhorst, a limp-wristed – no, limp-bodied – type who is usually all over me like white on rice, is border-line civil. 'How lovely to see you,' he says unenthusiastically. Clearly what he is thinking is how much lovelier it would be to see me dead.

Ursula is *molto simpatica*, which annoys John. My inner robot makes notes.

Ursula is wearing a deeply scooped tank-top. She has the kind of body which describes parabolas that are the object of worldwide distribution of male fantasies. Her face, at 50-something, is still fabulous.

'It's horreeble to get old,' she says. 'The skin is not elahstick. But vurs, even vurs than not having elahstick skin, is peeble. These days peeble have not time to be kind to each other. I am afraid of how peeble are behaving. All they want is power, success, money. You get success and in the end you're standing there alone and it's gone!'

As I leave she pushes a bouquet of flowers that has arrived for her into my arms.

*

It's a brand new year, 1989. On 21 January the world's press and a massive South African press contingent show up at the Pretoria City Hall where Terre'Blanche is to address the Executive Council of the AWB. The gates are manned by AWB men who carry shotguns over their shoulders. Keith Conroy, the former member of the SAS and chief trainer of the Aquilas, carries an M16 automatic rifle.

When the ex-AWB propaganda wallah rolls up in his wheelchair bearing a letter outlining his grievances about the organisation, he is forcibly removed from the premises.

Terre'Blanche compares his situation to that of Julius Caesar. He misquotes liberally.

'Et tu, Brutus. You also. You can plunge the dagger into the heart. Every day the press is fed. Stab him here. Perhaps he will bleed to death. Stab him there, here is a vein: poisonous swords have stabbed him in the kidneys, in the heart.'

Fortunately for the human colander, there were Mark Antonys.

'They stood around me and provided armour, a rampart, so that my heart was not touched. You were the armour that kept the swords from my heart. The heart that I gave you fifteen years ago and that is still yours.'

Terre'Blanche is carried out of the meeting on the beefy shoulders of his supporters. Two hundred and ninety-four out of 300 executive members have voted in support of his retaining the leadership of the AWB.

The next day Professor Bosch of distance-learning university UNISA's Theology Faculty also has the Roman Empire on his mind. He delivers a lecture in which he says that the conditions in South Africa are not dissimilar to those that prevailed in civilisations before they reached their decline and collapse. The wave of corruption among politicians is a manifestation of a moral crisis closely related to South Africa's political crisis.

'There was a time when the image of the Afrikaner was that of a person who may be difficult but who was at least known for his honesty and frankness. Now it's different. News manipulation and the concealing or distortion of the truth have become accepted practice. There is a cult of secrecy and a climate in which Afrikaner nationalists in all fields see themselves as immune to exposure as long as they profess to be acting in the national interests.'

*

My mantelpiece, once white with invitations, has become a place on which to stand candlesticks.

The cartoons of me in the papers haven't stopped and they have become increasingly cruel. Mostly I am portrayed as a deranged swizzle-stick. *Beeld* reports aggrievedly that their reporters remain banned from AWB meetings 'unlike certain English liberal reporters'.

When Terre'Blanche explains that he 'smuggled favourable stories about the AWB into the Sunday Times', Tertius Myburgh becomes apoplectic. He issues a press release saying that Terre'Blanche's remarks are so utterly preposterous as to be unworthy of serious comment.

'Suffice it to say that one should not look for too much veracity in the words of a fallen fanatic trying to ingratiate himself with his followers, who themselves are not known for their close contact with reality.'

Then he calls me into his office to tell me that I have become a serious embarrassment to him, to the *Sunday Times* and, more importantly perhaps even, his friends in Cabinet.

Myburgh's friends in Cabinet are embarrassed? The Cabinet friends who steadfastly denied South Africa's invasion in Angola? The Cabinet friends who deny any dodgy arms dealings in Middle Eastern countries? The Cabinet friends who are currently involved in such a spate of corruption scandals that no lesser person than General Magnus Malan was investigated by the Harms Commission because of alleged involvement with the activities of Albert Vermaas, a Pretoria businessman and friend of Tertius's? (It was alleged that R80 million in foreign exchange sent to the US by Mr Vermaas, and approved by the Reserve Bank to pay for aircraft and spares for his airline, had gone 'missing'. On the same day that the charges against Vermaas and Malan were dropped, a man who stole 48 cents' worth of salami was jailed for twelve months.)

All thought chases its own tail.

Geoff Allen and I go and see an art-house movie in Rosebank – black sub-titles against a black background. The film is about a man who, for 30 years, hides from the Russians by concealing himself under a pile of potatoes.

Given my current circs, 30 years under a pile potatoes is an attractive option.

*

In early February, in an unprecedented televised press conference, the Attorney General announces that Terre'Blanche is to be charged with *crimen injuria* and malicious damage to property. It is alleged that he rammed the gates of the Paardekraal monument with his BMW. Ten days are to be set aside for the trial. It's completely lunatic. The crime of malicious damage to property carries a fine of R50.

Life has become a tissue of impossibilities.

A newspaper billboard announces that I am to be subpoenaed as key state witness. Is that so? I wonder why I haven't been informed personally.

Terre'Blanche calls the *Sunday Times* in a rage, demanding to speak to me. When I refuse he ends up having an hour-long rant to Marlene Burger.

There are 27 messages from him on my answer phone when I get home.

*

I suppose the process of a nervous breakdown begins with the collapse of the will. When the will becomes passive, the vital forces sink and at a certain point physical health is affected. How close is the connection between man's state of mind, his courage and hope – and lack of them – with the state of his body?

I am the bed of a river and the current is all pain. My back is the worst.

'For God's sake, if your back is giving you so much trouble, go and see a doctor!' snaps Marlene, who by now has compassion fatigue.

That afternoon I am admitted to the Morningside Clinic. X-rays show that extreme and prolonged tension has caused my back to go into spasm, displacing three vertebrae. I am put into traction in a private ward, strapped into a pelvic harness onto which heavy weights are attached. I lie there, prone, and twice a day I have physiotherapy. At the end of two weeks I am fitted with an orthopaedic corset which I have to wear for the next four months.

The first newspaper I pick up on my return to the office runs a story about me being in traction. The pay-off line uses the Lexington cigarette ad slogan: 'After action satisfaction.'

20

FLATMATES FALL OUT

MEO PATACCA AND SUPPER WITH GORDON, who mentions casually that he has just bought a Lear jet and an island in the Bazaruto Archipelago.

When I return home I find Linda sprawled on the sofa chatting up someone on the telephone. I can tell when she's talking to a man by the way she titters and absentmindedly flicks cigarette ash all over the cream suede couch.

'By the way, that was Terre'Blanche,' she says when she rings off. 'He wanted to speak to you.'

Linda is having a spot of bother at work. Instructed to write a story about what people think about a new scent that's on the market and too lazy to canvass opinions, she simply invented names and quotes. Her editor Wynter Murdoch is taking a dim view and threatening to fire her.

I recall another night when I got home from the office to find Linda reclining on the couch like an odalisque.

'Rome was marvellous. Then of course we did Verona, Padua, Assisi ... of course I missed you. It was hell. Come around immediately, you luscious beast.'

She was reciting the itinerary from a trip to Italy that I had recently returned from. I had no idea who she was talking to on the phone that time.

That night her mating calls set the neighbourhood dogs off.

Another morning, only half-seriously, I suggest that she should have a turnstile fitted to her bedroom door.

One day I am almost relieved when I arrive home from work to find that Linda has moved out. The flat is as silent as if a lawnmower has broken down. A lone plastic spider sags from the lightbulb in her empty bedroom. That spider has probably seen more activity than a policeman's torch, I imagine.

A week or so later, I find a letter pushed under the front door. It's from Linda.

Since I am no longer rated amongst your ever-diminishing list of privileged confidants I am forcibly reduced to claim my position among the ranks of written correspondents (roughly 50 a day wasn't it?). So if I may, without usurping too much of your allotted letter-reading time, I'd like to enquire exactly what I have done to offend you. Or is it simply that I've served my purpose and am now redundant?

Please don't think I'm complaining! Nay, indeed! Allow me to say how grateful I am for the precious moments of your life granted me. And if you think I'm joking, let me put you straight before you charge off on the wrong track as usual. I'm actually fucking pissed off. I think you've got the most enormous nerve. And if this is your definition of friendship, I can't say I'm surprised your list tends to remain shorter than you might like. It might just be time you found out people are not in fact either commodities or doting slaves. Not all of them anyway. Perhaps you should stick to the other kind though. You seem happier with those.

Look, don't get me wrong. I'm not handing you the 'after all I've done' speech. And don't think I didn't expect this. I was just a little surprised at the crassness and abruptness with which I was handed – or rather not handed – my notice of termination. I was silly enough to think you'd be more subtle …

The letter ends by saying:

> Someone actually made a very astute comment about you. He said it is unfortunate your vanity exceeds your intelligence. He's right. It is unfortunate.
>
> Yours in obedience, Linda.
>
> Now go and show this around the newsroom, why don't you?

The last missive I'd received from Linda had had a somewhat different tone. In it she'd thanked me for being 'the best friend a girl could ever have'. She's also thanked me for saving her life.

Not long after Linda moved out, I relocated to a townhouse in a complex called The Birches, just below Sandton City.

21

MY APARTMENT IS BOMBED

I HAVE TO REPORT TO THE OFFICES of Johan Roussouw, Eugène Terre'Blanche's Senior Counsel, in Pretoria. He and Oeloff de Meyer are combative. From their mien it is obvious that they think I was 'part of the government's plan' to set up Terre'Blanche. They accuse me of 'infiltrating' the AWB.

When I get home there is a message from Pieter-Dirk Uys, the South African satirist. He is calling to advise me on what to wear for my court appearance.

'Go for the Greek widow look, sweetie. Lots of black and big sunglasses. The government has been looking for a chink in Eugène's armour for years. Who would have thought you were that honorary Chinese!'

*

Terre'Blanche continues to leave long drunken messages on my answer phone. Mostly he implores me to speak to him about the pending malicious damage to property court case, but on some of the messages Afrikaans poetry pours forth between the pips.

I remain on the down-staircase of apathy, probably because I am still in considerable physical pain. My back is giving me hell. I am re-admitted to hospital, this time for spinal epidural to relieve the pain.

Still the messages continue.

When I am back at work I tell Tertius I believe my phone has been tapped, that I think I am being followed and that Terre'Blanche is leaving endless messages on my answer phone. Tertius seems strangely elated at this last part.

'How do you know it is him?' he asks. 'Bring me the tapes. We'll blow this bugger out of the water forever.'

I tell him I don't think that's a good idea.

Apparently, I have also developed a bleeding ulcer and this time I have to be rushed to hospital. Geoff Allen drives me there and says nothing when I vomit blood all over his car. He handles all the admission stuff. I feel safe in hospital. All decisions are made for me. Nil per mouth. Ken Boffard, son of the more famous Ralph, tells me that when I was brought in I had had about two hours to live.

*

The calls don't stop. Desperation at its nadir, I make a call to Martie Terre'Blanche. I implore her to intervene, to stop Terre'Blanche from attempting to contact me.

Martie is deeply apologetic and pleads with me not to start legal proceedings against him.

'It's the court case,' she explains. 'It's working on his nerfs.'

During apartheid, Afrikaners living within the constraints of a proto-fascist state, the Dutch Reformed Church and the well-oiled propaganda machine that was the SABC were in a world in which male prowess was twinned with female abasement. Many women in this social group were morally paralysed, deeply self-censured and easily dominated. Masochistic subservience caused them to be bound to the hearth and the crib. Or, in Martie Terre'Blanche's case, to her woodworking (interesting choice – cutting without bleeding) and meticulous housekeeping.

Martie Terre'Blanche had been a beauty. She had once modelled Swakara fur in South West Africa. But now she was clearly beaten down by Terre'Blanche and probably unable to leave him even if she had wanted to. Why her husband was so drawn to me, I do not know. Maybe it was just because I was completely different to her.

*

On a day that sees the heaviest fighting in Namibia's 23-year-long guerrilla war, four South African Impalas take part in an attack in which 750 SWAPO insurgents are killed. Nineteen members of the South West African Police Force are killed. Foreign Minister Pik Botha announces that 'SWAPO's attack is illegal' and that he hopes 'that Sam Nujoma realizes he has made a complete fool of himself'.

On the same day government officials are alleged to have stolen some R47 million and yet another commission of inquiry has been set up to investigate the allegations.

This kind of thing will not be tolerated. Actually, South Africa is densely thicketed with people who say this kind of thing will not be tolerated and that kind of thing will not be tolerated, but the kind of things that will not be tolerated keep happening.

The press have bigger fish to fry, however.

They mass around the dreary magistrates' courts in Krugersdorp to watch the only show in town: The State versus Eugène Terre'Blanche.

The battered, rusty gates of Paardekraal have been lugged into the courtroom, along with two eyewitnesses, one Patrick Kearney and his daughter Wanda. Both claim to have seen Terre'Blanche smash the gates of Paardekraal with his BMW. Both allege that when I attempted to stop him, Terre'Blanche rugby-tackled me to the ground. One says I was wearing a long coat. The other insists that I was wearing a frock. One says I was toting an AK-47. The other says I had a pistol in my hand.

Kearney and his daughter contradict each other about virtually everything. At each contradiction the AWB supporters packing the court bray with laughter. When Wanda eventually bursts into tears and says that she hadn't wanted to come to the court in the first place, and begs that her evidence be withdrawn, there are wolf-whistles.

When it transpires that there is a third Kearney, Mr Kearney's son, who had written down the car registration number, and that the son is a dyslexic who is 'challenged', there are cat-calls.

'If people want to laugh, they can leave the court. This is a serious case,' warns Magistrate van Niekerk.

The hearing plods on. By turn, damage estimators, forensic experts, ballistics officials and policemen take the stand.

After three days the case is adjourned. I learn – again from a newspaper billboard – that I am now to be made available as a witness for the defence!

May 8 is a dramatic day in court. Again the rusty old gates are dragged in. However, forensic tests have proved that Terre'Banche's BMW was not responsible for any damage to the gates. Two young policemen, constables Page and Mitchell, confess that the whole farcical episode was a plot designed to discredit the right-wing leader. Both admit to lying.

The case is thrown out of court and Terre'Blanche, smugly porcine, is carried out, once more borne aloft on beefy shoulders.

*

It is said that people tell you the truth about themselves soon after you meet them. You may meet a man who says 'I'm basically a selfish person'. Then the relationship grows and he becomes unselfish. But when things go wrong it turns out that he had been frank and honest in the beginning. He IS a basically selfish person.

Terre'Blanche said 'they' would destroy me. How did he know that? And how did 'they' plan to do it?

I would find out before too long.

*

The paper has been put to bed. Marlene and I are at my apartment winding down, drinking a glass of wine and smoking. Circumstances create strange alliances. Marlene and I have become fast friends since we worked together on the Strydom shooting piece.

We are in the kitchen chewing the rag and going over the week's news when there is a polite knock on the door.

A couple of young men in khaki uniforms are standing in the passage.

'We're from the estate manager's office. Just need to check something.'

'Of course,' I say. 'Would you like orange juice? Coca-Cola?'

They decline but they walk into the sitting room and check the windows. Then they go into my tiny office and do the same there. Then they go through to my bedroom.

Marlene and I stand in the kitchen while the inspection takes place. We exchange puzzled looks. The men thank us and leave and I think no more about it.

I have other anxieties. I am still convinced someone is following me and that my phone is tapped. Tertius laughs and tells me I've been watching too many movies.

In the early hours of Thursday morning, long after Marlene has gone home, I am awakened by the sound of someone prowling around outside. Then a tap-tapping at the front door.

Frightened, I slide out of bed and lie down on the floor. The Roman blinds are open and I hope that by lying on the floor whoever is outside will think I'm not there. I will be safe in the bathroom, I think, so I start to leopard-crawl in that direction.

BANG!

The sound is massive! The windows shatter and so does the face of the alarm clock. My little cat Sylvester shoots out of my arms and into the night. It's 3:50 am.

Within minutes the estate manager is on the scene and the tenants of the neighbouring blocks in the townhouse complex gather anxiously.

It is discovered that a limpet mine had been placed outside my flat, but because of the lie of the land, the perpetrators had put it in the wrong position. They had meant to put it outside my bedroom window.

'Whoever did this knows about explosives,' the estate manager says. 'They knew exactly how long they had to escape before the fuse caused the limpet to explode. I used to be in mining. That's how I know.'

It is several hours before the police arrive.

Later, when I go in to work, Tertius asks me who I think was responsible for bombing my flat. I'm curious. How did he know about the bomb? The story was not out on Reuters.

✻

The posters read 'JANI BOMB RIDDLE'.

The *Sunday Times* runs the story as the front page.

'A bomb has exploded outside the apartment of Sunday Times columnist Jani Allan. She fears it may be part of a campaign of violent intimidation. A police spokesman said, "We have no reason to believe that this was the work of extremists on either the left or the right."'

I call my mother.

'Well, you *are* a very annoying person,' she says.

✻

Six months earlier the *Times* had run a story about dissent within the ranks of the AWB: 'SECRET SINS OF THE AWB'. The disenchanted complained of 'high-jinks parties with women and alcohol'. They also complained of active homosexuality in the ranks of ET's closest and demanded that ET step down.

It was against this background that I received death threats.

'Unless Terre'Blanche stands down, your life will be over,' said one.

✻

'I want you out of the country by Sunday,' Tertius tells me. 'You'll work from the London office in Hatton Garden.'

And so one Sunday night I find myself on a plane to Heathrow. I should have been suspicious. I was travelling first class.

I wasn't alone in my suspicions. My friend and colleague Geoff Allen, who was also a brilliant investigative journalist, told me many times before it was bombed that my flat was being watched. Mostly I thought he was being fanciful but it seemed that Geoff knew about Things, although he was never specific. He did tell me before I left

South Africa that Tertius had hired a replacement to write my column (despite Tertius giving me assurances that I could carry on with it from Hatton Garden in London) but I didn't believe him.

22

IN WHICH I LEAVE
SOUTH AFRICA

IT IS SAID THAT THOSE who have left the laager, who have left South Africa, suffer emotional imprinting that is called *mal d'Afrique*. A kind of madness of Africa, a longing for Africa. Africa, they say, is a bitch-goddess. Once she has you in her thrall, she won't let go.

Those that are left behind shake their heads.

'He'll be back.'

'It's just a matter of time.'

'They think they are big shots, but they all come back in the end. This is where they belong. They're South Africans.'

The description 'they're South Africans', in the '80s, has the same desolate ring as 'they're lepers'.

So the *verraaiers*, the traitors, those who go to the States or to Australia or the UK, find themselves in a place where people speak English but don't understand what they're saying. And despite the fact that they have a white skin they are rather surprised to discover that there are some places to which they will never be invited.

Nevertheless the *verraaiers* try to forget Clifton's beaches and the taste of biltong and rusks and Mrs Ball's *blatjang*. Actually, they even find a butcher in Highgate Village who sells *boerewors*. Well, they might call it *boerewors,* but it isn't the same. Maybe it's the different grass the cows eat in England. Plus it explodes. Takes forever to clean up the kitchen.

At the far side of the world, they even manage to smile when they remember the way the maid in the B block of flats used to carry on a conversation with her friend on the 4th floor of G block. They forget how much it used to irritate them. ('Can't you use the telephone, Gladys?') They denounce South Africa as small. The country is small. You only have to look at the newspapers. You know what they say. People get the newspapers – and the governments – they deserve. In Britain there are grown-up papers filled with words that are beautiful. The photographs accompanying the articles are masterpieces. The TV interviewers are sharp. 'That Jeremy Paxman. He said to a politician the other night "Come on! We know you're a politician and all politicians lie!" No one in South Africa would dare say that! Come on! Those doze-balls couldn't go two rounds with a revolving door.'

Still, the *verraaiers* keep remembering the smell of the earth after a Highveld thunderstorm. They even remember with something akin to fondness, the lunatic taxi drivers in Sea Point and the way *braaivleis* is on the breath of a summer evening in all their memories.

They fight it gamely, this disease of dislocation. They switch channels if there is a programme on South Africa on their televisions. And they search seas of pink-and-white marshmallow faces for one black face. Just one. (Oh, there's a difference between an African American, an African Briton and an *African* African.)

'It's just a matter of time,' say their friends. 'You'll be back.'

My mother used to say: 'Go back to Britain where you belong. There is nothing here for you. You like living in a car-wash.'

If Britain is a watercolor, Africa is a woodcut. Translate the hard edges of a woodcut into syllables and you have an explanation of the Katzenjammer accent. Sow Theffricuns are corlt things like Claafe (Clive), Jawtch (George), Ritshit (Richard) and Furllup (Phillip).

Writer Rian Malan and I are talking about South Africa. He has just returned from Uganda where, he reports, Museveni is facing three separate revolutions. He also has some insider gossip about Canaan Banana's rape cases, which makes us laugh, albeit in an appalled way.

'Whites are terrified of being branded racist, so they went along with the charade and became complicit in one of the disasters of our time,' he says. 'We live in a culture of "arwa rights" and "arwa demands" – but no responsibility.'

Rian left South Africa, went to live in LA, wrote a best-selling book called *My Traitor's Heart* – and went back to South Africa.

Just before I leave country I am sitting in a fast-food take-away joint in Midrand late one night when a gang of five men, all wildly brandishing AK-47s, bursts in. One of them grabs the manager and shakes him as though he were a maraca. The patrons who are waiting for their numbers to be called (the numbers attached to their orders, that is) shrink back against the walls.

'WHERE'S THE MONEY? WHERE'S THE MONEY?' are the words we hear, in between the deployment of much vile language. One of the AK-47 wielders takes a surprisingly accurate shot – WHIIIIIING! WHIIIIIIINNG! – at the till.

A handful of patrons who are sitting at the small tables gaze up in disbelief. Their heads swivel. No one dares to reach for a cell phone. It is as though they are frozen in aspic. When at last one man half-lurches out of his chair, he is swiftly punched in the jaw by one of the gangsters. BIFFF!!! You can almost see the think bubble over the man's head. 'Wha … the …?'

It's pure Robert Rauschenberg. Comic-strip crime.

Suddenly, another gang arrives. This lot are in uniform, but they're not the police. Their uniforms are black and have badges saying 'Rottweiler Patrol' on them. There are no Rottweilers in evidence, but they clearly don't need them. Within moments they have disarmed the first gang. As they are bundling them into a truck outside, the police turn up.

When I ask them why they took so long, they shrug. One of them indicates the manager, a man of small stature, who is now standing defiantly beside his bullet-dinged till.

'This bladdy Greek has been shot seven times,' the cop says. 'Do you blame us for thinking it was a false alarm?'

The take-away joint has emptied. You can dig spadefuls out of the silence. The roast chickens turn and turn …

Just another night in this gangsters' paradise.

✳

'Ag, there's violence everywhere,' say the South Africans.

'You go overseas. You'll come running back.'

'Every country's got problems.'

'At least the scissor freak untree' (This is a free country).

23

LIVING IN EPPING FOREST

GEOFF ALLEN WAS RIGHT, as it turned out. After six weeks in exile after my apartment was bombed, I returned to South Africa to pick up my job again. I hadn't been back very long before Smiling Death gave me the bad news and I was no longer Jani-Allan-of-the-Sunday-Times. I decided to go back to London.

I met Gillian Faulkner at the South African embassy in London in the winter of 1989.

Gillian was in her fifties. She had raven, rollered hair and a plummy accent. She must have once been a great beauty. She spoke often of having had a 22-inch waist when she was a young woman. She was married to a Mercedes Benz salesman called Terry. They lived in Dawes Hill, Chingford, in East London.

'It's only *postally* E4,' said Gillian. She was fiercely snobbish about where she lived. She would have preferred to live in SW1 but life hadn't turned out the way she thought it would.

The Faulkners' charming, large house was on the edge of Epping Forest. Soon after I arrived in London Gillian invited me to live with them.

I suspect that part of the reason behind the generous invitation was that she was attracted to drama, of which my life was clearly fuller than a pomegranate with pips. It was a good exchange. I provided the drama and she provided something else, something I craved: knowledge.

There is nothing I love more than learning and Gillian was always teaching me things. She was just so knowledgeable, about everything, it seemed to me – history, poetry, culture, theatre, mythology and music.

One November morning in 1990 we were walking in Epping Forest with Tassie, the Faulkners' German shepherd, when out of the blue Gill said: 'This is where Boudica fought her last battle.'

'You know about Boudica?' I was enchanted. 'The big bronze statue of the woman in a war chariot with the horses near Westminster Bridge and the Houses of Parliament? The one that's inscribed with the lines from Cowper's poem: "Regions Caesar never knew, thy posterity shall sway"?'

Gillian nodded. 'The Iceni were a Celtic tribe who were opposed to Roman occupation. So this broad, in AD 60 or something, led a major uprising against the occupying Roman forces of Gaius Suetonius Paulinus. Her warriors defeated the governor's legion and destroyed the capital of Roman Britain at Colchester. But later, while heading to London, she was defeated and she died in unknown circumstances. Some people say it was here, in Epping Forest. Boudica, or Boadicea. The name, translated, means "victorious". Boudica is still a heroic symbol of Britain. For me, she's a model of pure feminine courage.

'"Is it not much better to fall honourably in defence of liberty, than be again exposed to the outrages of Romans? Such, at least, is my resolution; as for you men, you may, if you please, live and be slaves!"'

Gill intoned Boudica's words with such emphasis that she became quite breathless. I put my arm around her. 'You're a one-off, Gilly,' I said. I meant it.

Gillian looked delighted. 'Did you like that?' she asked. 'Did you? Actually, you look a bit like Boudica. Tacitus said Boudica was of royal descent and that she was possessed of greater intelligence than often belongs to women.'

I giggled.

'Oh yes,' said Gill. 'She was tall and had hair described as red, reddish-brown, or tawny. Always wore a huge necklace and a tunic fastened with a brooch. Dio says that before the uprising apparently Boudica employed a form of divination to find out whether she should go to battle. She released a hare from the folds of her dress and interpreted the direction in which it ran. And she invoked Andraste, the Icenic war goddess.'

Gillian and I would listen to BBC 4 together and we would shriek at the pretentiousness of some of the items discussed.

'Come here! Come and listen to this, missy!' she would call as I sat typing in her study. 'Listen. Listen!'

'*The Trackers of Oxyrhynchus* is a hit play by English poet and playwright Tony Harrison. It's partly based on a satyr play by Sophocles. The play starts with the two archaeologists shown doing excavations in situ at Oxyrhynchus in 1907…'

We would sit at the kitchen table listening to the plot of the play on the radio. At the part when the papyrus jumps out of the crates, having been transformed into satyrs, we started snickering. By the time the satyrs were becoming unhappy because the gold bars they had received from Apollo had turned into gold-leaf-covered boom-boxes blaring a music they couldn't even dance to, tears of mirth rolled down our cheeks. 'Gold-leaf-covered boom-boxes!' we gasped.

One of Gillian's close friends was Roy Boulting, of the Boulting brothers, who used to be married to the actress Hayley Mills. Roy would come and weekend at the Faulkners and regale us with stories about the films he had made.

Once we went to the Italian embassy to meet Bernardo Bertolucci. The man who directed *Last Tango in Paris* explained to us how marvellous computers were for his art. His hands were doing a fair impersonation of a World War I pilot describing a dog fight. Roy gazed at Signor Bertolucci speechlessly for several minutes. He was clearly aghast. To purists such as he, films were plainly meant to be directed by a director. Laboriously edited even. Editing with a computer programme, as far as Roy was concerned, fell into the same category as that Japanese invention – praying by fax.

'My dear,' Roy said faintly later on when we were back at the Faulkners. 'Did you hear what he was saying? I blanched.'

Roy taught me about Stilton cheese. 'Fatal,' he said. 'Never put it in the fridge. It's fatal.'

Gillian had another friend, whose name was Trace, who was a vendor at Walthamstow Market. The pair of them would sit at the kitchen table and drink Scotch and scream with laughter over the stories Trace told Gillian about her life and her current boyfriend. ('If he says "Nice tuck" one more time, I'll kill him!').

One story was about how Trace had 'inadvertently' given her phone number to a bloke in a pub. 'What do you mean you "inadvertently" gave him your number?' asked Gillian. 'Inadvertently?' And they would both fall about. I envied their friendship. They were a pair of Londoners who shared a vernacular that was opaque to me.

*

Gillian and Terry led separate lives.

She and I would gad about in her Mercedes Estate car. She took me to Tikki Adorian in Sussex who owned Toy Horse International and bred tiny horses which stood no more than a foot and a half high at the withers. She would take me to cocktail parties in the Houses of Parliament. Some nights we would drive up to the West End for supper and come home as the commuters were on their way to work in the grey dawn.

We'd go to Le Gavroche in Upper Brook Street. Usually one had to wait three months for a reservation, but Gill had contacts. In 1991 it was the go-to haute cuisine establishment for a sophisticated, wealthy crowd. When we ordered the *millefeuille* of raspberries and gianduja and Gill told me that Terry called it Milly Filly, we laughed like hyenas.

*

I heard a story once about a couple who lived in Pittsburgh in the USA. The wife was a huge woman. Her husband was as small as a mouse's ear. A diabetic, he had had his lower legs amputated and used wooden prosthetics to get around.

They had Wagnerian rows. My friend Mike, who told me the story, said that he had peeped into their tiny sitting room when he was a small boy and saw the missus yelling and slapping her husband. He was horrified and ran home crying. When he got home and told his parents what he had seen, they laughed uproariously.

Apparently, Mrs Dowdy was forced to be the breadwinner when Mr Dowdy lost his job and his legs. However, as soon as she left for work at the steel mill he would strap on his legs and go straight to the nearest bar where he would drink her earnings. She became so infuriated with him that she confiscated his wooden legs and carried him down to the basement 'to think about things' while she was working.

Gillian liked to drink, too, and Terry was also infuriated by it. He had other ways of dealing with it, however: silence. The silence between them was a deep, passionless moat.

Gillian tried to hide her drinking from him. Once, when we were in London, she called the local cabbie and asked him to let himself into the house in order to top up the whisky bottle with tea so that Terry wouldn't notice how much of it she had drunk. When we got home she replaced the bottle. She would hide alcohol beside the dishwasher under the sink.

Gillian was extraordinarily kind to me. She would take me to the hairdresser, explain London and the Season to me and let me wear her earrings. She bought me my first Burberry raincoat. Before Derek Watts and a team from the M-Net television programme *Carte Blanche* came to the house to interview me, she found an Armani suit for me at the local consignment shop.

She drove us to Cambridge to King's College so that I could hear Evensong.

She also guided me through the intricacies of English pronunciation: 'Belvoir is pronounced Beaver. Featherstonehaugh is pronounced Fanshaw. And Magdalene, the college, is Maudlin.'

At night I would sit in her little study and type. She would come in and sit with me and start reminiscing about her days as a debutante. She'd start off a happy drunk, but after she had had a few she would become maudlin. Then she would start singing. She had a wonderful voice.

One of her favourites was Peggy Lee, especially the song that plaintively asks ' … is that all there is?' After listening to her singing it for the third time in a row, I would start to wonder if that was all there was too. When I told her this, she would pull my head against her vast bosom and stroke my hair.

*

Back when I was married to Gordon, he had bought me a Lancia Spyder. It was a post-box red convertible and I called it Valentine – because he gave it to me on Valentine's Day.

When I was instructed to leave South Africa, an acquaintance introduced me to someone named Manual Ramos. Manual offered to fly the car to the UK for a mere R1 500 (this was in 1989) courtesy of TAP.

'Eesa no problem. Lissabon. Lonnadon,' said Ramos impatiently when I hesitated.

For some reason the stipulated R1 500 was quickly inflated to R4 500.

'Eesa deposit.' Ramos looked irritable. 'You will get eet back.' He made the gesture beloved of London taxi drivers, the gesture that purports to mean 'Thank you' but actually means 'F✳ ✳ ✳ off out of my way'.

My hairdresser Debbie followed me in her car as I drove Valentine to a hangar at Jan Smuts airport in Johannesburg.

'Oy just,' she said. 'I wonder if you'll see that little car again.'

Weeks passed. Ramos failed to fax or phone me at any of the London numbers I had given him. Rumours festered. The car was spotted (they said) in Sandton City. In Italy. At the Oyster Box in Umhlanga Rocks.

Ramos's phone was ringing disconnected.

I called the acquaintance.

Somewhat disconcertingly, she began clicking her tongue impatiently when the pips alerted her to the fact that I was calling from overseas. 'Again with the car story …' She sighed heavily.

Two months later, the car was located in the port of Dover, strapped to the deck of a ship and thoroughly vandalised. The kelim rugs and other precious things Ramos had told me were 'quite fine' to stash in the trunk had disappeared.

Ramos, naturally, had disappeared, too, leaving not so much as a spot of grease.

I managed to drive the car to the Faulkners' house in Epping Forest. One of Terry's actor friends collected Italian sports cars and, reluctantly, I sold the car to him. I sent it along with a pathetic note: 'Please take care of my Valentine. If she should ever need a home I hope my circumstances may have changed and I can take care of her again.'

*

In those first months that I was in London I was happy. The patent leather shiny streets, the street names I knew from Monopoly – I was there! I was in Beauchamp Place! I was at the Hyde Park Hotel! There were pubs called witty things like Goat in Boots. England would make me, I thought.

When I was sent to cover the Caledonian Ball by the London *Sunday Times*, Gillian lent me an evening dress. It was moth-eaten in places and I felt ridiculous going to London on the train. One should go to a ball in a cab. As I was galloping up the stairs I bumped into Princess Anne. She was small as a dwarf's glove. After the ball I caught the Central line home and Gillian was waiting for me at Buckhurst Hill, eager to hear every last detail of my experiences.

When Steven Berkoff sent me tickets to his production of *Salome*, Gillian and I went together, and we saw him backstage. When Andrew Neil, the then editor of the London *Sunday Times*, asked me for lunch, it was Gillian who picked out an outfit for me and drove me there. (It was a brown suit and made me look as though I was a lady banker.)

We'd go to the local chippie in Buckhurst Hill and eat snowy white cod and vinegary chips.

She was mother/best friend/sponsor and tour guide.

I even got to go and see the Ceremony of the Keys at the Tower of London, the traditional locking up of the Tower that has taken place every night for at least 700 years. As one who has drifted and tossed, deracinated, for most of my adult life, I was mesmerised by the ancient ritual.

These are the things I love. Formality. Tradition. Predictability. In my fantasy life, I would know where I would be spending Christmas. And the next Christmas. And the one after that.

Gillian gave me a glimpse into a world that had existed for centuries. I loved her for that.

✱

I was with Gillian when I got the news that I had been on a hit list.

'There you are. Between Hitler and the Pope!' she said.

One day at the local newsagent we came across a magazine called *Options*. In it there was an article which implied that I had had an affair with Eugène Terre'Blanche. Gill went very quiet. We drove home in silence. Then she said, 'We really can't let this go on.' She looked at me with a serious expression. 'We have to put a stop to it.'

'The press has an obsession with me and Terrre'Blanche,' I said. 'Their preoccupation with what I am supposed to have done never gets old. What can I do?"

'Well, is it *true?*' she asked. 'If it's not, we have to contact Peter Carter-Ruck.'

I looked at her blankly.

'You know that actress,' she explained, 'the one with the teeth? Natalie Wood. And that politician Cecil Parkinson. Robert Maxwell and even Randolph Churchill used him when their reputations needed rescuing. He is fêted by the great and the good. He's acted for four prime ministers. Carter-Ruck's name is the writ writ large. Of course *Private Eye* refers to him as Peter ✱arter-✱uck.'

And of course I have never heard of him.

On Gillian's advice, I agreed to go and consult with the man.

Gillian knew what was best. We were the very best of friends.

✱

When Carter-Ruck leans forward and looks you straight in the eye, you understand why he is Britain's best-known and most feared libel lawyer, a formidable figure with a reputation for tenacity, cunning and aggressive tactics. Fleet Street editors are inclined to moan with dismay at the mention of his name.

Under the draconian libel laws of England and Wales few prisoners are taken, and huge costs are incurred. Carter-Ruck is as well known for his final bills as for his results but this is not something anyone shares with me at the time.

His offices off the Strand are functional but unimpressive. There are no overt signs of his success here. He has a Sloane Ranger as his junior. One Charlotte Watson. In her cut-glass accent she tells me that the offices of Carter-Ruck are the immediate port of call for politicians and celebrities as soon as they feel their reputations have been impugned.

We are shown into his spartan office, where everything has been laid out with the help of a set-square.

Close up Carter-Ruck looks like an undertaker. His words come out as though each syllable has been wrapped in cotton-wool. He tells us that his fascination with law began with an early sense of injustice. 'When I was told at aged six, in 1920, that I should have no haddock for breakfast because of something I hadn't done, I ran down the garden with the fish in my hand declaring that my sister couldn't have any either.'

Gill and I laugh. Peter Carter-Ruck laughs too. He loves his joke. He loves the fact that he was a precocious little brat. His laugh sounds like a small, rusty gate-hinge.

Then he adopts a very grave tone.

'My dear,' he says, 'you have been very seriously libelled. We need to send Options and the Evening Standard [which newspaper had also mentioned me in the context of a relationship with Terre'Blanche] one of my "Carter-Ruck Specials".'

Carter-Ruck's main weapon is speed. He sends forth his warning shots ('This unpleasant article for which you carry editorial responsibility ... a denigrating attack ... we invite your proposals for compensating our client for the distress this gross libel has caused him and his family…') within minutes of the decision to take action.

*

Carter-Ruck invites Gill and me to visit him in his home in Bishop's Stortford in Hertfordshire. It's a stone's throw away from where Cecil John Rhodes was born.

Everything is meticulously tidy. Even the wood outside the kitchen door appears to have been arranged with care. On the mantelpiece are photographs of Peter Carter-Ruck with the great and the good. He gives us a guided tour.

'That's the late John Eggar, whose son Tim Eggar is MP for Enfield North and until recently Under-Secretary of State at the Foreign and Commonwealth Office and now Minister for Employment. This is me with Armand Hammer. At the time of his death he had won the Soviet Union's Order of Friendship of the Peoples, the US National Medal of Arts, France's Legion of Honor, Italy's Grand Order of Merit, Sweden's Royal Order of the Polar Star … Oh, course Hammer hungered for a Nobel Peace Prize and was repeatedly nominated for one but he never won … You know his net worth was estimated to be $200 million?'

I don't. I try to look repentant for not knowing.

Even Carter-Ruck's home has a provenance. The previous owner of the house was Flying Officer Neil Lawson, a member of the Bar and later to become a High Court judge.

Nasty journalists have said that Carter-Ruck's tendency to drop names to dent a dance-floor makes them yearn for the kitchen-sink realism of *Jennifer's Diary*.

But I like him.

He's not just a clever-clogs who's turned into a name-dropper. He's commodore of the Law Society Yacht Club. He drives a Le Mans Bentley (Puerto Rican blue with a plate which says PCR1). He has a retreat on the Scottish Ardnamurchan Peninsula and an estate in Spain.

When he tells us that he lost his only son Brian in an accident, I like him more. It must have been difficult, but a lifetime of being discreet makes one only guess at how difficult.

Within months of him sending out his missives, both the *Evening Standard* and *Options* magazine settle out of court. They publish statements apologising for any wrong implication of a relationship between me and Terre'Blanche. Both organs had first sent spies and emissaries to South Africa to dig up any dirt on me. Both were unsuccessful.

I buy Peter Carter-Ruck an antique sailor's ditty box in Greenwich as a thank-you present.

And when BBC's Channel 4 airs a documentary in April 1991 that says much the same thing as *Options* magazine and the *Evening Standard* had said, it is to Peter Carter-Ruck that I will turn again.

24

THE RUNNING OF THE BULLS IN PAMPLONA

THE MORE FRAGMENTED MY LIFE became, the more I wanted to be in places of permanence. In the grounds of Hampton Court Palace I would sit on the jetty and imagine Sir Thomas More catching a boat to Chelsea after Henry VIII had demanded that he approved his divorce.

I would go to Greenwich and feel the *spiritus loci* of London's oldest Royal park and the place where hemispheres meet. I spent countless hours in the home of time (as Greenwich is called) gazing at the view across London from the Royal Observatory.

Greenwich became one of my grail places. It is where you will find the Prime Meridian of the world. Every place on earth is measured from here. The museums, the old Royal Naval College and the *Cutty Sark* enchanted me.

I also loved wandering around Earls Court. Once a verdant, rural area over which the Saxon thegn Edwin was lord, Earls Court is visible on maps of London dating back to the 1820s. The area was, for a long time, the place to buy and sell the ubiquitous VW camper van, no doubt because it was also the place that students and those who were on temporary visas would gravitate towards. Australians and New Zealanders, especially, seem to have made it their UK headquarters, causing it to be dubbed Kangaroo Valley. (Actually, after World War II a number of Polish immigrants settled in the Earls Court area, leading to Earls Court Road being dubbed 'The Danzig Corridor'.)

Many of the doors in Earls Court boast the blue plaques that indicate that someone of note used to live there: Howard Carter, who discovered Tutankhamun's tomb, lived at 19 Collingwood Gardens. Benjamin Britten, the English composer and musician, lived at 173 Cromwell Road, and Alfred Hitchcock at number 153. Freddie Mercury lived, and died, at a house at 1 Logan Place, just off the Earls Court Road. Diana, Princess of Wales, lived at 60 Coleherne Court, Old Brompton Road. Her parents bought the three-bedroomed flat for her as an 18th birthday present. The actor Stewart Granger was born in the same block of flats and spent most of his childhood there.

*

I saw the posters advertising the running of the bulls in Earls Court on one of my solitary walkabouts there: 'Pre-Pamplona Piss Up', followed by 'Pamplona Piss Up', and 'Post-Pamplona Reunion Piss Up'. Later, when I went home to the Faulkners in Epping Forest, I found Gill excitedly waving a telephone message pad.

'Some bloke called Bert was on the phone,' she said. 'He wants you to go with him to the running of the bulls in Spain.'

Synchronicity!

'Bert? Really?'

Bert, the man who had landscaped Gordon's garden, and with whom I had had a brief liaison. I was living with Linda at the time. She used to call him 'Vile Kraut'. I was surprised that Bert even remembered me, let alone found out how to contact me.

I reinvented him in my memory. I loved that Bert knew the Latin name of every plant and tree. I loved how he would leave dark chocolate truffles in the fridge for me when I wasn't there. I remember loving his smell. Loamy. Earthy. That's what it is all about, isn't it – scent? Pheromones. Scientists say that we respond to people's smell on a subliminal level. We are attracted to a person whose genetic make-up will be most compatible with ours in order for reproduction to be successful.

Part of my reason for accepting Bert's invitation to join him in Lisbon and then go on to Spain was curiosity. Curiosity about the running of the bulls, yes, but also curiosity to see how it felt to see him again. That, and a yearning to be stroked. It is always tempting to revisit an old flame. Will your wrists still get weak when you see him?

As long as I could remember, Pamplona had been a name with which to conjure. Hemingway heartland. In the subterranean ore of my imagination, it was a kaleidoscope of jewelled visions. Moons suspended like after-dinner mints in the vast goblet of a Curaçao night sky. Cathedrals made by lace-makers. Nights heavy with the fragrance of magnolia blossom.

Pamplona, I was sure, would be a place of machismo and moustaches and inverted question marks. There would be flawlessly mannered Iglesias *manqués* snaring girls with flashing smiles and the silk noose of murmured foreign promises.

The bullfight itself? There my imagination's rag bag was a jumble of swatches of glorious hues. Cerise silk, patent black satin ... The reality would prove to be something else, of course.

I didn't think it through. *I didn't think it through*.

How many bridges have been burned, how many forests, because we don't think things through?

Later, when I talked to Bert on the phone I told him about the posters I'd seen that very day in Earls Court, that I had always wanted to go to the festival of San Fermin. How marvellous that it would now be possible. And what a joyful respite from the stress of trying to find a life – *make* a life in the UK.

I realised I needed to spend time with someone who knew from whence I had come. I had been pretty badly shaken, what with the bomb and leaving South Africa.

Bert was part of a familiar landscape. We used to hang at little dives in Rockey Street in Yeoville before it became a no-go gangland. We used to go shopping at Thrupps for rose-petal ice-cream and drink coffee at a little coffee shop in the Carlton Centre when the Carlton Centre was chic.

I wanted to lean against him, that was all. Just for a few hours. Was that so bad? Yes, it was, I would come to realise. But not now. Not yet. I don't realise it yet.

*

We are to meet at the airport in Lisbon.

I spot Bert at once. He is as conspicuous as a Georgian bureau at a garage sale. He folds me into his arms and there is a diamond catch in my throat. I still love the way he smells. It's the smell of the woods in an early morning rain.

'Lisbon needs a coat of paint,' I say idiotically.

We collect a rental car and laugh at everything as people who are enchanted with each other do. A woman arguing with her husband while their children are opening a suitcase. A cute dog. A silly ad on the radio.

We drive to the Hotel Albatroz in Cascais.

'Dahling, I laff your shoes. I laff the way you dress,' Bert whispers in my ear.

I feel sure that everyone knows we are lovers. I feel loved and I look loved. Women who are loved have a certain air about them, a certainty that they are desired. It has been a long time since I had that feeling. An aeon.

When we attend a gala dinner at which George Benson is the guest artist, Bert takes a starched napkin and writes a poem on it for me. I will treasure that napkin for years. He gazes at me when George Benson croons 'In your eyes'. I feel like a dotty teenager.

At the Palace Hotel, a fairytale gingerbread architectural feat in the forests of Buçaco, where Wellington spent the night before defeating Napoleon's troops, we wander in a topiary garden which is shining like aluminium under a full moon. When Bert kisses my arms it feels like tracer bullets on my soul.

This is what happens when your life has been devastated. The smallest show of approval is monumentally healing.

In Coimbra, where Salazar was a professor at the famous university, we pack a picnic lunch. We eat chorizo with our feet in an icy crystal-clear stream. Bert even makes me forget how self-conscious I am about my hideous toes.

In Biarritz we lie on the beach and giggle as we watch a bunch of

Germans building a human pyramid as if their *Blut und Ehre* (blood and honour) depend upon it. We can hardly stop laughing when they run into the sea from great distances, splashing the French paddlers.

The drive from Buçaco in Portugal is long and sticky. The liquorice roads winding through the ochre countryside are hotter than a match-head. We are headed for the province of Navarre, the area east of Castille.

We stop at a roadside petrol station and restaurant that shimmers in the heat like cheap Christmas decorations. With gaits like tables – a dead giveaway that we have spent half a dozen cramped hours in a Golf – we stumble damply through the plastic fringe that serves as a door. A rusty fan twirls lazily. Even in the gloom it becomes clear that we have gate-crashed a wedding. Flies are jockeying for position on the fourteen-tier wedding cake.

*

Seven miles outside Pamplona the roads are impacted with vans plastered with 'I love Pamplona' and 'I love (shape of wine glass)' stickers.

Known in Roman times as Pompaelo (the city of Pompey), Pamplona was the capital of the Kingdom of Navarre from the 10th to the 16th century. The church of San Lorenzo in the middle of the Parque de la Taconera has a chapel dedicated to the city's saint, San Fermin, in whose honour the running of the bulls fiesta is held.

Asking the way to the Plaza de la Virgin de la O is an invitation for three enthusiastic Spaniards to climb into the car with us and curiously investigate the contents – and me.

There is a certain irony that the first phrase upon which my eye lights as I frantically consult my Spanish phrase book is '*Tengo dolor de cabeza*' (I have a headache).

Tourists come for the fiesta from New Zealand, Australia, America, Canada, Bavaria. The hotel is packed with foreigners who come annually 'to do their Spanish thing'. In the sitting-room, bedecked with plastic flowers and bulls, a Texas property tycoon and his wife, a

Canadian sociologist, are discussing the best vantage point from which to view the running of the bulls. Their chum is a swarthy Peruvian who looks like a cocaine dealer. A Spanish aristocrat has dragged his wife from the splendour of the Ritz in Madrid. Aggrieved in the extreme, her main concern is her hair. What is she to do without Faustus, the Queen of Spain's personal hairdresser?

The new part of the city is traffic chaos. The old part is merely anarchy. Garlanded with goatskin pouches filled with the local wine – a cheeky little plonk with an obnoxious nose – Pamplonans seethe through the narrow cobbled streets. Raucous bands and dancing of the variety that owes a lot to an Indian brave putting out a fire, they form human chains and do the *conga* and a clumsy can-can. By comparison the Rio carnival is sedate. Mardi Gras is a dirge. Everyone is dressed in white with red sashes, red neckerchiefs and a variety of black hats that range from matador to outsized mushroom.

The tourists are easily distinguished targets for the locals. They are at that silly-grin state of inebriation. More than stoic Basque blood is necessary to endure the festival of San Fermin.

The *encierro*, the running of the bulls (the word comes from the verb *encerrar*, meaning to fence in, to lock/shut up, to pen) involves running in front of a small group of bulls that have been let loose on a course of a sectioned-off subset of streets. These events are held in towns and villages across Spain and Portugal and even in some cities in Mexico. The most famous running of the bulls, though, is this one, in Pamplona, which takes place over an eight-day festival.

Bert attempts to tell me about its origins. 'It was from haffing to transport the bulls from the corrals where they had spent the night, to the bullring where they would be killed in the evening. It's a bravado thing. Young boys and reckless old men jump among them to show off.'

Actually Spanish tradition says that the run began in north-eastern Spain during the early 14th century. While transporting cattle in order to sell them at the market, men would try to hurry them up by using fear and excitement.

The *encierro* begins with runners singing a benediction, a prayer given at a statue of Saint Fermin, patron of the festival and the city, to ask for the saint's protection. 'We ask Saint Fermin, as our patron, to guide us through the *encierro* and give us his blessing.' It is sung three times, each time in Spanish and in Basque. The singers finish by shouting '*Viva San Fermín! Gora San Fermin!*' (in Spanish and then Basque). Most runners dress in the traditional clothing of the festival which consists of a white shirt and trousers with a red waistband and neckerchief. Some of them hold the day's newspaper, rolled, which is to draw the bulls' attention from them if necessary.

A first rocket is set off at 8 am to alert the runners that the corral gate has been opened. A second rocket signals that all six bulls have been released. The third and fourth rockets are signals that the entire herd has entered the bullring and its corral respectively, marking the end of the event. The average duration between the first rocket and the end of the *encierro* is four minutes.

The herd is comprised of the six bulls that are to be fought in the afternoon, six steers (castrated bulls) that run with the bulls, and three more steers that leave the corral two minutes later. The function of the oxen is to guide the herd, which goes through four streets of the old part of the city (Santo Domingo, Town Hall Square, Mercaderes and Estafeta) and a section called Telefónica, before entering into the bullring.

So it is on that on 7 July 1990 I find myself perched on a barrier filled with dread and anticipation. An old man next to me strikes up a conversation.

'You run with bulls?'

'No. My friend is.'

'You know before 1974 no women were allowed to run? Every year, between hundreds of people are injured.'

'Really?'

'You like animals?'

'Yes!'

'Then what are you doing here? These drunk people don't know what happens to these poor animals.'

In truth I have no idea what the reality of the running of the bulls will be like, but I will learn quickly. It will change my view of many things. I learn that it is a savage, brutal ritual in which animals are terrified and killed for man's amusement.

Watching torture is not a fun break.

✴

The penned bulls for the corridor are coursed through the palisaded streets of the town. Ahead of them run the youths of Navarre, ducking and dodging the crazed animals for the edification of the onlookers who are hanging from rooftops to watch.

There is a brief respite from the Taurine mayhem during which the crowds stagger through the knee-high piles of broken bottles, plastic cups and trash and gather at bars to drink sweet, thick hot chocolate and eat sticky pastries. They are evidently oblivious to the stench, the top notes of which are urine.

During the siesta the street and plazas are littered with revellers who have passed out in an advanced stage of inebriation. The occasional sound of retching accompanied by heartfelt groans of '*morto … morto*' – I die, I die – are heard.

After lunch the fiesta resumes.

As Hemingway wrote: 'It kept up day and night for seven days. The dancing kept up, the drinking kept up and the noise went on. The things that happened could only have happened during a fiesta. Everything became quite unreal finally and it seemed as though nothing could have any consequences.'

The processions, the puppets, and the hideous mask – I am starting to feel as though I am in a Goya painting from which there is no escape. I start to hate Bert for asking me to come and witness the spectacle with him. When I try to convey my feelings to him over supper he is scornful.

'You haff become an old stick in the mut,' he laughs. Then he promptly starts flirting with a nubile young Spanish woman at the next table.

Things have lost their lustre. I wander around the town and make friends with some Teutonic types who demand to know if I am English.

'We know Lineker! We know Lineker!' They are referring to the World Cup soccer player. It's not enough to forge a relationship.

For hours at a time I lose Bert. When we meet up he is distant. The curves and folds and ivory and patina of romance have gone.

*

This is what happens in a bullfight.

Before the fight, horses are blindfolded to prevent them from running from the bullring in terror. They're often injured during the course of the violence.

A picador on horseback plunges a metal lance into the bull's back. These armed men will twist and gouge the lances into the animal's flesh to impair his ability to move. A matador plunges a knife into the bull, who is already exhausted, injured and bleeding. Encouraged by the crowd, the matador prepares to strike the animal again and the bull goes down. Still alive, he lies on the ground, bleeding profusely.

With the help of the *banderilleros* and *picadors*, the matador preens and postures and performs the *veronica*, the *pase de pecho* and the *faena* – the rococo choreography with which the dignity of the animal is systematically undermined.

When the spectacle is over, the bull's suffering is not. He is dragged across the ring by his feet, leaving a trail of blood. A crowd – that includes children – looks on as the bull is hauled up by his foot. Then his throat is cut, and he is left to bleed to death. That's the end for this animal – and thousands of others will be killed in the same slow, terrifying and painful way in the name of a 'tradition' that most Spanish people don't want to preserve.

*

In the late afternoon I find myself alone at the bull-fight. In the huge crowd I can't see Bert anywhere but I suppose he is somewhere here. The excitement has reached frenzy level.

Some aver that the *corrida de toros* is a spectacle, an art, the essence of all things Iberian. It is a dark symphony played out in dazzling light.

Call it barbarism and you'll be scornfully pelted with sangria-sodden pieces of fruit.

I was.

The 50 000 spectators express their approval by spraying each other with cheap bubbly or the contents of the ubiquitous wine bladders. Or they roll another joint. Or they happily thunk each other on the head with baguettes.

At the end of each bullfight, six bulls have been killed.

✲

The fiesta goes on, but not for me and Bert. Castles in the air are all right until we move into them. Then the fragrance of magnolia blends uneasily with the smell of death in the afternoon.

We drive to Madrid in awkward silence. I resent Bert for exposing me to the horror of the bullfight. I can't un-see those images. We say our goodbyes outside the Ritz Hotel in Madrid. I try to be dignified but it is difficult.

Bert says, 'You know I will always laff you. Even if you think I am a saffage barbarian.'

Upstairs I order room service and cry into the best gazpacho I have ever tasted.

Many years later I receive an email from a woman in France asking me to help the fight against elephant poisoning in Zimbabwe. We have a mutual friend, she writes. His name is Bert. It would seem that straight after Bert had dropped me off at the Ritz he had driven to Paris to see her.

25

GLASTONBURY

SOON AFTER I RECEIVED the settlement from the libel actions against *Options* magazine and the *Evening Standard*, in 1991 I was able to move out of the Faulkners' home in Epping Forest. I rented a tiny flat in Wolsey Road in East Molesey, where the kitchen was the size of a throat lozenge but there were built-in cupboards and a view of a little yard. Hampton Court Palace was a stone's throw away.

I felt as though I had been given a new life – a life far from the haters and the bombing.

I was sure that it was as well that I was out of the country. 'There is nothing here for you,' my mother had said to me so many years ago. 'You need to find the world, even if it means losing this country.'

I was filled with energy and enthusiasm. Every day I woke up I couldn't wait to go and explore the country. I was *tidy*, for God's sake. In truth I became a little obsessive about keeping the flat tidy. It was my way of saying to me: 'You had no control over what happened to you, but in this way you can keep things in order.' I was rather like the anorexic who takes charge of her body because she cannot take charge of her world.

I would hang around the Palace and take endless pictures of the Queen's Beasts. On Sunday morning I would worship in the Chapel Royal where little boys with soprano voices and flower faces made me grateful to be alive. Late at night, I would trudge through the grounds of the Palace in the snow. I struck up a conversation with a guard one night. He told me nine out of ten ghosts preferred Hampton Court Palace.

How delicious it was to be able to walk around the village in the dead of night!

*

For many years I had wanted to visit Glastonbury in Somerset, and in particular the famous well which rests in a garden between Glastonbury Tor and Chalice Hill and whose water is said to have healing properties.

Some claim it to be the birthplace of Christianty in the British Isles. The historian William of Malmesbury wrote in his *Antiquities of Glaston* about how Joseph of Arimathea, the wealthy man who offered the tomb in which the prophet Jesus might be buried after his crucifixion, is buried there, with two silver cruets said to have been filled with the blood and sweat of Christ. Some believe that Christ himself came to England and drank the water of the well. Glastonbury's ancient names as recorded in medieval texts are not only 'The House of God' but 'The Secret of the Lord'. Legend also has it that Joseph brought the Christ child to Glastonbury and that when Jesus put his crook in the Tor, a thorn tree grew. Flowers from the tree decorate the Queen's Christmas table every year.

In 1582 Dr John Dee, mathematician and astrologer, declared he possessed the *elixir vitae* and that he had found it at Glastonbury and, 160 years or so later, some 10 000 people were said to have invaded the town in search of the holy water. Many cures were effected, a list of which was published in a book, with testimonies sworn before a magistrate as to the truth and genuineness of each case.

Like many romantics I wanted to make a pilgrimage to the Tor for lots of reasons, not least because of the Avalon of legend, Arthurian tales, and lives hidden and invisible to all but those who were said to have the key to the gates and vision. It is said that King Arthur and his knights lie sleeping beneath the Tor until their time comes again.

*

I set out at around 3 am on Sunday morning and stop at a filling station to stock up on *padkos* – Snickers and chocolate M&M's.

One takes the Great West Road and turns off at Chiswick. Wide skies and wind-swept roads, lead through the flat valley bottom of the Thames. The valleys give way to the sand of the Hampshire Barrens. Birch and fir replace solitary elms. Heather and gorse climb the rolling slopes. This is land haunted by the memories of highwaymen and heaven coaches.

Past the barrens is the rich farming land of the West.

A battleship-grey dawn. Stonehenge. The ancient monoliths brood in their impenetrable mystery. This is a heavy, cold place. A place of old gods. The earth feels heavy with death. Temple of blood, cold and sinister, and the dark side of the force.

A lone watchman with a German shepherd patrols the perimeter of the wire fence, balefully eyeing a few stray combis and their Arlo Guthrie *manqués*. The shredded denim-wearing travellers (ski-pants underneath to insulate from the cold) keep vigil. They are hoping to make a run for the stones. Just to touch them, it's said, will impart great psychic power. I ask the watchman if I can climb the fence to photograph the full moon, which is dawdling above the monoliths.

'Arrmmm. Sadly, no,' he says. 'We can't have people coming up close. We had twelve over the fence last night.'

I climb back in the Mini. The last barrier of hills. Then the road descends towards the alluvial levels that were once salt-marsh and tide estuary. Smoke hangs over the clusters of hamlets. On one side is the Poldens, the other the Mendips. Beyond is the sea, hidden by the grey mist.

In the middle of the plain rises the Tor. It's a pyramidal hill some 150 metres high, crowned by the tower of the 14th-century chapel dedicated to St Michael.

The first sight of the spiritual landmark, the holy hill of mystic focus, makes me gasp. The hill seems to radiate a strange and potent energy. As I drive into Glastonbury I see the sign: YOU ARE NOW ENTERING AVALON.

The morning sky is the colour of a Giotto fresco.

On foot, I climb and climb and climb, spiralling through strange terraces on the slopes thought to be the remains of a 3-D labyrinth. The Tor is lashed by icy winds. When the wind isn't howling in my stinging pink ears, the silence is deafening, save for the 'tisk, tisk' made by sheep pulling at the tender blades of hillside grass.

Above me is the tower. There is nothing but eternal blue and silence. I am in a Chagall painting. Far below is a tiny toy farm painted in the bright colours of childhood. The crowing of cocks, the barking of dogs and the faint, sporadic bleating of sheep are reminders that the mystic fugue of Avalon is played in harmony with this western corner of Somerset.

Finally, puffing like old boots, I reach the summit.

Timing has never been my strong suit.

Inside the tower is a group of Americans who have just gathered in a circle. They are wearing bulging anoraks and pristine white trainers. I have just stumbled on the Yonkers Chapter of the Amateur Aura Readers Association. Or perhaps it's the Muesli Cultivar Choral Soc.?

There is a lot of expectant squeaking from the new trainers. Then the Spiritual Tor Guide, a large person in glasses that look like reflector lights, clears her throat importantly. She steps forward and then starts circling the group. With her mittened hands she worries a brass bell.

Tinkle tinkle tinkle tinkle ...

'Now we are going to focus on the inner maze ... we're going to ... well, you know what we're going to do. Go into the maze. Work your way through the maze and find the inner temple. Leave a gift at the temple. Everyone comes to the Tor and takes from it. Leave a gift at the inner temple.'

The spectacle is hard to ignore. The large person continues.

'Leave your gift and put your focus on ... the Middle East,' instructs the Tor Guide. 'Ask the earth goddess to bring about peace in the Middle East. Put good in the heart of Saddam Hussein. Let there be peace in the Middle East. Let's hear those OOOOMs.'

I wander out of the temple and sit gazing at the 180-degree view of the Somerset countryside. The River Severn glints like a Christmas ribbon.

Having evidently left their gifts and secured peace in the Middle East, the Americans are now being urged by their leader to 'work quickly'. I hear a crazed clicking of cameras.

'Have you got a panoramic shot? Work quickly.'

I begin the descent. Halfway down I come across a creature that could have been a yeti. Dressed in a mouldy Barbour the size of a pup tent, he is poking at tufts of grass with a shepherd's crook and talking to himself in Standard Received BBC English.

How I love the eccentrics of this green and pleasant land!

I leave the Tor as if in a dream. It is a timeless and sacred place steeped in legend, symbolism and atmosphere.

Beneath the symbol is the Truth and to the pure in heart it shall indeed be revealed.

The poetry of the soul writes itself at Glastonbury.

I drive back to Hampton Court with a bottle of water from the Chalice Well. I post it to my mother in South Africa.

She is unimpressed.

FML.

26

MEAN GIRLS

THE WIKIPEDIA ENTRY for *The Sunday Times* (South Africa) includes this section:

Jani Allan sued the British broadcaster Channel 4 for libel over affair allegations involving her and Eugène Terre'Blanche. Allan had previously interviewed the AWB leader for the Sunday Times. Allan had already settled out of court with the London Evening Standard and Options magazine over similar allegations.

The then-news editor of the newspaper, the late Marlene Burger and newspaper astrologer Linda Shaw testified against Allan. Prior to the libel suit, Allan had published articles for the newspaper dismissing the affair allegations. Allan also allowed the newspaper to publish answerphone messages left by Terre'Blanche as well as her threats of taking legal action against Terre'Blanche for nuisance contact.

Allan lost the case; the judge ruled that she had not been defamed but did not conclude whether or not an affair had taken place.

The case became notorious for violence and a dirty tricks campaign. Publications such as the Financial Mail and Allan herself speculated that the defense witnesses were paid by the De Klerk regime in an attempt to destabilise the far-right in South Africa.

Shaw recounted her editor, Ken Owen's reaction to the case:

'When I came back from London, Owen stood in the middle of the newsroom and said: "You have single-handedly destroyed the reputation of every journalist in the country and we have become the laughing stock."'

*

Marlene Burger and I became chums after I was sent to interview Terre'Blanche about the Strijdom Square shooting and Tertius Myburgh had asked us to work on the story together. It was Marlene's job to approve the copy and she did so with a lot of 'he's damn right' mutters. 'He [meaning Terre'Blanche] is the only one who knows what is coming down the road,' she said.

Marlene's tacit approval of Terre'Blanche was understandable. She was an Afrikaner. She was part of his tribe. She spoke his language. She loved his poetry.

Her life revolved around the newsroom and her job as deputy news editor. From the moment we left the *Sunday Times* in the early hours of a Sunday morning until Tuesday morning when we reconvened for news conference, she spent the time combing every news publication she could get her hands for story ideas.

We were both in the habit of staying late at the office and soon she began inviting me back to her little home in Malvern, where she would polish off a box of wine and tell me about the man she had been in love with for some 20 years. They had met when they were working together at Armscor. Apparently for security reasons, involved couples cannot work together at Armscor and so she was let go.

He was married.

On Christmas Day she would put up a little tree and he would leave his bigger tree (and family) in Pretoria to spend a few stolen hours with her.

I knew nothing of his identity. I would hear her talking about the G5 rocket and how he was on some covert mission to Iraq – or, as he called it, 'Lapkopland'.

One night after visiting with her I drove back to Sandton and found a tiny kitten under a parked car. I called Marlene. She was my go-to friend. We were so close at the time that I asked her advice on everything,

'What should I do with it?' I asked her.

'Keep him. He may give you some love,' she said.

Thus I came to have a tuxedo kitty in my life. I called him Sylvester.

Marlene became my confidante. We were fast friends in the office – her office was next door to mine – and even closer after work.

We were an unlikely pair. She was short and stubby, homely in crimplene. I was going through my glamorous phase. We both smoked at least 60 cigarettes a day. In my case it was Camels. She used a filter. It was permanently plugged into her mouth.

Marlene was newsroom smart and down to earth. She seemed to 'get' me. She seemed to 'get' that I had been employed by Tertius Myburgh as a commodity he could sell every Sunday morning. She wasn't cultivated smart. She wouldn't know about *The Marriage of Figaro* or the Archaic smile on a Greek kouros figure, but she knew how a newspaper worked and what stories would get traction. She knew how to edit a piece without mangling it. She could write a snappy slug line. She had grit and guts and held her own in what was then a predominantly male-dominated world.

When I was admitted to hospital with my bleeding ulcer she was the first person to show up to visit me. And when I was released from hospital she would check on me every night before going to sleep. Hers was the last phone call of the day and the first phone call of the morning. She blamed Terre'Blanche for my fragile state of health. 'I wish he would fuck off and leave you alone,' she said. Marlene always swore like a sailor.

If Terre'Blanche had called and left a message (between the pips on the pay phone), I would play the message to her and we would giggle like teenagers. More than anyone, she knew how Terre'Blanche was fixated on me.

When I called Martie Terre'Blanche to beg her to tell him to stop phoning me, Marlene knew all about it.

'What the fuck does he think? Does he really think you would live in Ventersdorp? And how would you get your Estée Lauder delivered? Would it be air-dropped in?'

Laugh? We thought our knickers wouldn't dry!

Marlene was with me the day the 'estate manager's men' came to my flat to see where a limpet mine might feasibly be secured.

I left for London and didn't have access to my own phone, so we didn't call each other but there was never any bad blood between us. Or so I thought.

Was she toeing the party line? Was she advised by the government to testify against me in the libel case I brought against BBC's Channel 4? I don't know. What I do know is that I was beyond stunned that she insisted that I had confided in her that I had had an affair with Terre'Blanche.

That wasn't how the conversation went at all, Marlene. Wherever you are now, you know that isn't how it went down.

I heard of her death when I was in America. She died as she had lived. Alone. I wasn't surprised that she died of a heart attack. She was overweight and smoked too much. Even for a journalist.

When did the slow motor of hating me start?

*

Linda Shaw was the most obnoxious woman I had ever met. I liked her instantly. She had a smokey laugh, an exploded armchair hairstyle and long, long earrings that lurched and swung as she spoke. Her laugh was like blood gargling from a cut throat.

She called everyone '*ou bees*' and professed to hate babies. She carried a giant tote bag like an elephant's scrotum. She was an Amazon. She was reckless and fearless.

She lived in some undesirable suburb. Her flat-mate Alison was a dangerous girl too. It was rumoured that when Bonnie, some bloke she was dating, annoyed her, perhaps because she became pregnant, she and Linda smashed his motorbike.

I was married to Gordon at the time I met Linda, and living in manicured luxury in Linksfield. I drove a Mercedes 450SL and had ten perfect manicured nails. Gordon warned me about her. 'She'll get you into trouble,' was his prediction.

Tertius warned me about Linda too. 'She won't do your image any good,' he said, clamping on his pipe.

I ignored both of them. Linda was fun. She said unthinkable things. Whatever we did together would turn into an adventure. When she started working for the magazine section of the *Sunday Times* we shared a common profession.

We would go to Rumours in Rockey Street in Yeoville and scream with laughter. We went to gym together at Janis and Malcolm Dorfman's and afterwards we would lounge around in our leotards and suck Maynard's sour-balls and talk and laugh. Everything with Linda was unexpected and outrageous.

When I was invited to interview the actor John Savage at Sun City – the trip was a Sol Kerzner private plane job – I asked Linda to come with me. We went to many press junkets and lunches together, to fashion shows, movies, restaurants. Wherever I was invited, I asked her to come with me. Linda was my Plus One.

She would tell me about interviews that she had gone on and I would tell her about my experiences. At the time she was dating Trent, an art gallery chappie. One day Linda opened his mail and found a letter from a girl he was planning to marry. The girl was in England.

'There were even pictures of the wedding dress!' she wept. She was distraught.

By then, sadly, Gordon and I were over and I was looking for somewhere else to live. I imagined that by sharing a flat with Linda, I was saving her from suicide. It seemed like a good idea.

*

My half of the flat was cream suede minimal. Linda's was black and orange with crazy spiders sown on the curtains. We were so different that we had to have separate fridges.

Linda had a gorgeous singing voice and she would lie on the floor practising her breathing exercises.

I was the annoyingly diligent one, up at 7am, eating a poached egg on toast and at my VDT at the *Sunday Times* by 8:30 am.

Linda would invariably have been out partying the night before. There was a drum next to her bed in which she threw empty tequila bottles.

I have always been complicated about sex.

In my books it's either/or. Either love or sex. I am rather with Andy Warhol when he said, 'Sex is more exciting between the pages of a book than between the sheets of a bed.' Linda said she never trusted a man until she slept with him. I wouldn't sleep with a man unless I trusted him. Of course Linda's sexual behaviour was appropriate for the '80s and for the fact that she was a highly attractive, sexual creature at the time.

Stan Katz said that Linda was the roadie and I was the rock star. 'If you can't sleep with the rock star, you sleep with the roadie.'

Linda was interviewed by *Style* magazine once. She said this about me:

Jani's greatest weapon is her mind-boggling intellect which she employs with relentless stamina. Whether she uses it to convince you that the world is square or that you should feel guilt-ridden about some misdemeanour, she will stick to her point ...

People who claim to hate her (and there are many) find themselves falling in love with her.

Jani spends much of her time on her own, thinking or reading, or watching the same movie over and over. Her heavily painted image mostly serves to cover her innate shyness and fear of crowds. She often fails to arrive at functions because her courage has deserted her at the last minute ...

Her superbitch image has been fabricated for her own protection.

*

What wasn't I reading between the lines? When did Linda's motor of hate start?

I can only write about Linda as I saw it. If Linda saw herself as my acolyte or devotee, I cannot say that I saw this. Perhaps I embodied the Dionysus myth. I attracted devotees who in the end tore me to pieces. It is a precarious thing, being the object of someone's devotion or attention, because inevitably they will become disillusioned and then they blame not themselves but the object of their lost affection for the plight they find themselves in.

So it was, I think, with Linda.

I always thought that Linda had her own shimmering Neptunian magic, which exerted its unique seductive spell on men. Perhaps, as someone suggested, we were Rose Red and Snow White from the fairy tale, each with her own individual personality and personal destiny. Rose Red and Snow White. If I were rewriting that fairy tale, I would make a happy ending for both of those girls – because they both deserved one.

Linda was Rose Red and she chose to get bloody with me when she got cross.

I must have annoyed her no end. I can imagine the glee with which she invented the most ridiculous image she could – me underneath Terre'Blanche while two bodyguards looked on – to damn me forever.

When I said she should put a turnstile on her bedroom door, I didn't say it judgementally. Perhaps I said it half-yearningly. I wished that I could give myself over to abandon, like Linda could, but how could I with a mother like mine?

A friend claims about Linda that 'in her heart I think she has suffered terribly for having betrayed you as a friend'. (I am not sure about people 'suffering in their heart'. How does one ever know whether someone is 'suffering in their heart'?)

Some may say that it really doesn't matter, after all this time, whether Linda betrayed me or not.

But you see, dear reader, I think it does.

She destroyed my life. And my future.

*

A friend writes to me. 'Of course I am not dismissing the immense pain that Linda brought to you. But I have also read in a story Linda saying how the trial totally destroyed her own life and confidence too.'

Up to a point, Lord Copper.

After Linda delivered to the world that image of me flattened beneath a large white bottom, all hopes of empire collapsed.

The image has been an albatross around my neck for more than a quarter of a century.

'I know,' writes my friend, 'that Linda was flown in to give evidence against you and that she delivered damning evidence through her keyhole-peeping evidence but I know that you have maintained (and others have supported you on this) that Linda spoke before the trial of attempting to "get you" with her evidence. In that sense, she did destroy your life because she was one of the knife stabs against your own body of testimony at the trial.'

Of course Linda was not the sole agent of my destruction. There was also the apartheid government using me as a tool to demolish the right-wing faction. There was the vengeful right-wing faction itself that was furious with me for having supposedly compromised the reputation of their great Leader. And there was the mysterious and malicious person who stole my diary and delivered it to the courthouse in London. In fact there were many others with their own petty agendas who spoke against me. They were all like the assassins of Caesar, taking their opportunity to wield the knife.

I remain bemused by Linda's actions, however. What did I consciously or unconsciously do to elicit that kind of response from her at the trial? Why in the end did she come to hate me so much?

Linda was never vaultingly ambitious as a journalist. She did the least amount of work she could coast by on. She was more interested in her current boyfriend.

Soon after I interviewed Terre'Blanche for the first time – Linda even went to an AWB meeting with me as a laugh – she took up with

Martin Kahnowitz, who lived across town. The more involved she became with Martin, the more time she spent away from the flat. Soon she had pretty much abandoned the flat altogether and eventually she moved in with him.

There were no corridor wars, no angry notes left on the fridge. The most pernicious thing I ever did to Linda was annex my bedroom with the en suite bathroom.

27

THE COURT CASE PART 1

PREPARING FOR A COURT CASE is like wading through the Book of
Deuteronomy. Endless, time-consuming and, frankly, tedious.

There are endless communications from Peter Carter-Ruck, and
from DJ Freeman, the solicitors acting for Channel 4. Countless
faxes are sent to South Africa in search of documentation. I speak to
Charlotte, Carter-Ruck's assistant, half a dozen times a day.

The diary I had kept while I was in hospital is lost in the post. Dr
Stampanoni, my doctor in South Africa, reports that my files have
been stolen from his office. These files would have proved that I was
suffering from a bleeding ulcer and hospitalised dramatically during
the precise time it was said I was having sex with Eugène Terre'Blanche.

Twice a day I go for long walks in Bushy Park at Hampton Court
Palace. I try and remember what Sir Thomas More said:

*'God made the angels to show Him splendour – as He made the
animals for innocence and plants for their simplicity. But man He
made to serve Him wittily in the tangle of his mind! If He suffers us
to fall to such a case there is no escaping ...'*

Charmain Naidoo is now working in the London office of the
Sunday Times in Hatton Garden. She calls to find out what I will be
wearing for the court case.

'Armani on Monday? Ralph Lauren on Tuesday? Come on, sweetie.
You were the star columnist on the Sunday Times. We all remember
how you used to dress.'

Her glee at my impending ordeal is palpable.

'Don't worry about it,' says my friend Andrew Broulidakis. 'It's the old, "kill your idol" syndrome.'

John Souglides and his wife Christine have been infinitely kind. Christine used to ride my ponies in Bryanston. She has lent me an entire wardrobe of clothes to wear to court.

Carter-Ruck has advised me to wear black. 'And no make-up!' adds Charlotte sternly.

'My dear,' Carter-Ruck reassures me, 'I have never advised a client to take a libel action through to trial unless I considered the chances of success to be at least 85%. That's the highest percentage to which I would ever accord any case since of course in all litigation there is the elemental risk of the improbable emerging to defeat a case: a bad witness, apparent prejudice on the part of the judge, unexpected evidence emerging and, particularly in a case with political overtones, a prejudiced jury.'

Who am I to question him? After all, he wrote the book on libel. *Carter-Ruck on Libel and Slander.*

Moanday, Tearsday, Wailsday … the days fall soundlessly and impotently back to earth. The impending court case has cast a shadow over my life which has caused the days to blur. I am filled with trepidation and impatience in equal parts. I am impatient to be liberated from this prison of anticipation. The civil wilderness of sleep eludes me most nights until almost daybreak.

*

19 JULY 1992

The court case begins tomorrow. At sunset I go for a long walk in the Palace gardens beyond the Long Water. Even the trees seem to stand in mute prayer. Every instinct tells me that this court case will be a life-changing event. A thousand volts of longing shoot through me to be with my bossy, wise, strong mother who is in South Africa.

20 JULY 1992

Lord, let the truth prevail. My first thought on waking. As the sun rises like an orange monocle from night's waistcoat, I dress for the first day of the trial. I light a cigarette, listen to Bach, and breathe deeply.

Charles Gray is the silk who has been hired by Carter-Ruck. He is regarded as one of the most brilliant and venerated QCs in England. By his skill the reputations of some of the most famous in the land have been maintained or destroyed. His libel triumphs have included the biggest-ever jury award of £1.5 million for Lord Aldington, £200 000 for Jason Donovan against the *Face* magazine for homosexual allegations, and, perversely, the most celebrated £50 000 for *Coronation Street*'s Bill Roache for the claim that he was 'boring'.

Acting for Channel 4, George Carman's successes as a libel lawyer have been defeating the Yorkshire Ripper's wife, Sonia Sutcliffe, on behalf of *The News of the World*, defending Norman Tebbit against libel action brought by a Labour council leader, and winning £35 000 pounds for Jason Connery over claims that he had displayed cowardice.

As a criminal barrister, his triumphs have included successfully defending Jeremy Thorpe on his conspiracy to murder charge, and Peter Adamson on charges of indecently assaulting two eight-year-old girls.

*

Charles Gray gives his opening speech in which the identities of the lead characters are established and the plot broadly outlined.

'This is an action for damages for libel. The plaintiff who complains that she has been libelled is Miss Jani Allan. Miss Allan complains that she has been libelled in a programme broadcast on television by Channel 4 on 4 April 1991 and which was re-broadcast twice subsequently.

'The company responsible for those broadcasts is Channel 4 Television Company Ltd. They are the defendants in the action and are represented by George Carman.

'I will shortly show the whole broadcast so that you can see the parts complained of by Miss Allan in their context. I shall also explain what libel is and what questions who has to answer in this case. But first it is necessary to tell you about the background. Though the broadcast of which Miss Allan complains was transmitted in the United Kingdom, many of the events with which this action is concerned took place in South Africa.'

Charles Gray has a detached manner and a rangy, vaguely aristocratic bearing. It occurs to me that he is the kind of man you'd expect to see wearing a cravat to Sunday lunch at a rather posh pub in Esher. It's a pity that the members of the jury look as though they'd be more at home in the local in Tooting.

A brief biography of me follows. My academic qualifications – BA Fine Arts (Hons); post-grad high school teaching diploma; teacher's exam in classical music. Then my career as a journalist.

'Miss Allan will not seek to disguise the importance of her career; she was keen to succeed and achieved great success. She joined the Sunday Times in 1980. Probably it is the most influential Sunday "heavy" in South Africa with a circulation of some 4 million.

'You should also know that because South African politics has a part to play in this action, that the South African Sunday Times is largely controlled by the government. It has fairly been described as part of the apparatus of state in South Africa. Miss Allan had her own full-page column in the Sunday Times which consisted of comments, interviews, etc., called "Just Jani". "Just Jani" grew into "Jani Allan's Week" and then Miss Allan was given an even greater profile when her column became "Face to Face with Jani". Miss Allan not only wrote up interviews, but also took her own photographs. She developed her own distinctive style – a striking turn of phrase combined with a tongue-in-cheek/ironical approach. She was in no sense a political journalist but interviewed celebrities and politicians, both local and international.

'In 1989 she was voted the most famous person in Style magazine. Previously she was on a list of one of the most admired people in South Africa.'

Gray sails on. Each time I met with Terre'Blanche is described. The Paardekraal incident is included:

'Miss Allan drove to the monument as arranged on the 27th December. She parked her car in Market Square outside the Town Hall. The television crew was already there. Terre'Blanche arrived and, seeing Miss Allan's sports car, suggested that she get into his car in order to save her from driving over the rough terrain to the monument. The television crew went ahead and Mr Terre'Blanche and Miss Allan followed, stopping only to buy cigarettes.

'No sooner had they arrived at the monument than no less than six police vehicles dramatically appeared. Terre'Blanche was questioned and subjected to a body and car search. With equal suddenness the police left.

'The next day Miss Allan's editor instructed her to write an account of this bizarre incident.

'Going out of chronological order to complete the curious story of Paardekraal: after an interval of some three months, Terre'Blanche was charged with malicious damage to property. It was alleged that he damaged the gate to the monument. Miss Allan was subpoenaed to give evidence first for the prosecution and then for the defence. In the end she was required to do neither. The case was thrown out of court when the police admitted that they had lied and fabricated evidence and that there was no other explanation for the incident but that it was a plot to discredit the AWB leader.

'Going back in time to the end of 1988. What Miss Allan did not appreciate was that the incident at Paardekraal was going to provoke wide-spread gossip in the press to the effect that she and Mr Terre'Blanche were having an affair. In fact she was doing nothing of the kind but tongues started wagging – very likely encouraged by those anxious to discredit Terre'Blanche politically.

'Miss Allan was hurt by the publication of these wholly false rumours but at this stage was able to put a brave face on it. She expected the story would be a nine-day wonder and people would lose interest.

'Another unforeseen and certainly unwanted development after Paardekraal was that Terre'Blanche started to pester Miss Allan. It became apparent that he had developed an obsession with her, although it was not reciprocated in any way.

'From early 1989 Terre'Blanche began pestering Miss Allan, usually on the phone. Calls to Miss Allan were taken by others on instruction of the editor.

'Calls to Miss Allan at her flat were recorded on her answer phone. These taped calls were numerous and often in the middle of the night, when Terre'Blanche was obviously drunk.

'Not content with attempting to contact her by phone, Terre'Blanche plagued Miss Allan by leaving notes at her flat. On another occasion he turned up and when Miss Allan refused to open the door, he simply slept – passed out – on the doorstep.

'What effect did this have on Miss Allan and her health?

'Well, rumours of the affair did not die down. Journalists would not drop a juicy and titillating bone such as this was.

'The situation put intolerable strain on Miss Allan. She became physically ill. She decided to put the matter in the hands of the Sunday Times lawyers. But first she called Terre'Blanche's wife in order to beg her to get him to desist from pestering Miss Allan. Mrs Terre'Blanche was sympathetic but impotent.

'Miss Allan's lawyers then sent a letter to Mr Terre'Blanche threatening an injunction.

'Rightly or wrongly, Myburgh took the view that Miss Allan was there to report news and not to make it. Only when it became searingly apparent that the rumours were not going away, did he relent to the extent of publishing a story on 23 July 1989 which was headed "Enough is enough", recording Miss Allan's categorical denial of any kind of romantic entanglement with Terre'Blanche.

'The remorseless pressure building up over months culminated in the horrifying experience of having a bomb planted on the outside wall of her flat. Luckily she escaped injury. Myburgh saw the position had become intolerable and sent Miss Allan to London within the week to get her out of South Africa.

'The editor also saw fit to publish the contents of the message machine tapes. The Sunday Times saw political dividend in discrediting Terre'Blanche.

'Miss Allan's departure to London effectively marked the end of her career as a journalist in South Africa. She had reached full peak and her fall was correspondingly bruising.

'Add to this, the fact that within weeks of transferring her to the

London office, Tertius Myburgh called to advise her that he had hired another columnist and Miss Allan was fired.

'I apologize for the lengthy background. Now we move on to April 1991 ...'

At this point the court is shown Channel 4's film.

After the screening, Gray continues:

'You may feel that journalistically it was a worthless programme, but viewers were not left in much doubt that Jani Allan had had an affair with the repulsive Terre'Blanche. Why else would Terre'Blanche be deemed "sensitive" to questions about her? And what of the emotive language that was used – "*found* on the steps of Paardekraal with former model turned journalist"? There are blatant inaccuracies about Terre'Blanche being arrested. He wasn't arrested. Neither were they *found* on the steps.

'And finally we have "although the affair was never proved" – the implication being that it happened but no one can prove it.

'How does Channel 4 respond? In the beginning, Channel 4 says loud and clear: "We've never suggested any impropriety between Miss Allan and Mr Terre'Blanche. There was nothing sexual or romantic. The relationship between them was like that of a solicitor with his client."

'They insist that there is nothing defamatory about their programme. They then transmit a disclaimer of intention to suggest an affair ... So although initially Channel 4 says they never made suggestions of adultery, when the time comes to serve their defences they shift ground completely. They now say it is true and Miss Allan did have an adulterous affair with the neo-Nazi.'

Gray trailers the charges that Channel 4's witnesses will be making against me.

'First we have sex in the flat. This was supposed to have happened in May 1988. Please note the date.

'It is Channel 4's case that in May 1988 Linda Shaw, the then flat-mate of Miss Allan, looked through the keyhole of Miss Allan's bedroom door and saw Miss Allan naked having sex with Mr Terre'Blanche. Not only that but also in the bedroom, according to Linda Shaw, were two bodyguards of Mr Terre'Blanche.

'It is unclear whether they were watching or participating.

'One of the central issues, perhaps the central issue for you to resolve, is whether that incident took place ...'

As Gray concludes his opening speech I glance at the jury. I fervently hope that I am wrong, but it looks as if two of them have nodded off.

Politics in a country six thousand miles away. The Paardekraal episode. The ulcers. Published tape-recordings. The flat being bombed. It's a pretty indigestible menu that Gray has served up to what appear to be solid ploughman's lunch types.

Perhaps if I were one of the jury I'd have nodded off too.

21 JULY 1992

Gray's opening speech, which has been reported in all the papers, has piqued the media's interest. Today there are dozens of photographers waiting outside the High Court when Carter-Ruck, Charlotte and I arrive.

My cross-examination begins with the kind of chappy invitation to share an intimacy preferred by television agony aunts.

'Would you commit adultery with a married man?'

('Dial 070831222 if the answer is "yes"; if the answer is "no" dial 070831223 ... Meanwhile we have Babs on the line from Bermondsey to tell us about her experience ...')

The man inviting me to answer the question is George Alfred Carman QC. Carman is the most feared criminal barrister in England.

From the pulpit of the witness box I gaze down at Peter Carter-Ruck. With his lank hair, his black jacket and unmatched trousers he looks like a character from Dickens.

'Would. You. Commit. Adultery. With. A. Married. Man?' repeats my inquisitor with exaggerated patience.

Carter-Ruck's sepulchral face offers no clues as to how I should answer.

In the packed press benches puzzled looks exchange owners. No one has the least idea where this is going, least of all me. Is the question phrased in present indicative or past perfect? The silence in court is heavy as a water-logged boat.

I toy briefly with asking Carman whether he would ever kill someone, a question which to my mind raises equipollent conditional clauses, but I remember my barrister's caveat to answer only 'yes' or 'no'.

ALLAN: No [uncertainly].

CARMAN [smirks briefly]: Have you seen *this*, Miss Allan?

Like an amateur magician producing a rabbit from a hat he triumphantly brandishes a hard-cover notebook. Electricity runs through the court like a silent fuse.

My heart stops. Then it begins pounding in my temples. The last time I saw the notebook was in the room I was staying in at Gillian Faulkner's home in Epping Forest. I can picture it clearly. It was on the lower ledge of a bureau.

I desperately try to remember precisely what ammunition the notebook might contain. Since I had written it almost a decade previously, I can't. I do vaguely remember it to be filled with deeply personal, tear-stained scribblings.

Justice Potts peers down at Carman myopically.

JUSTICE POTTS: What is it that you have there, Mr Carman?

CARMAN: It's a diary, My Lord.

The word 'diary' is pronounced as if it were an unpleasant disease. The diary, Carman says, was delivered to the High Court by a motorbike messenger and addressed to him personally.

His professed mystification as to the origins of this manna from muckrakers' heaven is disingenuous. His intention as to what he intends to do with it becomes clear when the court usher, a kindly snaggle-toothed cove, hands it up to the witness box. The icy hand fumbling about my guts now finds a firm grip.

CARMAN: Turn to the back of the diary, if you will, Miss Allan.

GRAY: I object, My Lord ...

The proceedings have lurched from the trite to the shocking. Clearly it is time for the jury to be sent out. This will enable Justice Potts to pretend to preside authoritatively over the quarrel without any of its contents being either understood by the jury or reported by the press.

GRAY: My learned friend is proposing to cross-examine Miss Allan on the contents of a stolen document which has no relevance to the case and, furthermore, was not included in the submissions.

Carman bounces to his feet. Small, pointed pink hands make Uriah Heep gestures in the direction of the judge.

CARMAN: I humbly submit, My Lord, that my learned friends are, with respect, wrong on this matter. It is perfectly reasonable to cross-examine the witness on this notebook since it goes to matters of credit. But of course I am in Your Lordship's hands …

I fight the urge to scream. My learned friend. I humbly submit. The hypocrisy of the straight-jacketed language of the English legal system.

The judge glances at the clock on the wall. It's nearly lunchtime. He grants an adjournment until two o'clock. The feeling of disappointment in the courtroom is tangible.

✻

After the musty, cloistered cool of Court 14, the Strand seems like a fun-filled fairground seen from a spinning roundabout.

Charles Gray, his black gown flapping angrily like an un-guyed wigwam, strides back to his chambers in Gray's Inn. Carter-Ruck, Charlotte and I hurry after him.

How I envy the carefree tourists, the office workers popping out for a pint and a packet of crisps. I would gladly swap places with the beggar into whose hat I automatically toss a coin.

It was Charles Gray who had approached Peter Carter-Ruck and offered his services to me.

It was rather odd that on the three occasions that I had had 'cons' (as Charlotte calls conferences) with him, I had been left with the feeling that he disliked me intensely. His manner towards me was a mixture of scorn and distaste. The manner of a hairdresser faced with a particularly difficult head of hair.

At Gray's chambers Carter-Ruck, Charlotte and I are shown into his office. The diary lies malignantly on his desk, a time-bomb waiting to explode.

Magazine shoot for Fair Lady, *2000.*

Riding Emperor Maestoso in Kyalami, Laddie Chester trains, 1989.

With Barbara Ickinger and Melanie Millin-Moore, my PR friends.

With Chris Ball in London, 1990.

With MP Koos van de Merwe in London, 1991.

With film producer Roy Boulting at the Groucho Club in London, 1991.

All the money in the world! Spy wages! Hampton Court.

The Tor in Glastonbury, Somerset, UK, 1990.

In a fog outside Hampton Court Palace, London, 1990.

On the beach in Cascais, Portugal, 1991.

My mother arrives at Heathrow, London for a visit, 1991.

Punting on the River Cam in Cambridge, UK, 1991.

Biking with Jane Dutton in Epping Forest, 1991.

With Ria Saunders in the Yorkshire Dales, 1993.

Outside the High Court of Justice with Andrew Broulidakis, 1993.

With Cliff Saunders in Geneva, Switzerland, 1994.

I have just been given Tinytot How High T'
Moon! I am over the moon in Clifton, 1997.

At the Mount Nelson with Bantu Holomisa and Christo
Gerlach, 1997.

Up in the flying machine in Stellenbosch, 1998.

In Johannesburg at Kate's house wearing a long white dress and army boots – to keep it real – 1998.

With Mario Oriani-Ambrosini and Suzanne Vos in Cape Town, 1999.

With Kate Souglides in Johannesburg, 1999.

With Samantha Walt and Christo Gerlach doing a shoot on Clifton Beach, 2000.

*In Madison Avenue, New York, 2001.
Tiggy is in her little traveller.*

*Tinytot Miss Tiggywinkle – the heartbeat
at my feet.*

With Mark Lloyd in Clifton, 1999.

*With Tinytot Miss Tiggywinkle at ME, the local hairdresser in New Hope,
Pennsylvania.*

With China in Lambertville, New Jersey.

'This,' Gray prods the book distastefully, 'is Christmas for George Carman.'

Even the paper with which I had covered the book – an award-winning photograph from a De Beers diamond catalogue featuring a close-up of a bracelet and a pair of women's lips – embarrasses me acutely.

Gray's patrician demeanour has given way to pop-eyed agitation. 'What else will he come up with? What's in the diary?' he demands.

I shrug miserably. I can't recall. I had used the notebook to scribble random thoughts a decade ago. But one thing is certain: its contents have nothing whatsoever to do with Terre'Blanche.

'Carman will destroy you with that diary. You might as well give up.' Gray bites heartlessly into a sandwich. 'You'll lose the case.'

I turn to Carter-Ruck in desperation. 'How can anything I wrote in a personal jotter have any bearing on the case? I can't give up. I didn't have an affair with Terre'Blanche. We must go on.'

Carter-Ruck looks uncomfortable. The telephone rings. Gray takes the call.

'That was someone calling to warn me that if you go on with the case you will be killed.'

*

2 PM

Courtroom QB 14 is as packed as a Japanese subway.

I have been told that Carman spends weeks preparing his cross-examination. He even practises in front of a mirror before a case: a ham that can't be cured rehearsing his lines. One has serious doubts that he could ad lib breaking wind after a bowl of baked beans.

Despite having averred that he has only just received the diary, and despite the fact that many pages are tear-sodden and the writing illegible, Carman is remarkably familiar with its contents. I am in no doubt that he has been in possession of my scribblings – or leastways a photocopy of it – for months.

I had been warned that Carman combines the skills and manner of a Jesuit catechist – remorseless, icy and calculating.

CARMAN: Turn to the back of the diary, Miss Allan.

The invitation is poisonously gentle. I do as he says.

Stapled into the back of the diary is a yellowing telex message from an Italian pilot I had met briefly when reporting on an air show in Durban.

CARMAN: Read it aloud.

I feel as though the blood in my veins has been replaced with skimmed milk.

The message is innocuous drivel, but now that it is skewered on the spotlight, what might have been romantic once is instantly reduced to ridicule and elevated to the sinister Portent of Adulteries to Come. The stilted grammar, so charming when spoken all those light years ago, suffers in translation when exhumed so cruelly.

CARMAN [reading aloud]: 'Charles says Riccardo will get a divorce and marry me.' Who is Charles, Miss Allan?

ALLAN: A gay clairvoyant.

There are titters in court.

CARMAN: Can you read that sentence?

ALLAN: It says his wife has a weak heart ... I can't read that word.

JUSTICE POTTS: What word is Mr Carman thinking of, Miss Allan?

I have to concentrate fiercely on not fainting.

Shaw once noted that when man wants to murder a tiger, he calls it sport. When the tiger wants to murder him, he calls it ferocity. Carman was having a great sporting time of it.

The public rape of my privacy continues.

Mills and Boon descriptions about drinking Champagne on the beach, kissing, etc. follow. I attempt to explain that on finding out that Riccardo was married, I had, in fact, broken off the relationship which, in any event since he was living in Somalia and later Italy, had been mainly confined to telephone calls. But the facts are of jejune importance.

I can feel Dori Weil's eyes burning tunnels of pity through the air as Carman goes his leisurely way, gouging each fresh wound.

Dori is a clinical psychologist and an old university friend of both myself and my ex-husband Gordon. She was aware that my marriage had broken down largely as a result of my obsession with my column and my lack of interest in sex. She is aware, too, of the hiatus that exists between my public image and my private insecurities.

Dori flew in to London yesterday and she is here to give evidence on my behalf. I gaze down at her lovely, kind face. She is clearly stunned as to how Channel 4's solicitors have gotten hold of the diary and incredulous as to why it is being allowed to be used against me in court.

I am brought sharply back into focus with Carman's next question.

CARMAN: How many men have you slept with?

He holds up an X-ray for the jury to see. I recognise it as one taken when I was admitted to hospital for traction. How the hell he had got hold of it is mind-boggling, and what on earth for?

CARMAN: Why does this X-ray show that you have a contraceptive device?

No wonder Carman's tactics are deplored by some of his colleagues, who liken his advocacy to a music hall production in which he is the stage manager, the producer and the leading actor. He has an uncommonly brilliant common touch. He plays to the jury with all the nuance of a stand-up seaside comedian.

I feel nauseous. Right now my only thought is for my mother, six thousand miles away.

What Carman fails to point out, necessarily, is that had the defendants presented the diary at discovery, I may have been able to call Riccardo as a witness. Instead, Channel 4 has contrived to keep their knowledge of the diary secret until I am on the stand.

As a legal ploy it is a tour de force.

Hume's principle states that however a man strikes matches, there can be no proof that the next one will burn. In criminal cases the law decrees that however many crimes a man has committed, he is entitled to be judged on the one before the court and no other.

Libel is entirely different.

Events real or imagined in the distant past, alleged conversations, ironic remarks out of context – all are transmogrified into weapons.

Theatre is what a trial is all about. To a barrister like Carman, his entire mind's a stage and the facts of a case are incidental to the development of the plot. Carman's aim is to prove to the jury that I am the sort of woman who commits adultery with the regularity of a mother's phone calls.

I am leaden with despair. The jury, I am sure, are already convinced of my guilt and the cross-examination of my dealings with Terre'Blanche haven't even commenced.

Carman warns me that he will be suggesting that I fell for Terre'Blanche and wanted to marry him.

'We will dispute that tomorrow,' I say wearily.

I am Nosferatu – undead – seeing, hearing, feeling nothing. Only when we're in the cab and Dori reaches over and squeezes my hand tightly do tears needle my eyes.

I am furious with myself. One does not cry for oneself. One cries at the sight of great art, at bravery, at the miracle of animals, at humans behaving with nobility.

I know that if I am to start crying now, I might never be able to stop.

28

THE COURT CASE PART 2

IRONICALLY, THREE WEEKS BEFORE THE TRIAL, Carman had been surprised at the intrusion and unwarranted invasion of his privacy when the *Daily Mail* had run a story in which it was pointed out that although in *Who's Who* Carman had admitted to just two dissolved marriages, the *Mail* had excavated, as it were, a third ex-wife, one Ursula Groves. (No doubt under cross-examination he would be able to explain his Ursula amnesia.)

But for three days it has not been Carman in the box suffering 'intrusion and unwarranted invasion of his privacy'. It's been me.

When Carman is on less solid ground and the edifice of 'fact' that he has laboriously built up threatens to disintegrate, he retreats smartly into those technical safety zones from justice, i.e. legal argument. During the legal arguments the jury is sent to their room and the press is not at liberty to report what transpired.

JUSTICE POTTS: Mr Gray, on behalf of the plaintiff, seeks to adduce in evidence the transcript of a telephonic conversation which took place between the plaintiff and Mrs Martie Terre'Blanche on 25th April 1989.

Carman bounces to his feet.

Gray had submitted that he was entitled to adduce the transcript in order to establish the fact that when the defendants allege the affair was going on, I had had a conversation with Mrs Terre'Blanche begging her to use her influence to stop her husband from contacting me.

Carman bounces again.

JUSTICE POTTS: I will hear what Mr Carman has got to say about that.

CARMAN: My Lord, I strongly object to that conversation being adduced. I am at a loss to understand how the conversation is probative of anything. Furthermore, were the fact that the conversation had been taped to be laid before the jury, the jury might be tempted to ask if they could see it, with consequences that would be unsatisfactory. Wholly unsatisfactory.

JUSTICE POTTS: I have heard what Mr Carman said. I have to say I cannot see how the fact that the conversation was taped is material ... I am only too aware that were the fact that this conversation was laid before the jury, then the jury might be tempted to ask if they could see it, with consequence, if any ruling is right, which would be unsatisfactory.

❖

Wholly unsatisfactory, it has to be said, for Channel 4's purposes.

One of Carman's accomplishments is being able to bully a judge while letting the judge believe that he is making the decisions.

The phrase that I will forever dread is: 'I am in your hands, My Lord.'

More accurately, this meant that Justice Potts was in Carman's small, pink hands.

❖

JUSTICE POTTS: I am in your hands, Mr Carman. I am against you, Mr Gray. The answer is no.

GRAY [shrugs]: My Lord, I now know where we stand.

❖

24 JULY 1992

Channel 4 is seeking to adduce the statement of Kys Smit, an ex-AWB secretary. Kys claims that I was goose-stepping with Terre'Blanche. Whether this was before he saw Terre'Blanche wearing the famous green underpants and my size 4 jeans around my ankles is not clear.

GRAY: Smit, for reasons that are wholly unexplained and apparently unexplored by the defendants, refused to allow even a note to be taken during the interview he had with Channel 4.

The witness statement was served not only unsigned and therefore not in compliance with the order of the court concerning the exchange of witness statements, but Carter-Ruck had written to Channel 4's solicitors three times asking whether Smit had ever actually seen the witness statement before it was served. An answer was never given.

Gray calls Janet Tomelin, Channel 4's solicitor.

GRAY: Did Mr Smit explain to you why he was refusing to let you make notes when you had your interview with him?

TOMELIN: No.

GRAY: Did he explain later to you that he was not prepared to put anything in writing?

TOMELIN: No.

GRAY: Did you ask him?

TOMELIN: He said that that was just the way he wanted to do it.

GRAY: Did you not ask him: 'Why? We need a statement from you for the purposes of the legal proceedings in London?'

TOMELIN: No, I did not.

GRAY: Did he ever see the witness statement that was served in his name?

TOMELIN: No, he did not.

GRAY: Are you aware that no less than three letters were written by my instructing solicitors to DJ Freeman asking that question: did he ever see the witness statement, and we never had an answer?'

TOMELIN: Yes.

CARMAN: Hnnnnh! HNNNNNH!

JUSTICE POTTS: Yes, Mr Carman?

CARMAN: Well, My Lord, here is a man on my instructions now subject to police protection in South Africa and his life is under threat. It is perhaps not surprising my learned friend says that he was reluctant to sign the statement.

GRAY: As I think may already be apparent to your Lordship, there is some sort of conspiracy operating here.

CARMAN: I hear what Mr Gray says, but I have no idea what he means talking about conspiracy. I really haven't the faintest idea.

JUSTICE POTTS: I am in your hands, Mr Carman. I am against you, Mr Gray.

It is difficult not to be gobsmacked by Carman's *volte face*. While I was being cross-examined he ritually derided the notion that this trial could have anything to do with discrediting an unpleasant political figure, anything at all to do with politics. Surely Smit would not be 'under police protection' if he were merely a civilian telling the truth?

✳

An extraordinarily kind neighbour offers tea and sympathy. Apparently, she sent some photographer packing after he offered her £500 if she would allow them to balance a ladder against her wall to sneak pictures of me in my flat.

I am comforted by a string of kind and supportive messages on my answering machine. One is from the Cowards, a family in Yorkshire who have become friends.

'Hello, Jani, what have you been up to? Anything exciting we should know about?'

I have to laugh out loud. Since it *is* the silly season, the case has been exhaustively covered by every publication from the local *Kingston Gazette* to *The Times*. There is international interest too. Every time I enter or exit the High Court I am mobbed by some 30 or 40 photographers. *Private Eye* is hugely enjoying what they have dubbed 'The Libel Case of the Century'.

I am Ms Luni, Justice Potts is Potty-trained, and Carman is Car phone. I am accused of being infatuated with the 'notorious Pieter Carterre-Fuck of the AWB (Avaricious Writ Brigade)'.

The court case has been featured on every television bulletin on every television network in the land. I have had telephone calls from friends who have read about the case in Italy, Germany, Australia and America.

I speak to my mother every night to brief her on the day's events in court. Although my mother is in South Africa, the press reports that she has been in court every day, 'a fragile, white-haired old lady with a mouth that works furiously …'.

*

24 JULY 1992
Gray calls Dori Cara Weil.

Unlike Channel 4, I did not have the money to fly a plane-load of witnesses to London for an all-expenses-paid jaunt, plus walking around money. Dori's ticket was paid for by Zeno Souglides, a generous and decent gentleman (and until now a complete stranger to me) who has been following the case from Milos.

Dori has been a practising clinical psychologist for 18 years. She lectures all over the world and has a high media profile in South Africa as a result of her regular television and radio appearances.

We first met when I was at Wits but I started seeing her professionally in September 1987, some five months before I interviewed Terre'Blanche for the first time. Because of the confidential nature of the psychologist–patient relationship, Dori was party to my most intimate thoughts.

GRAY: Did you in the course of that relationship get to know Miss Allan well?

DORI: Yes.

GRAY: Were you able, during the course of that treatment, in your capacity as her psychologist, to form an assessment as to her sexual character?

DORI: Yes.

GRAY: Could you answer the question?

DORI: Yes. I found her to have major sexual problems, both in her sexual desire and also in terms of relating to men sexually.

GRAY: On the basis of your treatment of Miss Allan, did you form the view that she is a person of loose morals, likely to be promiscuous, have adulterous affairs with men?

DORI: No.

GRAY: Can you develop what you are saying?

DORI: Part of the content of what we spoke about during those sessions concerned difficulties in her relationships with men, meaningful long-term relationships, not only as far as her sexuality is concerned.

GRAY: And you are saying based on that sort of material you arrived at the conclusion that you did as to the likelihood that she would engage in a promiscuous fashion.

DORI: Yes.

GRAY: Did you know about the article she had written about Terre'Blanche?

DORI: Yes.

GRAY: Were you continuing to see and treat her over the following months and over the period when Mr Terre'Blanche was, as she described, pestering her?

DORI: Yes.

GRAY: Was that something that came up in the course of your sessions with her?

DORI: Yes, definitely.

GRAY: Pause before you answer this question. Did you hear any tape-recordings played while you were seeing and treating Miss Allan?

DORI: Yes.

GRAY: Do you recall a particular tape-recording?

DORI: Yes.

GRAY: Between whom did you understand the conversation to have been tape-conducted?

DORI: I recall two tape-recordings that I heard. One was a tape on an answering machine and the other was a conversation between Miss Allan and Mrs Terre'Blanche.

GRAY: Did she tell you about –

CARMAN: Objection, My Lord!

JUSTICE POTTS: Yes, Mr Carman?

CARMAN: I humbly submit, My Lord, but I object strongly to Mr Gray's line of questioning.

JUSTICE POTTS: If there are going to be submissions, perhaps the jury ought to go and have lunch.

[In the absence of the jury]

CARMAN: My Lord, the objection I make is that on what basis in law can my friend invite this witness who is not a doctor to say what the plaintiff told her? My Lord, that is hearsay evidence and, My Lord, inadmissible.

Gray points out that his learned friend is relying on all manner of admissions said to have been made to his witnesses, and in those circumstances, he feels that he is entitled to lead evidence from someone who had a close knowledge of and professional relationship with me.

He points out that Carman is relying on the evidence of one Stevie Godson, a confession, almost, a boast, which she alleges that I made to her, a stranger on a plane journey.

(A film producer I have never heard of had called Gray's chambers from America. He wished Gray to know, he said, that he had had supper with Stevie Godson in South Africa two weeks prior to the trial. At the supper, he alleged, Godson admitted to him that her evidence was fabrication but that she was keen to avail herself of a free trip to London. He was so outraged by the farce that was unfolding in QB 14 that he had telephoned Gray.)

GRAY: Is it not beyond belief that Miss Allan would have confided in Mrs Godson, a mere acquaintance, at the same time that she was seeing Mrs Weil? Is it not ludicrous to suggest that Miss Allan, described as she is by so many people as 'a very private person' who, as a result of her high-profile column, had experienced what it is like to be in the full glare of the public spotlight for a decade and who grew to hate it – would it not be ridiculous that such a person would choose to confide in a one-time gossip columnist with whom Miss Allan had only a nodding acquaintanceship?

Carman strikes a thespian pose in preparation to sucking up to the judge.

He complains that he can't meet a 'surprise' witness like Ms Weil. He argues his case for some 70 minutes. It is a performance that would make a conger eel arthritic.

GRAY: My Lord, my reaction to what Mr Carman has said is that what is sauce for the goose is sauce for the gander. Mr Carman produced out of his back pocket that diary. We had not advance notice of it at all … now Mr Carman wants to have provided to him in advance notice of the evidence we put forward in response to that wholly unpredicted and unforeseen evidence used by him against Miss Allan. My Lord, I do not see why he should have that unilateral advantage.

But the judge apparently does see why Mr Carman should have that unilateral advantage, although he doesn't share it with us.

Dori is dismissed from the witness box. With her, too, all chances of repairing the damage Carman has done to my case by producing a stolen diary which had nothing whatsoever to do with Terre'Blanche.

We are done for the day.

As I am gathering up my papers a pretty young girl rushes up to me and hugs me warmly.

'I'm Nicky,' she says. 'You won't remember me but I used to be a big fan of yours in South Africa. Hang in there. Sorry I can't stay. I work in the City and just dashed out of my office to give you a hug.'

Dear girl. Will she ever know how much her gesture meant to me?

*

FRIDAY AFTERNOON

CARMAN: My Lord, the jury is going to be very cross with me because legal argument once more rears its ugly head.

Charlotte writes me a note: 'Even Killer Carman is exercised about Andrew's impending evidence.'

Carman objects to several assertions in Andrew Broulidakis's statement.

Andrew has said: 'Both my family and I have known Jani for more than 25 years. We know her to have Christian values. Over the years I have known many people who have become infatuated with Jani and attempted unsuccessfully to court her. These included highly eligible bachelors who were suitable escorts … that they failed to win her attention makes the allegation that she would become involved with someone like Terre'Blanche nothing short of ridiculous.'

CARMAN: My Lord, it is all under the sweeping umbrella of opinion! It is absolutely wild speculation!

JUSTICE POTTS: But surely Mr Gray is entitled to lay the ground for making the point in his speech about this witness?

CARMAN: But My Lord, it is almost certainly hearsay …

'Wild speculation' aside, Andrew's statement, which explains the circumstances in which Linda Shaw's allegations about me were made, has been causing Carman some anxiety.

CARMAN: It does not relate to the issue in the trial. It relates to the creditworthiness of a witness I have yet to call.

GRAY: To suggest that that goes to credit is to overlook the fact that if Mr Broulidakis is right, this witness called by the defendant to justify the allegation of an adulterous relationship by giving first-hand keyhole evidence of what had taken place, admitting that Miss Allan was a friend … Anything further away from mere credit one cannot imagine …

When Justice Potts agrees that Gray may lead evidence, Carman suppurates poisonously. He rumbles on about how he 'may have some human problems in getting his witnesses into the box'.

Before the court rises we are told that certain witness statements have been leaked to the press, both in the UK and in South Africa. The Attorney General has been notified.

Though all the chief protagonists are questioned, the front page headline in the South African papers reads 'JANI ALLAN QUIZZED BY SCOTLAND YARD'.

I am interviewed by a personable young man, one Detective Shipperlee at New Scotland Yard. Shipperlee asks what I think Gillian Faulkner's connection with my stolen diary and leaked faxes may be. The telephone number at the top of the faxes is identical to hers – only two digits have been transposed.

I tell him that both Barbara Robb and Victoria Channon – two of Gillian's friends – have made statements to the effect that they had both seen the diary on Gillian Faulkner's kitchen table and they had also heard her having conversations with Ben Hamilton, Channel 4's researcher.

27 JULY 1992

Andrew is sworn in.

Gray asks him why he had taken it upon himself to investigate the case.

BROULIDAKIS: Jani had confided in me that Linda Shaw was making serious allegations about her that were untrue. I have witnessed Miss Allan being befriended by multitudes and seen them turn on her viciously.

GRAY: When did you first meet Miss Shaw?

BROULIDAIS: I first met her in 1984 when we had a brief affair. At that stage it would be no exaggeration to say she was in awe of Miss Allan. I knew that Jani had been a good friend to her. When I was in South Africa I called her and she invited me to her birthday party lunch.

GRAY: What happened during the lunch?

BROULIDAKIS: Linda asked me several times about Jani Allan. During the lunch she became visibly inebriated and sat on my lap. I was uncomfortable because her boyfriend was at the same table.

GRAY: Can you tell us what happened?

BROULIDAKIS: I took the unusual step of carrying a tape-recorder in my pocket. Linda was anxious to talk about Jani Allan. Over ten beers and a number of whiskeys she began to speak freely about the court case. After some more drinking we returned to her apartment. She left the room and returned wearing only a T-shirt. She said, 'I never trust a man until I've fucked him.' She asked if she had a better body than Jani Allan. I asked why she kept bringing Jani into the conversation. She said, 'Shit, I can't help it. After all this time I'm still obsessed.'

GRAY: Then what happened?

BROULIDAKIS: We had sex three times in five hours.

GRAY: Was there any conversation about the court case?

BROULIDAKIS: She told me that she'd seen Channel 4's solicitors and that they had been very nice to her. She also said, 'I told them that I'd seen Jani through the keyhole of her bedroom door having sex with Terre'Blanche and two other men.' She furthermore admitted that this was a fabrication but she found it amusing. She said that the lawyers had told her that she was of major importance to their case as she was the only witness who could claim to have actually seen them having sex. She then said, 'Wouldn't it be a scream to have that frigid bitch nailed for gang-banging Nazis?'

GRAY: 'Would it be a scream to have that frigid bitch nailed for gang-banging Nazis?' Were those her words?

BROULIDAKIS: Yes. Those were her exact words.

GRAY: What did you reply to that?

BROULIDAKIS: I remarked that anyone knowing Jani Allan would not believe the allegation.

GRAY: What was her response?

BROULIDAKIS: She told me that she had her story down pat and that she would 'bullshit' her way through.

GRAY: What else did she say?

BROULIDAKIS: She said that since Jani had left South Africa, she had 'replaced' Jani at the Sunday Times and was now getting all the invitations that Jani used to get. She said that men always regarded Jani as this 'untouchable goddess' and whom they proposed marriage to, while she was the one 'they just wanted to fuck'. She then told me she was a student of astrology and showed me that she had done Jani's chart.

Then Carman cross-examines Broulidakis.

CARMAN: Do you normally have sex with women in order to get information out of them?

BROULIDAKIS: No. In this case the end justified the means.

Andrew tells the court that he had been in a dilemma over the embarrassment of giving such evidence.

BROULIDAKIS: The reason I did it was that ultimately I believe for evil to triumph it is necessary only for good men to do nothing. By telling the truth I saw myself doing what any decent human being would have done – albeit you make it sound as terrible as it does.

CARMAN: Did Jani Allan promise you a reward for your secret mission?

BROULIDAKIS: No.

CARMAN: So she did know that you were trying to get information out of Miss Shaw?

BROULIDAKIS: Yes, but she didn't know how I was doing it.

CARMAN: You were using alcohol as one of the weapons in your armory to get this woman into bed and persuade her to find you attractive.

BROULIDAKIS: She didn't need much persuading … in fact if the truth be told it is the closest I have come to being seduced.

CARMAN: You were seduced! You with your tape-recorder! You were trying to get incriminating confessions from her!

BROULIDAKIS: And succeeding.

Carman is caught on the back foot. He does what any criminal barrister caught unawares would do: he goes for the witness. He calls Andrew a down-market James Bond of the Greek Orthodox variety.

Earlier Charles Gray had read out my ex-husband Gordon Schachat's statement in which he said that our marriage had broken up because of my obsession with my career and my lack of interest in sex.

'I do not think that she has a normal approach to sex [Gordon wrote] and her sexy public image is totally at odds with her real personality, which is in effect shy, withdrawn and quite anti-social. She has an inability to form relationships. She is not an extreme right-winger and certainly not anti-Semitic.'

✳

The South African media revel in the drama. South African journalists and broadcasters have paid more attention to the courtroom revelations about the sex-life of a former colleague than to the visit of the United Nations special envoy Cyrus Vance and the referendum.

The case is the dinner-table talk of the country. The *Sunday Times* in South Africa writes:

The Jani Allan libel suit in London is arguably the best thing that has happened since rain stopped play in the World Cup cricket semi-final match. In a country which, as Miss Allan unkindly remarked, is woefully short of celebrities, the keyhole evidence of the unusual private life of a beautiful woman is the perfect antidote to depressing news. In the politically fragmented and sexually repressed country, the very idea of a steamy love affair between the Boer fanatic and the blonde columnist is enough to send the Afrikaners to church on a weekday. They are also flocking to buy *Beeld*, the Afrikaans language paper which has gone to town on the tale. No doubt there is mischievous intent by the government-leaning paper to discredit Terre'Blanche for once and for all ... the newspaper has linked up a phone hotline to the High Court in the Strand for a minute-by-minute report.

When the newspapers catch up with Terre'Blanche, he brushes the case aside as 'filth'.

'I'm busy preparing my people for war. The witnesses are bad and evil people who were tempted by free trips to London and who have been paid money to lie.'

Peter Carter-Ruck decides it will be useful to subpoena Jane Dutton, who had accompanied me to Donkerhoek for the Day of the Vow celebrations. Jane refuses point-blank. Her previous devotion to me appears to have been long forgotten. I have seen her in court, sitting in the press box gloating with the other South Africans.

29

THE COURT CASE PART 3

29 July 1992

Linda Shaw steps up to the witness box.

Perhaps it's the hair, but something about her appearance is eerily reminiscent of Charles II. Charles II wearing a purple mini-skirt and fishnet tights.

Linda appears to be heavily tranquillised. She describes how through the keyhole she had seen me lying on the bedroom floor with a large white male bottom going up and down between my raised knees. She could tell that the bottom belonged to the overweight extremist Eugène Terre'Blanche. She could tell the feet were mine 'because of the gnarled toes'.

CARMAN: Tell us again what you saw, Miss Shaw.

SHAW: A large white bottom.

CARMAN: A large white bottom. [Pause] A large. White. Bottom. SO you saw a Large … White … Bottom … [Protracted pause. Rolls reptilian eyes about courtroom] And where [lip curled in distaste] was this Large … White … Bottom?

SHAW: It was between her two knees …

CARMAN: There was movement up and down?

SHAW: Yes.

Educationalists agree that the usual optimal concentration span of university students at any one point of time is 20 minutes. It is difficult to see how the average juror will take in all the thousands of pages of evidence in a trial that may last weeks. They may be preoccupied with their incomplete tax returns. They may find a caraway seed embedded in a tooth an attention-consuming diversion.

But Carman has taken all this into account. One of his gifts as an advocate is to plant a lasting image or phrase in the minds of the jury.

No matter what the facts of the matter regarding my alleged relationship with Terre'Blanche, Carman determines to make sense of the tidal wave of information with which the jury are deluged by simplifying and summarising. Carman's dictum is roughly the same as one I remember from teachers' training college: 'Tell them what you are going to tell them. Then tell them. Then tell them what you've told them.'

Then there is the old canard that people who love sausages and jury decisions should never watch them being made.

*

Shortly after he has begun cross-examining Linda Shaw, Gray produces a lock with a keyhole, through which he proposes to invite the jury, and Miss Shaw, to peer in order to prove that it would have been physically impossible for her to have seen what she claims she saw.

Carman bounces to his feet like a midget Harlem Globetrotter.

CARMAN: OBJECTION!

This is the by-now familiar signal for the jury to leave the courtroom.

CARMAN: We all know how perilous it is to invite the jury to become involved in experiments of this nature.

The jury file out dutifully.

The lock and keyhole are not identical to the lock and keyhole on my bedroom door in the townhouse Linda and I shared in Johannesburg. Neither is the lighting the same. The conditions here in the London courtroom are different.

What Carman is saying may be valid for a *criminal* case, but what Gray was attempting to do was to illustrate the average view afforded through the keyhole of the average door. There must be such a thing as an average door or else locksmiths surely wouldn't be in business.

Carman's squabble in Latin is protracted and effective.

Again, the judge rules against Gray.

The most damning piece of evidence against me – Shaw's claim – the piece of evidence on which Channel 4's case hinges, is left unchallenged and untested.

I dig my fingers into my palms, willing myself not to start crying tears of sheer frustration. Despair at full throttle! The injustice of the justice system!

✻

The second Tom Sharpean set-piece concerns the attempt to squeeze a huge, drunken neo-Nazi into the dickie-seat of a sports car.

Although Shaw at first claims that the fatty and I had had sex in this minute car while she watched the proceedings demurely from where she was perched on a nearby wall, when pushed by Gray she reflects that intercourse itself had probably been impossible.

But, she insists, even a fatty like Terre'Blanche, when well oiled, could be squeezed into the luggage compartment of a tiny sports car.

She herself, she says, is capable of anything when she is drunk.

On the way home, she also says, the drunken racist had leaned over into the front seat and started whispering into her ear and stroking her hair.

At this point, according to my former flat-mate, I had thrown up.

✻

I spend the night in Knightsbridge with Christine and her husband John. When I return to my Hampton Court flat in the morning, I find it has been broken into. Both the sitting room and the study are awash with documents. The manuscript of *White Sunset*, the book about South Africa that I have been writing, has been taken.

Esher police station is notified and detectives are immediately sent round to take fingerprints. They ask me if I have reason to believe that Anthony Travers, the self-styled South African government spook who had attempted to befriend me is, involved.

31 JULY 1992

A statement from Terre'Blanche and his bodyguard Dave Barnett is faxed to Carter-Ruck's offices!

What finally prompted Terre'Blanche to swear to an affidavit was what he called 'the despicable attack on his character by Mr Smit'.

JUSTICE POTTS [to the jury]: Would you like a little break?

While the jury are drinking their 9 000th cup of tea during the trial, Carman explains to the judge that the late arrival of Terre'Blanche's statement is a 'wholly intolerable situation from the defendants' point of view'. Why, the defendants have themselves been trying to contact Mr Terre'Blanche to see if he would assist their side.

JUSTICE POTTS: We are talking about the exercise of my discretion to admit this evidence and surely the circumstances in which it was obtained must be relevant to that exercise, must they not?

I listen in utter disbelief. Why was my diary admitted, despite the fact that it was stolen and that its prejudicial effects outweighed probative value, and Terre'Blanche's statement might not be adduced?

Carman grizzles and says that efforts were not made to obtain a statement from Terre'Blanche.

What of Channel 4's convenient tardiness with regard to Smit's statement, I wondered?

GRAY: Between January and June Mrs Watson was given to understand by a number of people (and they are identified in a letter written in response to DJ Freeman's letter) that Mr Terre'Blanche was not willing to give evidence or become involved. The first indication that he might be willing to assist came from a South African lawyer, one Oeloff de Meyer, in July. As your Lordship will see –

JUSTICE POTTS: I intervened because you appear to be taking me to task –

GRAY: My Lord, I would not dream of taking your Lordship to task.

JUSTICE POTTS: You were very politely rebuking me, Mr Gray.

GRAY: My Lord, I hope it was polite …

Terre'Blanche's statement is read out in court.

I. I have been the leader of the AWB since 1973.

II. Following the despicable attack on my character by Mr Smit, I now wish to submit this affidavit as regards the true facts relating to Miss Allan.

III. Mr Smit was forcibly obliged to resign from my organization following confirmation that despite my trust in him he had exported confidential AWB information to the forces against us. An internal investigation established this to be true.

IV. Mr Smit's attack on my character is consistent with the ongoing plot by the government and the media to discredit myself and consequently my organization.

V. It is a well-known fact that the AWB represents an ever-increasing proportion of the volk.

VI. Miss Allan was the first English journalist to give us an objective hearing.

VII. I categorically refute the scandalous allegation that I have ever had any kind of sexual relationship with Miss Allan.

There is more about the AWB representing the heart of Afrikanerdom, etc., etc. but Gray and Carman – at this stage their relationship is curiously cosy – agree to exclude certain points.

The points they agree to exclude are the ones that will make the jury understand why Mr Smit had turned against his leader.

1 AUGUST 1992

Gray requests permission to recall Linda Shaw.

GRAY: Miss Shaw, do you remember when I was cross-examining you I asked about what appeared to be a change in Channel 4's defence? You remember that originally the defence read that when they were in the Lancia together Mr Terre'Blanche and Miss Allan had sexual intercourse?

SHAW: Yes.

GRAY: But that was changed, altered, amended by Channel 4 … when I asked you about that. Let me refresh your memory as to what your answers were. You gave this evidence to his Lordship and the jury: 'I at no time said that sex took place … I think the Channel 4 lawyers misunderstood. I never saw the statement before it was sent to me … it would have been impossible.'

GRAY: So you are saying that it was a misunderstanding on the part of the Channel 4 lawyers?

SHAW: Yes.

Then Gray questions Shaw about a statement that she made on 22 October 1991.

SHAW: The statement was based on a lunch that I had with Jan and Ben. There was no mention of a statement being made at that time. I told them it was off the record. Halfway through lunch, Jan asked if I minded if Ben took a few notes. This was made from his memory of what I apparently said. The lunch was very lengthy and this is what he remembered.

GRAY: You signed it.

SHAW: Jan read it to me or something. I was not interested in the case at that point. I was not interested in any of it. I wanted nothing to do with it. I was not even listening.

GRAY: I am sorry, let us just see what you say, Miss Shaw. You describe how the two of you went to Krugersdorp and then you say this: He, that is Terre'Blanche, started drunkenly molesting you. That is immediately he gets into the Lancia for the first time – is this right?

SHAW: This is Ben's recollection. I didn't say that.

GRAY: This is him getting it wrong?

SHAW: That was Ben's memory of a very long lunch. There was nothing written down at the time.

GRAY: And when it was read to you, you did not spot the error?

SHAW: I wasn't even listening. I said to Jan, I don't want anything to do with this. She said, 'Just sign it as it is. We'll put the proviso at the bottom saying that nobody else will see this.' I see that this had not in fact happened and now everybody's seen it. It was not supposed to be a factual statement. This was just a sort of basic pre-run of the whole thing and I had no intention of being involved. This was not supposed to be a statement.

GRAY: 'I rejected his advances' and then these words, Miss Shaw: 'I then saw clothes flying around inside the car, which was obviously Jani Allan and Terre'Blanche having sex.' We all know what the phrase 'having sex' means, do we not, Miss Shaw?

SHAW [sobs noisily]: How much longer is this going on? This is such a nightmare.

GRAY: I am sorry that you are distressed, Miss Shaw, but you probably appreciate that I have a duty to put Miss Allan's case. Did you say that to the Channel 4 lawyers or is this a misunderstanding?

SHAW: What?

GRAY: Did you tell the lawyer –

SHAW [very distressed, loudly sobbing]: Oh GOD!

GRAY: – and Ben the researcher that you saw clothes flying around inside the car and that there was –

SHAW: I don't remember what I said! This is what *they* remembered I said! I don't remember what I said! I wasn't even opening the statements. I was just leaving them and hoping the whole thing would go away. I don't remember what I said.

A barrister sitting in the court remarks to a colleague that based on Shaw's meltdown and complete self-destruction of her credibility, I have won the case.

Later, as we leave the offices in Shoe Lane, Carter-Ruck calls me aside. He says Gray will not sum up the case unless we are able to give him £20 000 (which is owing to him) by Monday morning.

Where am I to get such a large amount of money? Apart from the initial £5 000 deposit, Carter-Ruck has never asked me for money. There is something strange about this. All the bills I have had from Carter-Ruck have always been accompanied by a covering letter which states 'For your information only' and 'Payment pending settlement'.

I spend the weekend throwing up blood.

Before Monday morning my mother is magnificently resolved: there is nothing for it but to give me her entire life's savings.

30

THE COURT CASE – FINALE

THE FRONT PAGE SPLASH in all the papers today is that Channel 4 has been fined £75 000 for refusing to reveal the source of a programme they made. An ironic twist to the saga apparently occurred when the very man whose identity they went to court to protect condemned their programme as little more than a collage of unsubstantiated rumours and fabrications. An Ulster Loyalist has claimed that a hoax he set up to discredit the Royal Ulster Constabulary became the basis for the controversial Channel 4 Dispatches programme 'The Committee'. The man who would not allow his name to be published, and who was described as Witness X during the High Court proceedings, was interviewed in a hotel near Belfast by Chris Ryder, the Irish correspondent of the *Telegraph*.

In a voluntary statement made to the RUC in the presence of a solicitor, the man from Portadown, County Armagh said:

'The whole story of the Inner Circle and the activities I described were a complete fabrication. I was tricked into appearing in the programme. I was offered £5 000 to recite a prepared script about events on which I had heard rumours but about which I had no personal knowledge.'

Six men whose on-screen interviews were used to support the programme's thesis all said that they did not believe the film's central allegations and that their doubts were edited from the final version.

Source A said that in 1991 a journalist called Martin O'Hagan had asked him to meet a television researcher called Ben Hamilton.

'Martin asked me to tell Ben the rumours. He said Channel 4 would look after anyone who helped them. He mentioned £5 000 and that seemed like a lot of money.'

Sir Hugh Annesley, the RUC Chief Constable, said that the allegations, as portrayed by the programme, were without foundation. 'The programme, in the view of the RUC, recycled damaging and untrue allegations and should be exposed as such.'

Channel 4 defended the programme as 'a model of hard-hitting investigative journalism'.

'These smears have no foundation,' said Liz Forgan, Channel 4's director of programmes.

It's one name that leaps out of me from the article: Ben Hamilton.

The self-same Ben Hamilton who had been in South Africa gathering 'evidence' for Channel 4's case against me.

The self-same Ben Hamilton who, in Linda Shaw's own words, 'got it wrong'.

Four solicitors I speak with agree that the script and the sequence of events have a ring of familiarity to them.

*

3 August 1992

At 1:50 pm the usher's office at the court is telephoned by a woman who tells them that Peter Carter-Ruck has been stabbed and will not be appearing in court.

This cannot be true. Peter Carter-Ruck is sitting beside me. Within moments detectives arrive and call Carter-Ruck out of the courtroom to interview him. Carter-Ruck is visibly perturbed. 'I must go off and telephone my wife immediately,' he says.

It transpires that at 1:39 pm Mark Lehane, a newspaper seller, had seen a man staggering down an alley from the side entrance of The George, a public house opposite the High Court. The same man was seen by two jurors. He had blood oozing from his mouth and a knife wound in his chest. Just before he collapsed in front of Lehane, the man gasped, 'The bastards stabbed me in the lavatory!'

Ambulancemen identified the man as Anthony Travers.

Travers claimed to be the AWB's Northern Europe representative and was monitoring the trial for the AWB. Later he made a statement to the Bow Street police, describing his attacker as white, aged about 50, heavily built and wearing a blue suit.

I am sure it was entirely coincidental but people thought the description matched that of Kys Smit.

5 AUGUST 1992

The French word for the whole process of litigation is *chicane* – from which the word 'chicanery' is derived. The thesaurus offers the following descriptions of chicanery: deception, trickery, verbiage, flim flam, underhandedness, double-dealing, smoke and mirrors.

CARMAN [in the absence of the jury]: My Lord, I have asked the jury to be kept out in the light of your Lordship's comment yesterday …

Carman is quibbling that in the judge's summing up he used the phrase 'on the balance of probability' and he wants the judge to say 'more probable than not'.

CARMAN: It's just that the phrase itself might be a little confusing.

JUSTICE POTTS: Absolutely. I regret that. What I was proposing, almost as my last words to the jury, was this: Has the plaintiff proved that the words complained of meant she had an adulterous affair and were defamatory? Have the defendants proved, on balance of probabilities – that it was more probable than not.

(Charlotte explains to me what this means: in other words, he is modifying the defence. If I did not have an affair with Terre'Blanche, then the relationship was more than merely professional.)

The jury is brought back in.

Then, curiously:

GRAY: My Lord, might I suggest that all the exhibits … go with the jury?

CARMAN: My Lord, I am content that the jury has whatever they want.

JUSTICE POTTS: Yes. What I would suggest, members of the jury, is this: that you take the notebook with you now and if there is anything else you want to see, then let me know.

The theory is that beneath that ludicrous half a pound of permed horsehair there should exist a mind free of prejudice and capable of cool judgement. At the very least, one hoped for old-fashioned common sense. It was not so, in my experience.

When I hear that the diary is going to be taken into the jury room, I know the case is lost.

The jury retires to consider its verdict at 10:42 am.

After three and a half hours the verdict is returned.

The jury finds for the defendant. It is a sentence that slips underfoot like a bar of soap.

A collective gasp goes up in the courtroom. Channel 4's solicitors leap up and hug each other like triumphant football players. Mechanically, I turn around to thank Gray and shake his hand.

When we leave court we are mobbed by photographers and journalists. Carter-Ruck is knocked down and the waiting taxi-cab is dented.

'Miss Allan! Miss Allan! This case will cost you £300 000? Do you *have* £300 000?'

'Not on me,' I say.

31

In which I am unwittingly
recruited as a spy

For 20 years, a South African television journalist named Cliff Saunders was an institution at Dithering Heights (the South African Broadcasting Corporation headquarters in Auckland Park, Johannesburg).

Beneath a hairdo that owed more to a hardware store than a hairdresser, Cliff wore a permanently furrowed brow. His was a heavy responsibility. Every night before the national news, he waged a one-man onslaught against communism and the ANC with the fervour of a televangelist. He delivered his speeches leaning forward earnestly, rather like a man selling insurance polices.

'We're not going soft on the ANC. In fact the ball is on the other foot.' (This would have been a perfect candidate for a 'Quirks' R5 prize in 'Just Jani'.)

Cliff finally moved on and he turned up in London, which was where I met him after my mishap in the High Court. I was doing a post-court case satellite link-up for the SABC and Cliff conducted the interview. The one-man onslaught looked a little more leathery but the helmet hair was still in place.

'Why don't you come and visit us in Surrey?' Cliff suggested chummily once the interview was over. 'Come and meet my wife Ria. The two of you can go to Bible study together.'

Privately, I was annoyed at the suggestion, but this, in fact, was how my unlikely friendship with Ria Saunders began – and we did go to

Bible study together. Ria was the perfect Afrikaner wife. She cooked and cleaned and prayed. She was a kind and thoughtful soul. She invited me to Christmas Carols in the Royal Albert Hall, expeditions antique hunting in the Cotswolds, and once we even took a bus trip to Scotland to see the Edinburgh Tattoo.

The Saunders had a comfortable home with a garden in Kingston Hill in Surrey. Not only did they have a garden, they had built-in cupboards. Each was as rare as hen's teeth in London – having both was luxury. Ria even had a Salton Hostess hot tray, which she used frequently as the Saunderes entertained expansively.

Later I learned that they didn't only have a Salton Hostess hot tray. They also had a ski boat. This was high living indeed for a transplanted South African family.

I became a family friend and I was often there for dinner. Before each meal we would join hands and Cliff would bow his head and pray. After he had had a few and the air was heavy with cigarette smoke and sentimentality, Cliff would talk about South African politics. He would tell me how he admired the 'prince of the Zulu nation', Dr Mangosuthu Buthelezi, how Pik Botha had betrayed Jonas Savimbi (he had tapes to prove it, he said), but mostly he grieved about the ANC being a bunch of Commies and how he hated Nelson Mandela's guts. When Cliff got going like this, Ria would look as though she was sucking on an aspirin but she said nothing. She idolised Cliffie. She didn't even mind when he absentmindedly stubbed out his cigarettes on his dinner plate.

After a vigorous work-out with weights every morning, Cliff would type furiously on an old typewriter in the study. Ria's days were mainly occupied with taking care of Cliff and with her Bible studies. If I wondered what her husband was typing all day, she didn't seem to. Cliff was also constantly travelling. He spent a lot of time in Russia, America and Switzerland doing 'consultation' work.

When his contract with the SABC expired, Cliff and Ria decided they wanted to move from Surrey. I had a friend who was an art critic and was moving to Australia at around the same time. His flat in Riverbank in East Molesey overlooking Hampton Court Palace,

I thought, would be perfect for the Saunderes. It even had a garden. Everything came together and I was happy to have been able to help. Cliff and Ria moved into the flat, which was just around the corner from mine.

At this time in London I was freelancing as a journalist. I wrote pieces for the London *Sunday Times*, the *London Telegraph*, the *Daily Mail* and the *Spectator*. When Cliff asked me to help him open an office for the new consulting group he was setting up, Geofocus, which provided information for potential investors in South Africa, I was glad to accept. A steady income was attractive. I asked him about my duties and he waved his hand vaguely. 'Routine office work,' he said.

The next day Cliff, his buddy David Bamber, another South African journalist correspondent, and I went to buy computer equipment for Geofocus. Price was no object. Computers, modems, printers, fax machines, desks and printers. Cliff paid for them all from a bulging roll of cash. It never occurred to me to ask questions about the company or its ownership, but its offices were not exactly prestigious and my 'routine office duties' turned out to be doing everything from installing the telephone lines to putting up book racks.

Geofocus was half of a grubby semi-detached house in Raynes Park, a working-class suburb in South East London. Opposite us was a funeral home. Two doors down was a liquor store. Every day I was dispatched to the latter to replenish supplies of expensive Scotch and cartons of cigarettes.

'I am what is known as MBIQBE,' Cliff would say, dragging on his 80th cigarette of the day. 'Master of Bar Room Intellect and Qualified by Experience.'

While I dragged desks around and installed computer terminals, Cliff sat with his feet up on the kitchen table. Cliff did a lot of sitting with his feet up. However, he did enjoy making popcorn on the tiny kitchen stove. He would throw a kernel up in the air and triumphantly catch it in his mouth. He seldom missed. He had the snapping skills of a crocodile.

After making a couple of calls, he would go and sit on the back porch and flirt with the next-door neighbour, Mrs Woolley, who was a sex worker. Every now and then he would bawl for more whiskey and Perrier water. When it was really hot he would pour the Perrier water over his tanned and muscular chest. He was as preposterous as a teapot with two spouts. He thought it was amusing to leave the bathroom window open with a notice which read 'EIGHT AND A HALF INCHES AVAILABLE. ENQUIRE WITHIN'.

David Bamber would visit often. When he did, the pair of them would sit in the back room drinking whiskey and talking in low voices.

One day I was informed that Cliff and David had established a company called Newslink International. Press accreditation cards had already been printed. We were to go to the United Nations Conference for Indigenous Peoples in Geneva.

Besides my skivvy office duties I was instructed to set up interviews with anti-fascist groups, fascist groups, and leaders of minority parties like the Vlaams Blok in Belgium. I was also to do research on methods of recruiting terrorists and the rise of Louis Farrakhan and Islam. In addition I had to interview South African politicians. The one person Cliff was extremely keen that I interview was Dr Buthelezi, leader of the Inkatha Freedom Party and a direct descendant of Shaka Zulu. Buthelezi and I were old friends, dating back to when I had interviewed him for one of my *Sunday Times* profiles. When he called me Cliff would clumsily eavesdrop on our conversation. Then he would retire to his office and type as though outboard motors were attached to his wrists.

A few days before the World Cup rugby tournament, Cliff asked me to clean his house. He'd had a few business associates over to visit, he said, and Ria was away in South Africa. I didn't mind. The 'business associates' had brought a suitcase of money with them and they certainly had been careless with it. When I went in to clean up the next day, I found pound notes strewn about like confetti. Some of them even blew out of the door. David Bamber and his wife came over for a *braaivleis* later on, and we all took turns photographing each other with money.

When Ria returned to London from South Africa, I noticed that she spent a lot of time scrubbing the floor and crying. A few days later, when I was tidying the office, I came across a letter Cliff had written to her. He was aggrieved that she was spying on him.

Ria had written in the margin: 'I am not a spy – YOU are.'

I was perplexed. I wondered what the exchange could mean, but more than that I felt guilty for having read personal correspondence between a man and wife. I didn't have much time to ponder anyway because I was kept busy at Geofocus.

Every day I had to write a report on my research and Cliff would add his commentary. It seemed he was also in endless correspondence with his employers in South Africa. The process of transmitting a document was elaborate. First Cliff would pick a sentence from James Michener's *The Covenant*. I would then type it into the computer and encrypt it. (Cliff's knowledge of computers was limited. As long as I knew him he was studying *WordPerfect for Idiots*.)

When I enquired why the research had to be encrypted he looked at me pityingly. Didn't I know that it was standard practice to avoid corporate theft?

He also warned me that it would be most unwise if I were to attempt to read any of the documentation.

One evening after a long session of drinking in the office, David Bamber asked Cliff straight out who was employing him. At first Cliff declined to answer the direct question, but when it was clear that David wasn't going to give up, he gave up a name.

'Mandela,' he slurred.

David went to the bathroom, where I heard him throwing up. As for me, I was shocked.

Mandela? Cliff was employed by Mandela? How could this be? What on earth was he saying? What about his avowed hatred of the man and the godless, communist ANC he was always going on about? Did Ria know? Was he saying he was actually working for the ANC under the guise of Geofocus? And what about Newslink International – where did that fit it? This was double-agent stuff and none of it made sense. By now Cliff, in his inebriated state, wasn't making much sense either.

Leaving him and David to it, I gathered my things and fled. I drove my little car home to my flat in East Molesey, my thoughts whirling all the way there.

But most of all I wondered how I fitted into this peculiar scenario? Were these people whom I believed to be my friends in fact traitors? Was I being used? Was my world about to crash yet again?

I will never know why, but some compulsion made me return to the office late that night. I had to know what information Cliff was sending back to South Africa. Terrified that I would be detected, I crept into the airless little office and with shaking hands I copied the encrypted files onto six disks.

The next day I caught a train to my friends the Turners in Shropshire. Colonel Turner had contacts in MI6 and he had the encrypted files decoded.

When I read the dispatches there was a taste of rust in my mouth.

In one transcript Cliff boasted: 'To use Miss Allan as a front person makes good sense... she is the perfect mole, practically a genius ... as far as she is concerned, she is busy helping me with one of my consulting projects. She knows nothing of the Broad Organization. When she starts getting monies for the work she is doing, she will be compromised and will not be able to refuse collaborating. The technique is well known, one that you yourselves taught me.'

In other reports he made reference to me being a 'kingpin' in future operations. 'She can be used to cover high-risk stories. She is sophisticated and well liked by British society. We can use her to persuade Buthelezi to open an office in London. In this way we will keep tabs on our – the ANC's – most threatening enemy.'

I was sick to the stomach. From the colonel's study in Shropshire I typed my letter of resignation to Cliff Saunders and 'the Broad Organization'. And I copied it to Buthelezi.

32

MY MOTHER DIES

WHILE I WAS WORKING as a spy (unbeknown to me) for Cliff Saunders in London, my mother took extremely ill. I was advised by a close friend of hers that I should return to South Africa to see her before she passed.

I made two trips to Africa.

On the first trip Janet Sophia was in the Johannesburg General. She was still feisty enough to poke at me with her walking stick because I arrived later for her visit than she had expected.

I arrived on a Tuesday morning. The nurses were striking and an old person had died as a result. I was horrified to see the state of the hospital. Like Groote Schuur, it had always been a teaching hospital, pristine and run like clockwork. Now, I was told, in Groote Schuur patients had to bring their own sheets and food.

In the Gen the elevators were used as bathrooms, it seemed, judging by the stench.

My mother was anxious to get out and go home. I plied her with her favourite treats: dates, dried peaches and raw unsalted cashew nuts. She was weak but resolute. She had to be back in Bryanston to see to her animals.

I consulted with Dr Stampanoni, our family doctor.

'She certainly shouldn't be on her own in that big house. She could fall and break a hip,' he said. 'On the other hand, old people are like trees. If you transplant them, they die.'

I begged my mother to let me get her a nurse.

'No! They steal!' she said. 'Get back to London where you belong.'

I filled the fridge in the Bryanston house with food and left. There was nothing I could do. My mother had placed herself beyond my help.

Five months later I got a phone call from her friend. There had been a home-invasion (at that time we called it a burglary) and almost everything from my mother's house, *including the Bechstein concert grand*, had been stolen.

My mother was too enfeebled to do anything, but a neighbour who had seen a pantechnikon outside had alerted the police.

The next time I saw Janet Sophia was in the Hospice. I looked down at the frail husk on the hard, white bed. I believe she was already being inexorably swept out by the high velvet tide of death by the time I got there.

She looked at me without recognition.

I sat at her bedside for a night and half a day.

'She hasn't got long to go,' said the nurse. 'I can tell by the colour of her skin.'

Like litmus turning pale green, my mother's soul entered into immortality at ten past one on Monday afternoon.

I walked out of dimness into the ram's-horn blast of a hot summer's day.

33

MARIO AND THE INKATHA FREEDOM PARTY

EVER SINCE I HAD INTERVIEWED Dr Buthelezi for one of my *Sunday Times* profiles, we had stayed in touch. I regarded him as a friend and we would talk on the phone from time to time. He and I were brother and sister in Christ. He encouraged me in my faith and I marvelled at how his faith enabled him to endure the deepest personal tragedies. I envied his absolute trust in the Lord.

Our friendship endured, even after I had moved to London. Usually when we spoke on the phone it was just chit-chat. I would make him laugh by telling him vignettes about living in London. Once I saw a man with a beard wearing a summer frock at Wimbledon station. I told Buthelezi that it wasn't even a great frock, just some Dorothy Perkins high street fashion. He laugh delightedly. He loved my stories.

He told me that he had a brilliant young Italian constitutional lawyer working for him by the name of Mario Oriani-Ambrosini. I wondered if Ambrosini had been captivated by the mystique of the great Zulu nation the way many foreigners are.

Later that year, on one of my trips to South Africa to see my ailing mother, I flew to Cape Town to meet Dr Ambrosini.

We met at the Cape Sun Hotel. I thought him attractive but arrogant. We spoke about Inkatha and Dr Buthelezi and I asked him how he came to be in South Africa. He told me that just as some people are said to have had 'a good war', so the Zulus had had 'a good history'. Among all the black nations of Africa, he believed, they had most captured the imagination of the Western world, helped along considerably, it had to be said, by Michael Caine in the classic film *Zulu*.

Mario told me that in his view Dr Mangosuthu Buthelezi, the minister for Home Affairs, was increasingly being treated as, at best, a semi-detached member of the ANC-dominated Pretoria government.

'He has also been badly treated by the world outside South Africa. While bravely refusing to have any truck with the apartheid regime so long as President Mandela remained in prison, he nonetheless stood out against demands for sanctions on South Africa. He understood that those who would suffer most from them would be South Africa's black people. But instead of earning gratitude and plaudits, he has mostly been cold-shouldered by the international community. Under the pressure of political correctness, they have found it more convenient to buy the ANC view of the Zulus as trouble-makers.'

When we parted we shook hands.

＊

The next morning I flew to Durban to the Royal Hotel. Buthelezi had invited me to attend the Shaka Day celebrations along with John Aspinall. 'Asperse' was passionate in his admiration for the Zulus and devotion to their cause, and they in return regarded him as a 'white Zulu'.

When I returned to the hotel, Mario was waiting for me.

What could be more romantic than an Italian-American con-stitutional lawyer fighting for the Zulu nation's right to self-determination?

Although Mario was Italian-born, he hated everything about Eedally. There was too much drama in Eedally. Most of all he hated his mother Berenichay – Bernice. To prove that he was American through and through, he aggressively ate KFC, despite the fact that it was rumoured that he was so highly paid he could have had his caviar monogrammed.

Mario calls me in London about a dozen times every day.

Before too many weeks have passed, he has almost convinced me to return to South Africa and work for Shenge (Buthelezi).

He finally persuades me on New Year's Eve. I have been with friends at Annabel's, the famous London nightclub. We return to Johnzi's flat in Knightsbridge at about 3 am. Before we'd gone out on the town, I had put my washing in the machine, but someone forgot to switch the dryer cycle on. I have to bundle a heap of wet laundry into a bag. I stuff it into the Mini and pootle home to Hampton Court.

There I struggle up three flights of stairs. As I am draping the wet washing all over the radiators, Mario calls.

It is as if time has cleared its throat and is tapping a brand new watch.

I must come to South Africa, Mario announces. He will get an apartment for us wherever my heart desires – Clifton beach is even a possibility. I will work for Buthelezi – whom we both admire and love greatly – and he will take care of me.

I feel as though I have been sentenced to heaven.

I start to pack.

✻

On the way to the airport, I gallop to a delicatessen in Kingston upon Thames where I buy a bucket of baby mozzarella cheese. Mario loves his baby mozzarella cheese and you can't get it in South Africa.

I totter onto the plane at Heathrow, looking like a refugee from a third world country. I am garlanded with so many bags and carriers that I can hardly manoeuvre down the aisle. I do a lot of 'Excuse me'-ing. People glare. I smile back beneficently.

The first fern-growths of love, tender and fragile, are starting to grow in my heart and oh how beneficent that makes one feel.

By the time we reach Charles de Gaulle airport in Paris, where

I must change flights, the baby mozzarella bucket has leaked onto my Armani blazer and has formed a puddle in the bottom of my Louis Vuitton tote bag. (In the interests of accuracy and for clear understanding of extent of damage, I feel I have to name names.)

As a going-away present, Johnzie had given me six Xanax to help me sleep on the plane. During the course of the flight, I will take all six and remain completely wide awake.

When I arrive at Cape Town airport, an elderly customs official recognises me.

'Welcome back, Miss J. Is that yours?' He laughs gummily – 'hehehehe' – his shoulders jiggling as he points at the leaking plastic bucket of baby mozzarella.

I have spent days working on shopping for my wardrobe. How do I want to look when Mario first sees me? What perfume should I wear? Hair up? Chic? Casual? Casual chic?

Mario evidently hasn't shared my sartorial concern. He is wearing grubby shorts and the kind of sandals that look like toe cages.

On the drive from the airport to my new home – the promised beachfront flat in Clifton – he takes seven calls on his mobile phone. It is not terribly reassuring. Have I given up a rather nice life in London for someone who is going to be perennially preoccupied with party political matters?

We have lunch at Blues, a restaurant that overlooks Camps Bay beach. Mario eats his food in the American way, skewering the meat with a fork, which he holds in his right fist as though it were a dagger.

When he looks at me it is rather like an empty apartment with one ineffective nightlight left on. He's there, but he's not with me. He is in a fugue. He gazes out to sea a lot.

When he interrupts his private moment, he chides 'Eh! Sweedart. You really must stop to smoka. Let's go for a walk on the bitch.'

The Cape Doctor blows up and sand stings my face.

The flat in San Michele is furnished with garden furniture. It has a side-view, rather than a sea-facing view. Mario goes back to Parliament as soon as lunch is over.

I speak to Johnzie in London.

'You just be happy,' he advises. 'You've been through a lot with that Saunders character. Let this man take care of you.'

'I'll try,' I say gamely. Already I am feeling as lonely as a pair of gloves left on a train.

*

Mario and I settle down into domesticity.

Actually, I settle down on my own. He is always flying off somewhere for various meetings. Monday, Caypa Towna. Tuesday, Doorbin. Wednesday, Johannesburga.

When he goes on his business trips he doesn't pack clothes. He puts his peellow in a suitie-case. Hygiene is not a priority.

At first I offer to drive him to the airport and fetch him, but he becomes irritable.

On the rare nights he is in the flat, he likes to leap about, miming to his opera CDs. He is particularly fond of Wagner's *Parsifal*. In truth, he emits vulpine bays rather than sings, but at least he is home.

When I ask him what he'd like for supper he ignores me for the first three requests. This is a small price to pay, I tell myself, for being with a genius who is going to save the Zulu nation.

When I go to his office in Parliament, he is striding up and down, dictating – declaiming, more like – speeches to his secretary. His voice booms and thuds down the corridors like a cement mixer:

'UNLIKE the sainted Mandela, Bishop Tutu and all the other Marxists, Buthelezi TODALLY rejected violence during the apartheid years ... PARAGRAPH.

'It was because he refused to join the armed wing of the ANC, Umkhonto we Sizwe, that the ANC toorned [*sic*] against him and called for his assassination. PARAGRAPH. Without Buthelezi's campaigning, Mandela would not have been released from jail. Period!'

New Paragraph. [Unscrews top of expensive fountain pen.]

'PARAGRAPH! More than 600 Zulus – IFP office bearers – have been systematically assassinated. Period!'

To emphasise the import of what he is saying, the cement mixer delivery escalates to a near-shriek pitch.

'The GENOCIDE that is being visited on white Afrikaners is following the pattern set by the ANC in the eighties. PERIOD!' [Shrieks. Screws lid of expensive fountain pen back on.]

'In a low-level CEEVIL war more than 15 000 Zulus have been killed. ANC leader Harry Gwala, now thankfully departed, used the tried and trusted Communist method: systematically he would target each Zulu village. In a war of attrition the will of the Zulus was worn down. The process of THREAT, murder, rape, pillage and burn gradually split the Zulu nation. Now the great Zulu nation, the fearless nation that defeated the British Empire at Rorke's Drift, is cowed ... PARAGRAPH!'

[Unscrews lid of expensive fountain pen.]

If the truth be told, I'm pretty cowed too. I feel as though I am drowning in an ectoplasm of over-long sentences. Leading off the back of his office is a narrow room containing files which, he boasts, are the history of the Constitution. I am not allowed into the back without dispensation. Neither am I allowed access to his computer.

When I accidentally stumble upon something on his computer about the constitutional talks that I am evidently not supposed to know about he shouts, 'OUD. Oud. Get oud! Of thees OFFEES.'

Now there's a question that hangs in the air like barbed wire poking.

Is Mario really devoted to the Zulus? Perhaps engaging in the constitutional negotiations is simply a bloodless intellectual exercise for him. After all, as a member of Human Rights Advocates International, he had litigated and lobbied in respect of Nicaragua, the Russian Federation, the Indian tribes in Canada, Uganda, Fiji, Romania, Poland, the Moluccan Nation, the Cuban shadow government ... Why, he had even acted as constitutional advisor to Sir James Mancham in the Seychelles, and the Rehoboth Basters ...

✳

Mario grows angry when he learns that the Zulu prince calls me at home.

'You donta talka to heem unless I say you can!'

Finally, timidly, I ask him if he is working for the CIA.

'They don't pay enough!' he snaps.

I seem to irritate Mario a lot. One morning he becomes so exasperated with me that he pours a cup of coffee over his head. He refers to my belief in God as 'bourgeois superstition'. He advises me to read *The Chymical Wedding of Christian Rosenkreutz*. He also advises me on my television and radio appearances. He deems me unqualified to speak on most subjects.

The parliamentary grapevine is filled with rumours about a colourful and comprehensive love life.

I can hardly believe it.

When Mario kisses me it feels like he's doing it only to take his mind off something else.

When he's not declaiming in the halls of Parliament and dictating pompous briefs and unintelligible speeches to his secretary, he is attending constitutional talks.

His trademark behaviour is to shred paper serviettes and eat them. There he is on the national news – Dr Buthelezi's extremely highly paid adviser chewing paper napkins!

The 'constitutional talks' he is always attending, evidently don't take up all of his time.

I am doing a television shoot for the BBC when I stumble on the truth. A cameraman tells me that Mario has been seeing a stripper. He visits her in his American pimpmobile. He has also secretly rented another flat.

I swim in swirls of nausea.

I find out where the stripper is living and press her intercom outside the building. I want to hear her voice.

I grow thinner and thinner. I sit on the couch for days. My friend Peter, a tiny gay man, asks me: 'So how long are you going to sit there?'

I keep pestering Mario, begging him to speak to me.

'Fuck off. Stop bothering me!' he shrieks.

My days curl into each other like defeated acanthus leaves. I live somewhere between now and then.

34

BETWEEN DEVIL'S PEAK AND
TWO DEEP BLUE SEAS

SOME MONTHS AFTER ABANDONING ME, Mario sends me a Pomeranian puppy. He bought Tiny Tot How High T'Moon from a breeder in Johannesburg and had him flown down to the Cape. I suppose the Pomeranian is to be my consolation prize. I called him Teddy.

I had set out with the faith of a saint in a coracle in coming back to South Africa for Mario. I had risked becoming, yet again, the cynosure of the media. I had been prepared to fly in the inhospitable sky of their unreasonable, unfathomable, inexplicable, seemingly endless fascination and apparent hatred for me. For Mario.

But, consolation prize or no, I grow to love Teddy more than is possible to understand. I will always be grateful to Mario for giving him to me.

✻

When Pieter-Dirk Uys asks me to play a small role in *Going Down Gorgeous*, despite deep misgivings I allow a friend to stay in my flat overnight with Teddy and I fly to Johannesburg. I ask my friend to make sure Teddy is not off his lead when she takes him to the beach for his walk.

We have wound up shooting at the Rosebank Hotel and I am sitting at a Sandton coffee shop with Yvonne when the call comes. She doesn't have to say anything. I can hear by her voice. Teddy has been killed on the beach by a Staffordshire terrier.

I cannot speak. Grief closes the back of my throat like gravel. I can't walk either and Yvonne has to help me to the car.

Only those who have loved a pet as one would a child would understand my pain.

I fly back to Cape Town in a cathedral of grief. When I get to the flat, the woman I'd left in charge of my dog has removed all Teddy's toys. I ask her if I can have them back, trying to explain that it is necessary for me to have them.

Taryn James, the manager of Cape Talk, the radio station where I do a late-night show, is kind. Jane Raphaely sends flowers and a lovely portrait of me with Teddy.

Noseweek, the *soi-disant* investigative news magazine, however, deems that the death of Teddy warrants my being on the cover.

HOW HIGH T'MOON?
JANI ALLAN WAS IN GAUTENG [on a film shoot with Pieter-Dirk Uys, my dears], when, at 7.15 pm on Monday October 19, Sea Point dog lover Karl Haupt called her to tell her that her toy Pomeranian had just died. One of Karl's Staffordshire terriers had frightened it to death while the dogs were playing on Camps Bay beach.

As it happened, Jani was spending the night with dog breeder, Yvonne Meintjes of Tinytot Pomeranians, Vorna Valley. Jani shrieked and dropped the telephone receiver. After a suitable pause, it was retrieved by Ms Meintjes, who immediately accused the unhappy caller of murdering Jani's doggy – stud name [stud name? – Ed.] Tinytot How High t'Moon – before slamming down the phone.

Another to call Jani with the sad news was her instantly ex-friend, Tina Wappenhans, who had been baby-sitting Teddy, and had taken him to the beach for an evening run when it happened. She had wanted to tell Jani how several little dogs had been playing happily on the beach, when suddenly round the corner, as if from nowhere, a Staffie hurtled down on Teddy. "Teddy just collapsed. How clever, he plays dead when frightened, I thought."

But Jani refused the call.

Both Karl and Tina tried repeatedly to speak to Jani. She refused their calls and didn't reply to their messages on her cell phone.

So they never did manage to tell Jani how they had rushed the limp dog to Cape Town's most fashionable veterinary clinic, where Dr Michael Vries immediately took it into intensive care. The surgeon placed Tinytot-etc in an oxygen tent and gave him an adrenaline injection in the heart. Unfortunately, however, this was, as the saying goes, a very dead parrot. Jani's dearly beloved Teddy was departed – for t'Moon.

While Karl's Staffie had stood over Jani's Pom, and had held it in his mouth, the doctor could, in fact, find no sign of injury to the deceased. Tinytot had died of a heart attack from shock, was the doctor's conclusion. He added: "These dogs tend to be pretty inbred ... delicate stomachs, weak hearts ..."

Late that night Jani had recovered sufficiently to make an abusive call of her own to Karl Haupt. "Do you know who the fuck I am?!" she yelled – then told him anyway and announced that she intended calling down the wrath of radio, press and TV upon him.

Her Cape Talk show was devoted to the subject on more than one occasion; The Atlantic Sun, Die Burger, The Sunday Times, SAFM and her personal web page on the internet – all broadcast her rage and accusations. The ageing Jani's fading celebrity status was briefly restored. Her facelift, compliments of Femina, had been completed in the nick of time.

The infantile cruelty of the media.

Still, I don't allow myself to hate them. That, as someone once said, is like burning down your house to get rid of rats.

35

IN WHICH I AM HELD
UP WITH A MAGNUM .44

THERE HAVE BEEN MORE CHANGES in my life. I now have a three-hour late night talk show slot, 'Jani's World', on Cape Talk, whose studios are in the city. I have a new dog, another Pomeranian, whom I have called Miss Tiggywinkle. I am still living in Clifton but in another flat from the one Mario had rented for us when I first returned to the country. The flat had been sold and I was hoping to stay in the area, which I had grown to love. When a listener from the Domestic Animal Rescue Group heard me on the radio one night saying that I was looking for an apartment on Clifton beach and was prepared to pay R7.50 a month for it, she thought it was pretty funny and she called me up. When she saw Tiggy, she told me, she was won over. I began to do some work for DARG, including cleaning kennels over the weekends, and bullying people to donate when I was on the radio.

*

I am in Cape Town. It is the early morning hours of Saturday in mid-June. Outside the Ferrari dealership a handful of homeless people are sleeping in rubbish bins that have been laid on their sides. The majestic colonial building that houses Parliament and that last bastion of British imperialism, the Mount Nelson Hotel, loom in velvet silence. The stars look like God's jewellery display. This is when I love Cape Town the most. In the middle of the night, uncluttered by the racket of taxis, newspaper vendors yelling 'Ar-gie! Ar-gie!' and the angry tangle of humankind.

When I get home I plan to take my usual walk on the beach, my ritual unwind after doing my talk show.

I nose down deserted Bree Street towards the docks and then I turn left to Sea Point. The main road is empty. The drug-dealers in their BMW Z3s, the prostitutes teetering in their high-heels, the ubiquitous beggars – all have gone to wherever people of the night go in the middle of the night. The only noise is the rattle of a tin can as it blows across the road.

Beneath Lion's Head I follow the curve in the road to Bantry Bay and then Clifton.

This is the Cape Riviera, with its multi-million dollar beachfront apartments and homes, some of them with infinity pools cantilevered over the ocean.

As I turn into the driveway of mine, I notice a young man walking towards me with a jaunty gait. He is wearing an expensive leather jacket. I wonder for a second what he is doing walking at this time of night and when he comes closer, for some reason I assume he is trying to help me open the boom gate. 'Shukran, shukran' (Thank you, thank you), I say, sticking my head out of the driver's window.

Still he comes closer. I urgently fish around in my bag to give him some money. 'Shukran …' I begin again. But now I know he isn't looking for a tip. He is standing a yard away from me, right up at the half-open window of the car. I can smell him. It is the acrid smell of evil. His face is expressionless. Only his eyes move like those of a lizard behind a crack in a stone wall. He reaches down into the front of his jeans.

Oh my God he's a flasher. The thought crackles through my mind like electricity. Slowly he reaches down and pulls a huge gun out of his trousers. Terror rushes through my body and floods my brain, roaring in my ears. He shoves the gun against my right temple.

'Give me the car … the cell phone … the dog …' he says, cocking his head to where Tiggy, my three-pound Pomeranian, is lying in her little traveller bag on the seat beside me.

All that stuff about seeing your life flash before your eyes is more or less true.

My mind goes into slide-show mode. I see the inside of the car spattered with blood. Half my head is blown away. Next is the dashboard flecked with gobs of flesh … then an image of a tiny little auburn dog lying in a pool of maroon congealing blood.

It's pure *Pulp Fiction*.

Before any of these images can become a reality my left arm swings up and with all the force I can muster, I hit the gun away from my head, using the heavy bracelet I always wear. At the same time I hear an eerie screaming, which grows louder and louder. It is an ancient siren, a banshee wail that swirls around the car and swoops down to the crashing waves and then drifts up to the mountains.

'Noooooo … oooooh …'

The Munch-like scream is coming from me.

The man with the gun looks as though he has seen something he was not expecting to. His eyes widen. In truth, he looks frightened. He turns and lopes off into the night like a jackal. A jackal in an expensive leather jacket.

I open the car door and flee across the rooftop parking, stumbling down the stairs like a drunk. At the flat door, I am shaking so violently I can hardly put the key in the lock. I hold Tiggy close to me, rocking back and forth.

'Bastard! Bastard! Complete bastard!' I repeat it like a mantra. 'Complete *utter* bastard.' When that doesn't allow me to vent enough I resort to 'What the fuck! What the FUCK!'

I want to call someone. I need a witness, but whom? My mother is dead. My friends are in other countries. I dial my producer Dion's number. His mother answers the phone.

'I just want you to know I have been held up at gunpoint,' I quaver. I feel slightly foolish. 'You don't have to do anything. I just wanted someone to know. No, no, I'm all right. I just wanted someone to know …'

'Call the police,' suggests Dion's mother. 'Report the incident.'

I call the Camps Bay police station. After an age, the phone is answered.

'What do you want?' demands the sergeant who picks up, unsettling me all over again. I begin to explain but he cuts me off. 'Why are you telling me these things if you don't have this man's address?' He is clearly annoyed. Judging by the noise in the background, I get the feeling that I have interrupted a party. 'What do you want me to do? You want ... you want me ... I must find this man with *a gun*? Ah noooo. It could be dangerous!'

I hang up.

The next morning the national news reports that I have escaped an attempt to hijack me. Everyone tells me how lucky I am, that the first rule is 'to give them whatever they want'. The consensus is that it is better to allow yourself to be raped than resist, if it comes to that. Most hijack victims are shot if they resist in any way.

For several days I have no voice. I suppose it is delayed shock.

The incident has revealed two – no three, no *four* – things to me.

The notion that you can 'ward off' attacks by generating strong and benign energy is a myth. I used to set great store in believing that if you put out good vibes, they will be returned to you, and if you project strong energy, you will be safe.

The second revelation that the incident provides is that I know with frightening certainty that I would rather shoot my attacker than submit to being raped. It is not a pleasant thing to know on some level, that given certain circumstances you would, if necessary, kill. The self-realisation rises in my throat like bile.

Thirdly, not only has the incident capsized my anti-gun stance, but I start pestering a local gun dealer to sell me a SIG Sauer or a Glock. I change the screen saver on my computer to Glock. Drastic plastic.

Lastly, but most regrettably, I know that I can no longer safely walk on Clifton's silky beach alone at night. I will never again have the mystical experience of paddling in the shallows and watching a pod of dolphin playing in moonlight.

I may have escaped literal rape but another violation has taken place.

36

EXILE IN AMERICA

I SUPPOSE IF IT WERE BOILED DOWN, the reason why I was exiled to America was because I had outstayed my welcome in South Africa.

I understood that the talk show platform I had on Cape Talk was a rare gift for a 40-something white woman in a media industry undergoing the growing pains of transformation. And now the station was 'letting me go'. They said it was because they thought I had been too soft on some guests and too hard on others. Many were the times that the station manager would come in to the studio in her pyjamas to tell me to get someone off the air.

One guest the station decided I had been too soft on was Keith Johnson of the Militia of Montana. My producer and I had decided it would be interesting to interview the American right-winger and so I got him on air. During the interview Johnson expressed offensive views, among other things, about homosexuality and Judaism. In retrospect I should have cut him dead. By not doing so, I was accused of supporting him. The *Cape Times* sprang into action with posters saying 'JANI ALLAN DOES IT AGAIN'. Johnson's views were, not then and are not now, mine. The next night on air I made a heartfelt apology to anyone who had been offended but it was an inoculation that didn't take. I was called in to the station manager's office and told that Friday would be my last show.

The greatest regret of losing Cape Talk was not the platform of interviewing the rich and famous, but losing an important platform for animal advocacy, which by then was my greatest passion. When

I had had Aloudien Ahmed from the Cape Horse Protection Society on air one night, for example, I had managed to bag a fully equipped animal ambulance for his organisation. And probably one of the most important stories I did (in my view, at least) was one that highlighted the horrific tortures inflicted on horses as part of gang initiation on the Cape Flats.

During my last show the electricity suddenly cut off – just after I had announced that this was to be my last 'appearance'. In Hebrew there is no word for 'coincidence'.

South Africa was in a state of flux. I didn't recognise the country. I had been absent for seven years. I flew from London into a crisis. For me there was no gradual transition. The crime rate was soaring and corruption scandals were growing like Hydra's heads. Victims of crime were no longer friends of friends: they were friends and colleagues. And then it was me.

In many ways South Africa's growing pains in 2001 reflected my own mental anguish.

M-Web terminated my: 'CyberJani: On Line and Off the Cuff' column after I penned a piece on infrastructure development in colonial Africa.

I loved that column. It was a gorgeous, cutting-edge website, the kind of website I imagined Andy Warhol might have designed.

Perhaps I was too irreverent for the times. Perhaps my political philosophy of libertarianism was misconstrued as coldness or elitism. Certainly I was a different writer then. But I thought some of the pieces I wrote were hilarious. Many of my readers apparently thought so too.

Whatever you want to call it, the signs were there. Rug after rug was being pulled out from underneath my size 39 feet.

The biggest rug to be yanked from under me was Mario Oriani-Ambrosini falling out of enchantment with me, although by then I knew not to take it personally. Mario could be dating someone with the brains of Marie Curie, the body of a Victoria's Secret model, and the wit of Joan Rivers and his eye would still be on the next conquest.

I thought about London again. All in all I had been happy there, even after my experience with Cliff Saunders (who I'd heard had returned to South Africa and was apparently running a successful vulture restaurant in the Magaliesberg).

My little flat in East Molesey had been up three flights of stairs and was so small that a Pomeranian would have to wag its tail up and down. But when I'd looked out of the skylight I had been able to see the chimneys of Hampton Court Palace. I could walk down the Long Water and get lost in the Maze. On Sunday mornings I went to Henry VIII's private chapel …

And I had been getting work from London publications, proper newspapers like the *Sunday Times*, the *Daily Mail* and the *Evening Standard*. But could I take Tiggy and go back and live there again?

✳

After I got held up at gunpoint Mario summoned me to his opulent home in Tamboerskloof. He had imported the family furniture from Rome. There was an oversized, heavily embroidered American flag in his study, prominently displayed.

Mario had a fantasy relationship with a mythical place called America in which America was a mistress who could do no wrong. I should have been alerted when we first started dating and I realised that his preferred food was KFC – which he would wolf down by the bucket as a sign of his continuing affair with the New World.

Mario decided where I would go next.

'You-a will-a go to my friend Peter Knop and write a book about his Christmas tree farm in Virginia,' Mario instructed me. 'I have booked your teekit. You will go to the American embassy and get a visa. I will write you the letter.'

His current 'love interest' (at my age one doesn't like to use the term fuck buddy), was sitting in the kitchen reading a newspaper. She rustled the papers angrily as Mario went to his preposterously pretentious desk (all his furniture looked as though it were from Versailles) and commenced to write a letter to the American embassy there and then.

Knowing my poverty-stricken state, he then went to his overstocked freezer and picked out some frozen meat for me. He did this in the impatient way one might give a beggar a few coins – partly to assuage your guilt for their situation (you are poor because I am rich) and partly because you just want them to get the fuck out of your space.

Miraculously, I got the visa.

In exchange for the cost of the plane ticket – or as a gesture of misplaced gratitude, since I didn't know what the hell he was sending me into – before I left the country, I gave Mario an antique mirror which had belonged to my mother. It was a large, handsome walnut Georgian triptych, the size of a small family-sized car.

That left me with three pieces of her antique legacy: two small silver salt dishes with silver mice feet and a two-carat diamond ring.

I recall Linda professing to 'adore Americans because they are so confident' but in truth I wasn't excited about going to America. America was second from last on my list of least desirable travel destinations, just slightly ahead of Papua New Guinea.

I was to learn that Americans are indeed confident, if that is another way of describing a collectively bossy, self-opinionated nation – a 13th century culture with big trucks – who learn geography by invading countries and prior to the Gulf War thought Iraq was the past tense of Iran.

I had not the slightest curiosity or interest in America.

'Ah. You're going to Washington. *Wasblik*.'

'There are potholes in the road,' my friend Georgia volunteered.

Mario put it another way.

'You are going to the capital of the world. Don't fuck it up. This is your last chance to re-invent yourself.'

Personally, I am not big on re-inventing myself. I like to think that the older I get the more unapologetically me I become. I like to believe that I am a congruent person – what I feel inside is what is expressed outside. I have no desire to be someone else. I would just like to be me. With more money and slightly better press.

*

Mario gave me one week to pack up my flat in Clifton. Part of this was easy, but another part not so much. I shall not forget the gut-wrenching feeling of loading my dozens and dozens of boxes of books onto the back of my friend Shirley's bakkie, destined for her house in Hout Bay.

Books are sacred. They are my constant friends, my messages, my therapists, and the reassurance that I am never alone. Through books I learn that other people have had the same feelings as I've had. Other people have wondered why it is that our beginnings never know our ends. Other people have been disappointed in the same way that I have been similarly betrayed and, hell, they survived. And they wrote about it. That is why writers are my heroes.

Shirley and her partner Joe came to fetch me to take me to the airport on a scorchingly hot day in March 2001. All my possessions were in a blue tin trunk that I had bought down the bottom of Diagonal Street in Joburg years before. On the top of the trunk I had pasted the 'JANI ALLAN DOES IT AGAIN' poster from the *Cape Times*.

I had Tiggy with me in her little denim carrier. If people had no idea who *I* was, I made sure they knew who she was. I had had her name embroidered on the side in red.

'Tinytot Miss Tiggywinkle'.

My heartbeat at my feet, little Miss Tiggy was the only familiar being I had in the world.

I knew no one in America. At least during Exile One, I had been bound for my beloved Londinium, which is densely populated by the spirits of the writers I know and love so much. The New World was all new to me.

*

The night before I was to depart for the colonies I prayed and asked the Lord to fill me with His spirit and give me courage.

Of all the biblical characters, I have always loved Joshua the best:

As I was with Moses, so I will be with you: I will never leave you nor forsake you. Be strong and courageous ... be very strong and courageous. Be strong and courageous. Do not be terrified. Do not be discouraged, for the Lord your God will be with you wherever you go. As I was with Moses so I will be with you.

So I crossed my personal Jordan – the second Jordan, or was it the Rubicon again – into another kind of hell.

Only in this hell, one drove on the right-hand side of the road.

It is not the sound of victory; it is not the sound of defeat.

It is the sound of singing that I hear.

I kept telling myself.

I was trying fervently to believe that this was another adventure necessary for my soul's growth. I was born to be alone. When one is a foundling, one knows aloneness.

As the plane took off from Cape Town, bound for Atlanta, Georgia, and then Dulles International in Washington DC, I feared that my aloneness would suffocate me. Like Spanish moss suffocates the tree it grows on.

37

MÉSALLIANCE

THERE WAS NO ONE TO MEET ME at Dulles Airport in Washington DC, so I hung around, waiting and wondering whether I should hail my first American cab.

Finally, Mario's friend Peter Knop turned up and he drove me to the apartment in which I was to live. Prospect House had spectacular views of the Jefferson Memorial. But not my apartment. Mine overlooked the parking lot.

I felt desperately alone.

I went to every museum in Washington and practically became *une habituée* at the Smithsonian and the Pentagon. Tinytot Miss Tiggywinkle was my companion. She and I walked around Arlington Cemetery until I felt I knew every grave. I sat for hours and looked at the Iwo Jima Memorial. I walked to the Jefferson Memorial every day.

I was so starved of human company that one morning I went to the convenience shop in the basement of Prospect House to talk to the shopkeepers. That was a failure. They were Asian and, I discovered, could barely speak English.

Peter Knop, whose book I was supposed to be writing, had given me an ancient computer, which kept shutting down. He also gave me endless video tapes. After not too much research, however, it became clear to me that I could not write the book he envisaged. He wanted a whitewash. When I told him this, he became angry and got the Christmas tree farm manager to tell me that he had lost interest in the project.

Meanwhile Mario, he of the double-barrelled name who had sent me to America in the first place, had little time for me.

'You-a get-a off-a your skeeny ass-a. Find-a something to do. There is nothing, I repeat, NOTHING in Soud Africa for you,' he told me. He always lapsed into Henry Kissinger-speag [sic] when he was angry with me which, come to think of it, was most of the time.

When I feebly protested, Mario yelled at me. I was supposed to be reinventing myself, he reminded me, so I had better call in all the contacts I knew. Knowing I was out of options, I tried my best and eventually, at the end of March, I got a call from a chap I had had as a guest on my show on Cape Talk, one Dr Fred Bell. Fred suggested that I call his friend, Dr Peter Kulish. Kulish, he told me, was looking for someone to handle his company's PR.

Peter was a leading light in 'alternative' healing therapies and his research in the field of bio-magnetism and the development of bio-magnets (which was what his company sold) was groundbreaking, apparently.

I didn't know much at all about bio-magnetism, which is all to do with tapping into the electro-magnetic fields the body produces naturally, but I have always been drawn to the alternative and so I was intrigued.

On the phone Peter Kulish had a charming manner and he was compassionate about my plight. He told me that although his bio-magnets were hugely successful commercially, not only in America but internationally as well, his real vocation was that of healer. I enjoyed talking to him and gradually a phone relationship evolved, to the point where we were talking every day.

He sent me a copy of his book, *Conquering Pain: The Art of Healing with Bio-magnetism*. I was almost moved to tears when I read the introduction, in which he describes how he diagnosed his daughter as having elephantiasis, or Elephant Man disease, and had cured her by using his magnetic therapy. He told me that I should wear a magnet close to my heart every day in order to keep my organs operating at optimum level. He said I should attach them to my 'undergarment'. Undergarment, not bra. His formality pleased me.

We would speak on the phone for hours. He spoke my language. He understood about things like the Divine Matrix, about HAARP, about spirit animals. He told me he used to carry a lop-eared rabbit around with him ...

Suddenly life was bearable. Even the potholes in the road stopped annoying me.

Instead of being a sinister place because it had been laid out by the Freemasons, Washington DC became a glamorous stage-set accessorised with black patent leather limousines.

Within weeks Peter suggested that I move to New Hope in Pennsylvania and work for him. He needed someone to redesign the look of his company and, given my qualifications (my Fine Arts degree) and my journalistic experience, he knew I would be perfect. He also seemed impressed with the kind of people I knew and suggested that we might utilise them in future business ventures. (I'd told him I'd once received a fax from Prince Charles's equerry at Buckingham Palace and it seemed to knock his socks off.)

*

I spoke to my friend Katiemou in Greece.

'Hell, you're lucky someone is interested in you,' she said. 'Go! GO! You've got nothing more left to lose.'

Nothing left to lose.

Nothing *more* left to lose.

It is said that a large part of our time is spent remembering the past. Except what we remember are more often than not images fabricated by our internal dialogue about what has happened to us. We don't remember the facts. Rather, we remember interpretations of the facts. Usually we are too involved in repeating to ourselves a mythical history that our ego has developed to justify its existence.

I spent hours walking around Washington DC thinking about my life, about the court case, about my apartment being bombed. I replayed each mental video until I realised I was driving myself a little crazy.

I prayed. I meditated. I read my Bible. Especially the Book of Psalms. The Psalms always comfort me.

Then I decided to embrace the unknown.

I accepted Peter Kulish's offer to send me the money for a train ticket to Pennsylvania. New Hope, Bucks County, Pennsylvania.

I took the name of the town as a sign of good things to come.

*

Peter was waiting for me at the Trenton train station. I saw a short, tubby man with spectacles the size of a small car's windscreen.

On the front seat was a gift for me: a carton of Camel cigarettes. At that time I still smoked and I was grateful for the cancer sticks. It had been a long time since anyone had given me a gift of any kind. Many, many years since the diamonds, the flowers and the Champagne.

We drove through bucolic Pennsylvania in Peter's old white Cadillac, which he called 'the angel car' because of the winged figure on the hood, to his home. The house, which turned out to be a modest ranch house, was situated at the end of a long driveway.

Peter carried my red suitcase inside and I followed him. Immediately, I was almost dumbstruck by the untidiness and the countless *tsatskes* from Hammacher Schlemmer mail order catalogues all over the place. I was also somewhat taken aback by the poster-sized photographs of his seven-year-old daughter which, shrine like, adorned every wall. Peter told me that he and his daughter were 'very tight'.

Then he showed me where I would be sleeping.

'I'm warning you. It's rustic!' he said playfully.

He wasn't kidding.

It seemed I was to live in a wooden shed a couple of hundred yards from the house. There was a futon on the floor. There was no bathroom or running water.

The guest bedroom in the main house was taken up with the daughter's toy hoard.

Really, Lord? REALLY? You knit me in my mother's womb. You knew me before I was born ... and now this?

The next morning Tiggy and I present ourselves at the main house at 8:30 am sharp. I am wearing an Armani suit and ready to set off for my first day of work.

Peter's daughter is sitting sullenly in the front seat of the Cadillac. There is something bizarre about this but I brush the thought aside and assume that all American children are free range. I don't say anything. Hesitating just a moment, I get in the back. After we drop her off at school, Peter invites me to sit in the front.

At the office I get on with the staff and become instantly indispensable to Peter. Or so it seems. When my friend Fred calls to see how things are going and to ask me to come to Laguna Beach, Peter tells him, 'Jani is the greatest thing that has ever happened to this company. She's not going anywhere.'

However, within a week one of my co-workers takes me aside and tells me things about Peter that I find hard to believe and to reconcile with the caring, middle-aged, grey-haired doctor we both work for. There are apparently dark tales of Peter's past relationships, a custody battle over his daughter, brushes with the law, and more.

Much more.

I am baffled and uneasy. Why is this man telling me these things? Is he deliberately trying to sow seeds of mistrust? Could he be jealous of Peter?

I push what I've been told to the back of my mind. Or at least I try to. But the words sink into me and I live with them inside me, eating at me, slowly and gloomily sometimes, but at other times they surface and I am wrapped in tentacles of icy worry.

When one goes to another country – in my case, my third country – one loses frameworks of reference. Had I been in Johannesburg, Cape Town – or even London – my ear would have been attuned to the phony baloney, but in America I am on far less certain ground. I worry that taking this job and moving to a state where everything and everyone is unfamiliar to me might not have been the smartest idea, but I try to suppress these negative thoughts. I hear Mario's words about reinventing myself over and over, hollowly echoing. I am fully aware that my choices in America are less than limited.

I decide to trust my initial instincts. And so far Peter Kulish is very impressed with me.

In fact I am enjoying being useful to Peter's company. Every suggestion I make to improve the company's image is met with enthusiasm and approval. He and I work 16-hour days, redesigning sell-sheets, websites and liaising with press. After working hours we don't do very much of anything else except, occasionally, go to his aged parents for supper.

Each day is a lithograph, a copy of the one before.

Shed, work, shed, work.

*

Gradually, as we work together we eventually become more involved, but it's not a passionate situation. Rather we are two middle-aged people, having come together to work 'for the benefit of mankind', as Peter modestly describes his bio-magnets business.

The first occasion that Peter makes physical advances on me, and I refuse him, he hurls a lamp across the sitting room.

I choose to interpret this violence as proof of how much he wants to be with me.

A few months later – about five altogether since I arrived in the States – I become very ill. Although he is not a medical doctor, Peter diagnoses my condition as Lyme Disease. Lyme is a disease carried by deer ticks and since there are herds of deer in Pennsylvania the disease is fairly prevalent there.

Peter transfers me from the shed to the couch in the sitting room, where he proceeds to administer IV vitamin C 'pushes'. With a cigarette clamped between his teeth, he curses and mutters, unable to find a vein – this despite the fact that I have veins like windswept branches. At one point he makes a telephone call to his friend Tom – a real doctor – who instructs him over the phone.

For days I am semi-delirious but Peter refuses to take me to consult a medical doctor. He tells me that I will be fine, he knows what he is doing, and, too weak and sick to know different, I believe him. If he says I have Lyme Disease, then that's what I have. (In retrospect, I have no idea what made me so ill.)

Slowly, I get better and then, one morning out of the blue, Peter suggests we go to Maryland and get married.

*

Looking back, it seems completely daft. Maybe I was grateful that Peter had supposedly nursed me back to health with such care. Probably I believed I had no other options. I was in a foreign country with no support system and, without Peter, no money and no job. Although my heart wasn't in it, marrying him didn't seem to be such a terrible idea.

I wore jeans and a faux tiara belonging to Peter's daughter for our wedding. Not the kind of Pamela Anderson 'look at me I'm fabulous' jeans. Sad, defeated jeans.

There was no one but us at the ceremony. I felt as though I was in a dream. I struggled to keep the trembling parcel that was my face together with a tight smile.

For the wedding 'feast' we went to McDonald's. Peter assured me that it was inverted chic. I remembered dining with Mandy Rice-Davies at a smart London restaurant once where there was a piano-player in a tuxedo and bangers and mash on the menu – now that *was* inverted chic. Still, I didn't protest and McDonald's it was.

Afterwards we went back to Pennsylvania and got back into work. Peter's promised salary to me of $125 000 a year had become $500 a month, but after we married, it ceased completely. Somehow I couldn't bring myself to bring this up.

In the early days of the marriage I noticed that Peter was very short-fused, especially with those people to whom he owed money (and there seemed to be many), but he was always courteous with me. He seemed even to be in awe of me and somewhat astonished by my professionalism, my past achievements, the people I knew. He loved to boast about me. But not quite as much as he loved to boast about himself.

He never tired of telling me how he was fêted by royalty and about his international fame as a healer. (Again with the healer story!). He claimed to be the sponsor of the Tesla Society and spoke of how he was received as a pop idol in India, Thailand, the Philippines.

Trapped in his car going to and from the office, I was a captive audience. I was told unceasingly about his personal brilliance, about all the famous people he knew, of how he had 'turned everyone onto acid', in New Hope, how he'd spent time in solitary confinement 'speaking the truth' (whatever that meant), about how so and so had stolen his technology/film script/something else.

His stories began to sound far-fetched – even for an American. One of his favourites was how he had hitched to Las Vegas and was 'hanging' with famous musicians when he was ten. On the sixth telling when I asked him mildly why he hadn't been in school, he grew very angry.

He had a Harley Davidson and insisted that we go for long, hellish rides on it together. After a couple of narrow escapes, I became reluctant to go. This also made him angry.

One of his 'business partners' was a chap called Baba who, so Peter said, was the leader of the Sikh nation. Baba averred that Peter's daughter was the incarnation of the Indian goddess Kali. Peter, of course, was the incarnation of St Peter. Peter was so flattered by these pieces of spurious nonsense that he immediately sent a large donation to Mumbai. When I suggested that Baba was playing him like a Stradivarius, his rage was frightening. He shouted and screamed at me and ended up throwing my little Pom Tiggy across the room.

Then he grabbed me by the throat. Ah, the throat. Why do so many violent men want to crush the throat? Is it because they want to smash the chakra of speech? Is it because they want to snap the tender Modigliani vulnerability that reminds them of a past palimpsest of gentle kisses? I don't know. I do know it hurt like hell.

The police came. They examined the marks on my neck.

The police were to become regular visitors.

I had no friends in America. Peter had no friends either. No one came to the house. I became increasingly isolated. To say I had no independence would be an understatement. I was a virtual prisoner. Fear, someone once said, is pain arriving from the anticipation of evil. In truth, I lived in fear.

On the occasions that I needed to see a doctor, Peter would make the telephone call for me and sit in the doctor's room with me. When I wrote to friends overseas he got into my emails through the company server and took it upon himself (without my knowledge) to respond in vicious ways. He presented himself as the sane person. I was mad and delusional.

Once we were married and as the weeks became months, Peter's initial infatuation with me was spent but his anger and reign of terror grew. His rages were terrifying. Whenever anything displeased him, he would kick doors, overturn coffee-tables, smash laptop computers or throw things.

The things that displeased him most were imaginary slights to his ego. His narcissism was such that he demanded utter obedience. If I showed any reluctance to be intimate with him, he would rip the duvet off the bed, overturn the night-stand and stomp out of the room, cursing me.

He controlled everything I did. He demanded that I turn out the light when he wanted it turned out. I was not allowed to spend any time alone. He would go into a fury if I spent time on the computer. In the evenings I had to sit beside him and watch whatever he wanted to watch on TV.

When one of the women in the office suggested that I have a lunchtime coffee with her and the other girls, he would not allow me to go. He said I had no understanding of the American class system and that it was entirely inappropriate for me to become familiar with the office staff. To this end, he would police the hallway outside my office to check who was coming in to see me. When the art director came in to talk with me, Peter would leave the intercom on and eavesdrop on our conversation.

Whereas in the beginning I could do no wrong, now it seemed that

I could do no right. We argued about everything. He even forbade me from wearing certain colours. Anger rose from him like a molten corona.

Despite everyone's best efforts, the business was not going well. Whether this was as a result of Peter's pomposity and narcissism (as I suspected) and that his biography and his boasting didn't really match, I don't know. I was not privy to the finances. But, as the business deteriorated, so did our mésalliance – our misalliance – and his violent rages grew. I became the proverbial punching bag wife.

As things slid financially, Peter began to bring up the possibility of the house having to be sold, and so it came to pass and we packed up the ranch house and moved, deep into the Pennsylvania countryside. Our new home was a renovated silk mill that dated back to the 17th century.

Perhaps the stress of moving contributed to Peter's *agitato* state, but when, in November 2002, my friend Georgia and her husband Louie came to visit me from South Africa, Peter went ballistic. The visit had been planned months in advance, but he was unable to contain his rage. He hated having 'intruders' in his home. He accused me of being a lesbian. Georgia, he said, was ruining our marriage. Once he pushed her so hard she nearly fell down.

One morning he flung open the door of the guest bedroom and swore at Georgia and Louie. 'Get out!' he shouted at them. Then he threw their suitcases down the stairs. They were fearful – for themselves and for me.

I never thought I was being abused. I always thought it was my fault. When my friend sent me a book about abuse and Peter came across it, he tore it up.

As time went on I became so depressed that eventually I couldn't drag myself out of bed. This made Peter curiously cheerful. The more my 'learned disability' increased, the more empowered he felt. I cried and cried and it went on for weeks until, irritably, he took me to see a counsellor, Dr Paletz. When the doctor saw the condition I was in, he said, 'You are going to slide over the edge and no one will be able to pull you back.'

Sleeping in the same room as my husband became impossible even to contemplate. I would lie beside him with a pounding heart. When he started snoring – actually, it sounded more like a string quartet tuning up – I would sneak out of the bed and go upstairs to my little 'office', where I would sleep on the floor. He complained bitterly about this, referring to my 'English' ideas and saying that this wasn't a marriage.

I couldn't help it. I was too frightened of him to have any feelings for him. I was nervous as cellophane all the time. At times I would lose my voice from sheer terror.

When I saw him crouched down, in a rage, his eyes popping, it looked to me as though he had been taken over by some demonic force.

I took to sleeping on the far side of the house and propping a heavy steel ladder against the door so that Peter wouldn't smash it in when I was sleeping. He refused to give me money to buy food. I felt that he wanted me dead. I was utterly alone with a deranged man in an isolated mill in rural Pennsylvania. Since hardly anyone even knew I was there, he was not answerable to anyone for what he did to me.

The beatings and punishment I took became so bad that I was admitted to the local hospital. After extensive tests – blood work, CAT scans and psychiatric examinations – the doctors told me that I was physically manifesting all the signs of a traumatised, abused wife. I guess, like many an abused women, I was in denial but all I felt was shame and embarrassment. I didn't know what I was supposed to do, where to put myself.

At night I took to walking to the local cemetery where, among the graves of the Celtic mill-workers from centuries past, for a few hours I knew I would be unharmed.

It was not a life, but I continued trying to live it, to get better at it, to hold my head up.

38

MISS KATE

I MET KATE – MISS KATE, as I called her, and still do – in a moment of
such chance that we talk about it without ceasing. Uncharacteristically,
I was taking a walk along the river one day with Precious, a little dog
I was taking care of for Catherine, an acquaintance. Catherine was on
her annual pilgrimage to India.

Personally, I thought Catherine's guru was as phony as a replica
Rolex. He lived in an upmarket condo – completely at odds with his
tofu-eating, cheesecloth-wearing constituents. When I saw one of his
acolytes lovingly painting his toenails while he imperiously told them
about God, I felt vaguely uncomfortable. When, after *satsang*, they
would prostrate themselves before him, I felt distinctly uncomfortable.
He would fly first class to the ashram in India, courtesy of his disciples,
who all flew cattle class.

Anyhoozelbees …

As I was crossing the T-junction a kindly faced woman in a PT
Cruiser drew up beside me.

'My, what a pretty little dog,' she said, looking at Precious. When
I opened the traveller in which I carried Tiggy, she gasped. People
gasped a lot when they saw Tiggy. She was a tiny (two pounds) orange
Pomeranian, cute as a Beatrix Potter hedgehog (which was why I
named her Tinytot Miss Tiggywinkle, of course).

'Come and see me sometime,' the woman said and she told me
where she lived.

For some reason I took her at her word. Before too many days had passed I went to call on her. I took her some flowers. I remember being astonished when she opened the door – she was scarcely five feet tall. But, as I was to discover, there was nothing else that was small about Miss Kate.

'I can't have those flowers in here!' she said immediately. 'I'm allergic!'

A few months later, in the middle of the night – it was 14 May – Peter was raging around so much that I feared for my life.

At four in the morning I took Tiggy, snuck out of the Mill and fled. My heart was beating in my throat as we escaped onto the hilly, gravelled road, with the stars crowding in on us. I didn't have a plan, but somehow my feet took me to the door of Miss Kate's house and I dredged up the courage to knock on it until she came. She stood looking up at me, this small woman I barely knew, and opened the door wide.

For six months I slept on a couch in her living room.

*

I was to learn that Miss Kate was allergic to many things beside flowers. Fresh newsprint (the ink made her fingers swell), the smell of Earl Grey tea – and, of course, cigarette smoke. She claimed that she could smell it if the people two cars ahead of us in the traffic were smoking.

Above Miss Kate's little house was a tiny apartment, with two dog-house windows. When it became available I moved upstairs. There was a waist-high wooden bed, a table, a chair, and a hideous kidney lamp.

To me it was luxury. My prayer for a different kind of solitude had been answered.

Miss Kate made porridge for me every morning. 'It's good for your ulcer,' she said.

'Yoodleloodleloodleloo! Yoodleloodelloooo!'

I would awake to hear her at the bottom of the stairs. There was no way round it. I would drag myself out of the waist-high bed, scoop up Tiggy and go downstairs.

Mission: to find a job, a writing job, any job, without a Green Card.

39

In Which Hopes of Being on Oprah are Dashed

Barry Farber is an American radio talk show host, author and language-learning enthusiast. In 2002 *Talkers* magazine ranked him the nineth greatest radio talk show host of all time. He also writes articles for the *New York Times*, *Washington Post* and the *Saturday Review*. He is the father of two grown daughters, Celia, a journalist and Bibi, a singer-songwriter.

Barry is one of my telephone friend Jeff Nyquist's contacts.

According to Jeff, Barry is a charming Southern gentleman and something of a radio personality legend. 'Farber is easily identifiable by his unique combination of drawn-out Southern drawl, intense delivery, verbose prose, and quick wit. Sponsors love his ability to deliver a live commercial spot, often ad-libbed, and make whatever the particular product was sound tantalising; he always sounded like he truly believed in the product,' Jeff tells me. 'Ten years ago he was named "Talk Show Host of The Year" by the National Association of Radio Talk Show Hosts. You should go and meet him. He's a good contact to make.'

'Bah Fah here!'

I am talking on Miss Kate's handheld telephone, standing under the street light in Old York Road. I introduce myself.

'You sound like Julie Andrews!' Barry exclaims.

He certainly is personable.

We arrange to meet for lunch in Manhattan. He lives on Broadway in The Apthorp, a building on the Upper West Side which, he tells me, is bristling with celebrities. Cyndi Lauper. Nora Ephron. That other rock musician. You name them, they're at The Apthorp.

Miss Kate drives me to the bus stop in her Peanut Butter Cruiser. It's a palaver for her to get out of the house and more of a palaver for her to get into the car and settle herself. There are a series of cushions and buffers that have to be arranged. I could have walked the mile to the bus station by the time she switches on the engine, but I am grateful. Her middle-aged son Danny was at the house earlier. He didn't recognise me with my maquillage.

I catch the bus from the Donut Shop in New Hope to the Port Authority in New York. Then I take a taxi to Broadway. I have to wait in the street while the concierge buzzes Bah Fah. The building looks a bit like the Pitti Palace. I peer past the concierge into a paved atrium the size of a tennis court. It is filled with magnolia trees and topiary that has obviously been snipped with a pair of nail scissors.

Barry appears suddenly. He is tall, lean and pleasantly gnarled like the trees, but slightly less manicured than the topiary.

'Wow! I thought you had sent your daughter!' he greets me. He proceeds to lay the compliments on with a trowel. 'You're fantastic. Mind you, all the best women are in their seventies.'

'Thank you,' I say meekly, but my heart sinks. Already he's coming onto me. Or is he? Perhaps I shouldn't flatter myself. After all, he lives in the deeply desirable Apthorp which was built a hundred years ago. (What kind of a name is that for an apartment block anyway? It sounds like one of those unpleasant growths chemistry professors have on their chins.)

I don't point out that I am not actually in my seventies.

We walk to a riverside café and Barry buys me a hamburger. He can't stop paying me compliments. I am starting to wonder if he is going to ask me for receipts. He eats like a hungry wolf. He tells me that with my accent and experience it will be a matter of time before I am on Oprah. Or have my own talk show. On radio. Or TV. Or both.

'Wayall, Ah cain't say other than Ah will knock on avery door Ah know to see that you are where you deserve to be. Ah'm as happy as a billy-goat in a field full of clover to have met you. You and me together – we are a forest fah!'

As the bus leaves New York, a huge pantechnicon passes alongside it. On it is written the word GOD. A sign! Never mind that the letters stand for Global Overnight Delivery. I believe that the Universe/God sends us signs and I take it as one. I seem to have forgotten that I was drawn to a town called New Hope not so long ago.

I can hardly wait to tell Miss Kate that things are looking up. Someone believes in me.

On the way home I am elated. I don't even mind that the bus driver misses the stop and I have to walk back to South Sugan Road. My little green suede ballet shoes clip-clip happily on the pavement as I trot home.

'Start spreading the neeews,' I warble to myself under my breath. 'If you can mayayayayayake it here you'll mayayayayayake it anywhere … it's up to you Noo York, Noo York …'

*

It is arranged that I will broadcast with Barry first – just to test the waters. Again I make the trip in to New York. First we have lunch at a diner. Barry brings his own grits. Then we repair to his apartment in The Apthorp.

Judging by the furniture, I think Barry's apartment must be a rent-controlled one. Once you get past the faux Renaissance barrel-vaulting of the entrance, it is sparsely furnished with masculine furniture. A glimpse into his sleeping quarters reveals a mattress propped against the wall.

He leads me to his 'studio'. Actually, it's a room that has been turned into a radio station.

Everyone I have met in the States seems to be into home broadcasting. If it's not from the kitchen table, it's from a room in the Upper West Side. At The Apthorp, no less. There are stacks of unread books – oh the perks of being a media person.

I put on an ancient headset. The controller is in some undisclosed location. Barry starts rabbiting on and on. Information practically leaks out of him. He comments on the politics of the day (prudently taking an extreme centre position) and adds all sorts of interesting things, about Ava Gardner and Tracy Spencer – or it is Spencer Tracy – and Humpty Go-kart.

I am nervously fingering my notes. I have carefully planned what I will talk about on this my test broadcast. I want to talk about how the wildlife in Africa is being destroyed. I have arranged to have Johnny Rodriguez of the Zimbabwe Conservation Trust Fund on the line.

Bah Fah introduces me as JA – a journalist who had her apartment fah-bombed! Then he rips the cans off and disappears into the next room to watch a football touchdown, leaving me to rant on solo.

I wonder if anyone is listening.

'Mah deah, they don't even know where Zimbabway is, never mind care about it,' says Bah Fah later. 'Now are you going to meet my daughters and their husbands for supper?'

I explain that I must return to New Hope.

'But you will come again. On Yom Kippur,' Bah Fah makes me promise. 'While Ah'm in shul, you can do the shows.'

Things don't go entirely as planned, however. I become ill – recurrence of The Ulcer problem – and want to cry off the trip, but Barry is determined that I come to the city. He will come to New Hope to fetch me, he announces. He arrives in a VW bus with a mattress in the back and curtains in the windows. The bus is driven by his plumber. Barry offers me an Oxycontin. 'Take one of these and you will be seeing double and feeling single,' he says.

I take the Oxycontin and promptly fall asleep. On the way back to the city Mr Bah Fah and Mr Plumber stop and have a drink. While they are womanising, I am in a coma on the mattress. When we arrive at the apartment I am installed on the couch in the study. I meet Barry's two daughters, who are intelligent and intense. I am given another Oxycontin and then they all go out together because Barry has to 'grandfather in' a date, whatever that means.

The next day everyone departs for shul, leaving me and Tiggy alone at the apartment. I stroll around before I sit down in the 'studio', noticing that there are pictures on the walls of Barry looking very handsome indeed. When I look closely I see that they were all taken about 30 years ago. While Bah Fah is making atonement, I am making no headway with the controller-of-undetermined-location. If the truth be told, he isn't too keen on me broadcasting anything without Mr Farber's say-so, so it's a non-starter.

Barry returns from shul and waves away my anxieties. 'We'll broadcast together tomorrow.'

While the daughters prepare a traditional supper, they ask me if I know there is an elephant in the room.

I look blank. I don't know what they are talking about.

The daughters explain. It seems that (a) their father is very keen on me and (b) their father likes to drink.

As the evening wears on it seems that Barry does indeed like to drink and very soon he is drunk. Moreover, he is an angry drunk. After making sarcastic comments about everyone, he abruptly leaves the room and goes to bed. The daughters start arguing about what the purpose of atonement is. I take yet another Oxycontin and promptly fall asleep.

The next day is the broadcast. When I seem to be doing rather well, Barry gets annoyed. In fact he becomes almost angry with me. After the broadcast he demands to 'see me in the study'. While he is drinking copious amounts of the hard stuff he demands to know why I didn't get up earlier to spend time with him and his family.

'Why weren't you like a puppy dog, running around and greeting and kissing?' he demands.

'It wasn't proper,' I said. 'I am English. We think that house-guests should stay in their rooms as long as possible.'

'Don't you know how much I want you? Didn't you feel me licking your clothes off with my eyes last night?'

I stare at him with a degree of horror. The thought of Barry *sans* clothes is like Tutankhamen without the bandages. If the truth be told I am rather afraid. I am alone in an apartment in New York – by now the family has departed – with a bitter old man who may or may not decide to throw me and/or Tiggy out of the window. When we project our attractions onto someone, especially someone who isn't reciprocating them, there is always disillusionment on the part of the projector and distaste on the part of the projectee.

I explain to Barry in a very level voice that I am still in the process of getting divorced and my priority is getting a job. I am not ready for a romantic relationship.

I don't want to tell him how desperate I am; how I have taken to compulsively crunching bags of ice. I crunch so much ice that my teeth are becoming worn down, rather like the Ancient Egyptians' teeth were ground down by the desert sand. (In attempting to understand why I am compelled to crunch ice, I discover an ice-crunchers' bulletin board online. That there are other crunchers out there doesn't comfort me, however.)

I don't want to tell Barry how much I weep into Tiggy's fur every night. I can't tell him how I can't imagine ever having a proper life again. Right now all I am is a bit player in Miss Kate's life. I don't have my own friends, my own car, my own space – or a job. But I am not crying in front of Mr Bah Fah.

He gets drunker and drunker. I am like a deer in the oncoming headlights of a car. When he shouts at me to go and get take-out from the chicken place on the corner of Amsterdam and Broadway, I scuttle away gratefully. The New York sirens and night sounds are merely background to my pounding heart.

At first light I make an urgent call to the plumber. I beg him to return me to New Hope soonest.

'I'll see you again,' I lie to Barry, waving goodbye.

'The good-looking ones always say that,' he says viciously. 'All dreams of empire are over.'

How silly I was to imagine that there were no strings attached.

Buh-buh, Oprah.

*

When I first moved upstairs to the tiny apartment above Miss Kate's, when I wanted to smoke I used to hang out of the dormer window upstairs, or else I would walk down the road for my cigarette fix, where I would get bitten by mosquitoes the size of sanitation trucks – no one told me Pennsylvania was a jungle. But soon, a result of poverty – and out of respect for Miss Kate – I stopped my packet-of-Camel-a-day habit.

Miss Kate and I, though different in many ways, were – and continue to be – firmer friends than is possible to describe. We would go together to Giant, where she would ride in the electric cart and point with her cane at things she wanted. 'There! No, not that one! *Behind* that one.' And she'd poke the offending carton or can until I got it.

We never spoke about my traumatised state, but she would drive me to the women's shelter, where I had started seeing a domestic violence counsellor after I had been hospitalised before I escaped from Peter. The first time I went there I cried tears like rain rivers on bony land. I cried with relief that I was not to blame for everything in my marriage. Miss Kate would also drive me to the lawyers in Doylestown. I would cry in various offices, but when I came out and saw her sitting in the car with little Tiggy on her shoulder, I was always comforted.

It turned out that we shared curious connections. Books. Movies. A mutual fascination with Tibet. Even music. I remember the first day I sat at Miss Kate's kitchen table. She was modifying a pizza (she always modified food). She took the pizza out of the box, pressed paper towels onto it to soak up the excess grease, then fried it in a pan. It was delicious.

*

I started writing a monthly astrology column for an online magazine. The first one I wrote was when Pisces was at Seven Degrees. The symbol is a challenging one:

> Illuminated by a shaft of light, a large cross lies on rocks surrounded by sea and mist. This symbol shows the ability, or the need, to be able to stay firm in one's faith and belief in life

even when one's hopes and dreams take a battering. There may be feelings of chaos and misplaced loyalties in your life, like something has been sacrificed for no real cause and some things have come to nothing.

At such times in your life, you may want to see if perhaps your aim was too high and things came crashing down as a result of a lack of care, by yourself or others, or through people opposing your objectives or success.

[Damn, skippy, it was accurate!]

Having faith and a positive end in sight, you can experience a wonderful spiritual awakening – reconnecting with your spiritual ideals. Concentrate on the 'Shaft of Light' as this can show you that white light is all around you.

I was able to come to terms, most of the time, with the loss of a country, a career, a marriage and a home. There were times, though, that I would break down and cry. Not in front of Miss Kate. But when I was sent on an errand to Staples or to the post office. Once, one of the sales persons in a shop pushed a $20 note into my hand. I think she did it just to get me to leave. There is something alarming about a woman sobbing in public, especially if she is wearing a Bloomingdales cashmere sweater which has holes in the elbows.

✳

Danny, Miss Kate's son, was gay. We called him the Tree Nazi because every weekend he and his partner would come and inspect the trees in his mother's garden, which were being attacked by Japanese beetles. He would inspect them with increasing agitation. But he was just as agitated about Miss Kate and became more and more nit-picky.

'She used to look like Gina Lollobrigida,' he told me. 'Now look at her!'

Personally, I thought Danny was exceedingly cruel and superficial. He nagged his mother about her weight, about the number of times she used the washer-dryer and and about all sorts of other minutiae, until finally she decided to pack up and go and live near her daughter Laurie in Missouri.

I helped her pack her things. When I watched her drive down the road, I knew I was truly alone in America.

✻

I moved into an apartment in Waterloo Street in the spring. It was a bedsit with a tiny kitchen and, although it did have a balcony looking out over the Delaware River, from the get-go it was a nightmare.

The landlady, Gail, was one of those Christians who like to tell you how the Lord has blessed them. This has the effect of making you feel suitably insignificant, and unblessed.

'Look at this house! Has the Lord blessed me or what?'

Gail was an insufferable landlady. She refused to give me a key to the apartment, so in effect I was living in a large room in her house.

As such she thought it acceptable to traipse up the stairs from the kitchen through my bedsit several times a day. I was not allowed to feed the seagulls because they would foul her deck. I wasn't allowed to bring my books to the apartment because they were too heavy and might collapse the ceiling. I was obliged to put them in storage.

When she was renovating her bedroom at one end of the house, she lived in another suite. She slept in a boxed-in bed and cooked her food in a microwave that she kept in the lavatory. Her voice boomed through the house as she instructed the workmen and the kids from a local church group who would come to do her gardening chores and other handiwork.

When the Delaware was predicted to flood its banks she instigated a double-pronged resolution: first, she called in the local church people – and a couple of Catholic nuns for good measure – and they all prayed in the sitting room.

'Please, God, we raise Gail's house up to You and ask You to intervene, Lord and we ask that You spare her home, Lord ...'

After prayers she reclined like a queen on the sofa, from whence she directed a team of people (Christians) who were tasked with moving everything from the downstairs of the house to the waiting moving vans. 'How the Lord has blessed me having all these friends,' she said as she serenely directed the traffic.

Unfortunately, when it came to averting the flood, on this occasion the Lord had other things on His mind and we were advised to evacuate the house. We were billetted at the Holiday Inn, which was giving special rates to flood victims. A flood victim! This was a first for me.

Eventually the river subsided, but not without doing millions of dollars of damage to many properties. The roar of jet skis on the river was now accompanied by the roar of water pumps at every house as desperate owners tried to suck the water out of their basements.

Gail's house was badly damaged and so, once more, I was homeless. I needed a job – any job.

40

GIMME SHELTER

GETTING DIVORCED IS FAR MORE than a legal, public statement. There is a shift in the inner world and morphic field. Perhaps women feel this if they have an abortion. The pregnant mother is prepared, expecting, anticipating and then life is yanked from her womb. Life has been terminated. Ended. Cancelled. Halted. How does she feel? Certainly she will never be the same again. Even if the abortion was a necessary escape, she is a changed person.

Divorce makes you a changed person too. You had been meaning to, planning to, preparing to and expecting to spend the rest of your life with one person and the plans have been aborted. Although some might trot out the old canard about a bad marriage being like a lukewarm bathtub is true (it's still better being in it than heaving yourself out of it), this wasn't an option for me.

I was adrift between identities. I had been one person in South Africa. I became another when I married an abuser. Now I was entirely on my own in a nightmare-laden dark place. TS Eliot's words about our beginnings never knowing our ends are with me again.

Women from all strata of society are abused. Perhaps the ones with money can hide their circumstances better. Perhaps they can fly to a rich aunt in Laguna Beach and see a therapist at some high-end nursing home. Have a little Botox while they're there to make them feel better about themselves. Others go to a women's shelter.

If anyone had told me that one day I would find myself with no place to go but a women's shelter, it would have seemed preposterous.

Unthinkable and unthunk. Spit three times. Hush your mouth. But that is what I did. The one in which I sought refuge was an ugly building with tiny dormitories and communal bathrooms. A kennel, really, for junkyard bitches. There was a television room with old magazines and games. Down a hallway were the volunteer therapists.

The women I met there were untainted by education and most of them were on the poverty line. They were coarse in feature and behaviour. We had two things in common, though: we were all female and we had all been abused.

Each abuse is unique but there are tell-tale signs. I remember bursting into tears of relief when one of the therapists showed me a diagram indicating the different kinds of domestic abuse. It started off with ambient abuse, which is slamming doors and throwing things. Then it moved to verbal abuse, and then finally on to full-blown physical abuse.

I hated the women at the shelter. I hated myself for hating them. But mostly I hated myself for being there. I would open my Bible and stare at it sightlessly. The meniscus in the bowl of my faith, once so full, was gone – like water tipped out of a dish.

One's aura, or as I understand one's aura, communicates everything about what one has learned on the soul's journey. It's an etheric compilation of everything you know and are. Your aura influences everyone around you, whether they know it or not. I remember how I had once been in an audience with the Dalai Lama. I didn't know then why he was so attractive, why his disciples yearned just to be in his presence.

My co-abused at the shelter were lumpen, overweight and inked up. I suspected their lives were stunted and brutal and devoid of beauty, but that would be my innate snobbishness talking, wouldn't it? They must have been interested in beauty of a kind. Why else were they tattooed? How did they find the money for these tattoos?

Once a week there was Food Bank. I would pick listlessly through the donated food and what were called 'creature comforts' for something that might comfort me. Tins of tomatoes, packets of cheap spaghetti, no-name brand peanut butter, toothpaste and hair combs. No-name brands for no-name people. When it came close to Thanksgiving someone donated a lorry-load of turkeys. I offered one to Miss Kate but she declined. It was too big. Or too small. I can't remember which.

Seeing my gaunt, tear-stained face, a woman at the turkey shelf said, 'Youse gonna be all right. We all gotta be in the bottom of the barrel at some stage and youse in the bottom of the barrel now. Don't axe me how long youse gonna be here, I'se don't know.'

I looked at her, saying nothing.

There was nothing to say.

*

It's always the same dream. I am struggling. Struggling to escape from the invisible cords that want to bind me to an old identity. I am struggling to find my way into a castle. The castle is a synthesis of the house I lived in when I was married and part Scottish castle. It is visible but impenetrable. Night after night I attempt to gain access to the fortress – without success. I wake up exhausted, sweating and weeping.

Always seeking, I am always seeking Jehovah Shammah, 'The One Who is with us everywhere for He is Omnipresent'. The Jerusalem of Ezekiel's vision. I want so much to believe in the text of Isaiah 60:19–20:

The sun will no more be your light by day,
Nor will the brightness of the moon shine on you,
For the Lord will be your everlasting light,
And God will be your glory.

Like Perceval, I feel as though I am wandering in a forest, lost and unclaimed.

According to legend, after the death of his father, Perceval's mother takes him to the forests where she raises him ignorant to the ways of men until the age of fifteen. When King Arthur's knights ride through the woods – through the acton (as a clearing in the woods is correctly called) – Perceval is captivated by their heroic bearing. He leaves home and travels to Camelot to prove his worth as a warrior. The tale ends with him being knighted and invited to join the Knights of the Round Table.

I had become caught up in the brittle shell of worldly success and materialism. Now the shell has been broken and I am in the forest, wondering what I failed to do or what I didn't value sufficiently and lost.

I know that the forest is a place of soul growth. I know that I have learned a great deal about humility and humiliation. The desire to be real and true to myself is becoming urgent. For too many years I have allowed myself to be like the handless maiden who agreed to have parts of her cut off in exchange for an authentic life.

Philosophical ramblings and existential angst aside, I have to get out of the shelter. I have to find a way of supporting myself.

The man who had redesigned and brought his children up in the Mill where I had lived with Pol Pot in the Pennsylvania countryside owns a restaurant in Lambertville, New Jersey. On the off chance that he might be able to help me, I go and see him.

For $12 an hour, off the books, he gives me a job answering the telephone.

I introduce myself as Juliett.

41

IN WHICH I BECOME A SERVER

JIM HAMILTON MUST HAVE BEEN wildly attractive when he was younger, judging by the pictures of him posing on ski slopes with his arms up in a kind of joyful crucifix. There are other pictures too. Jim tossing pancakes. Jim tap-dancing with three other blokes. He had the kind of face that was a weapon with which, I suspect, he cleared his way in the world.

'I worked with all the big names on Broadway,' he told me soon after I started working at his restaurant. 'Designed sets for Ringling Brothers and Barnum and Bailey. Once we did a snow scene with snowmen … carrots for noses … and then the snowmen started dancing.'

Gabrielle Hamilton, his youngest daughter, owns Prune restaurant in New York. She wrote about her father having a 'design and build' studio in Lambertville, the pretty historic river town in which he had grown up. She remembered visiting her dad in an old skating rink at the dead end of South Union Street, the building in which he would build huge stage sets that would be shipped off to New York. 'Prying back the lid on a fifty-gallon barrel of silver glitter … and shoving your hands down into it up to your elbows is an experience that will secure the idea in your heart for the rest of your life that your dad is, himself, the greatest show on earth.'

These days Jim's achievements are not known by the younger people who patronise the restaurant. His glory days are worn, by him, like ancient shrouds. These days his voice is no louder than rustling parchment paper. He may be frail and sometimes cranky, but his is an indomitable, an obnoxiously indomitable, spirit.

There is a theory in the restaurant that Jim is always moving, always creating, always devising because he fears death. He is perched on his architect's chair before rosy-fingered dawn pulls back night's bedspread. He keeps chickens in a coop on the deck of his loft. When it gets so cold that they might freeze he totters outside, scoops them up in a black plastic bin bag (with holes) and puts them in his shower cubicle.

The ventures he prefers are those that are (1) guaranteed to lose money and (2) as inconvenient and impractical to implement as possible.

Of course I want to work for him. Of course he will become the father figure I never had and that I have been seeking my whole life. And of course Jim is the father figure that I can never please.

*

Soon after I start working at the restaurant Jim asks me to be his assistant at a series of cooking classes he is giving at a local Wellness Centre. The people attending the class are in the Metallic Age: silver hair and golden teeth. I assume Jim is going to teach them something practical, something they can go home and do for themselves. Perhaps a demonstration on how to make an omelette. Jim has other ideas. He is going to show the old-timers how to make Lobster Thermidor.

On the afternoon of the class I report to Jim's loft apartment to do the prep. It's a converted loft which Jim is pleased to call a *pensione* when he's doing an Italian cooking class and an *atelier* when he's doing the French stuff.

The loft is a gorgeous open-plan space decorated in pure Hamiltonesque fashion. There is a Nakashima coffee table, a shabby chic sofa and a view of the canal.

A repurposed antique work bench serves as the kitchen sink and prep table. Copper pots hang like chandeliers. *The World at War* is blaring from the television set in the living room. Jim loves that stuff.

I am tasked with peeling potatoes and extracting the meat from lobster claws. When I drop the claw meat on the floor, Jim bends down creakily, picks it up and tosses it back in the bowl. His generation isn't as germ phobic as the current American one.

I have to pack up everything we need for the cooking class into Jim's VW which is parked in the lane. There are Sterno burners, pots and pans, spoons, knives, forks, plastic bags of mirepoix (Jim is not the Tupperware type) and a bottle of cooking wine.

Jim spoons himself carefully into the driver's seat. I squeeze onto the passenger seat. My knees are at chin height because I have to rest my feet on the lid of a giant pot filled with par-boiled lobsters.

As Jim reverses down the lane he wings the mirror of a parked car but carries on, oblivious. We pootle down the tree-lined avenues to the Wellness Centre, where I have to do all the heavy lifting in reverse.

Everything must be carried into a set-up in one area of the gym. My job is to assist Jim and hand him whatever he needs. Actually, my job is to be the fall guy.

The class watches in fascination as he prepares to make a Lobster Thermidor. Mostly I think they are fascinated that someone so super-annuated should be allowed to handle sharp knives and hot flames.

'Juliett,' he says stabbing in my direction with a knife, 'she can't peel potatoes. She fondles them.' He savagely cuts open a lobster.

The class titters, embarrassed. They are Jim's fans, his constituents. Lambertvillians who were probably brought into the world by Jim's father, the local doctor. Though considerably enfeebled these days, Jim is still at the throbbing aorta of the community. When someone dies, he sends over roasted chickens. When the Buck County Playhouse reopened, he donated food for the party. He's designing a park for the residents. On holidays he comes into the restaurant wearing his Ralph Lauren suit (the suit he wants to be buried in) to 'schmooze' people. They like to have him come over and shoot the breeze with them.

While I play fall guy to his straight guy with as much humour and dignity as I can muster, I sense there is a degree of *Einfühlung*. I feel waves of compassion wash over me as he pokes fun at me.

'Can you pass me the mandolin? Do you know what a mandolin is, Juliett?'

*

Jim Hamilton slots neatly into the space in my psyche that is father-figure shaped. I want so much to please him but I keep falling short. Actually, everyone falls short. When he calls a staff meeting and tells us that we have to work on Thanksgiving, he feigns surprise at our disappointment. 'I didn't stop you from going to medical school!' he says.

Over the years, Jim will fire me several times. It's an inoculation that doesn't take.

Once it is because I give him the wrong count on the number of diners we are expecting for his tableside cooking.

Another time – another Thanksgiving – I seat an 80-year-old divorcée who has had a crush on Jim for years at his table.

'You're fired,' says Jim. 'You ruined my Thanksgiving putting that bitch at my table.'

'I thought she was your friend?' I say.

'Of course she's my friend. That doesn't mean you have to ruin my Thanksgiving by putting her next to me.'

Americans and their Thanksgiving. It's only an eating holiday, for Chrissakes.

A story that has become part of the mythology of Hamilton's is the time that Jim's VW Beetle was driven down the road and pushed into the canal.

'Joy riders,' Jim explains. 'Silly kids. Took the car for a joy ride.'

Personally I think they were probably disgruntled former employees.

*

'Behind you! I'm coming around. Hot plates! Get the fuck out of my way.'

'That's *steamed* clams, not clams on the half-shell! Burro! When are you going to learn?'

'Your food's not up yet! Get out of the kitchen!' Two seconds later: 'What's wrong with you? Get your food out of the window! Your food is *dy-ing* here, Brouja!'

Thus, as a newbie server, having graduated from answering the telephone, am I yelled at by the Guatemalan line chef and Irma, the *garde manger*.

The temperature in the submarine-sized kitchen is over a hundred degrees. At any given time eight servers and runners will be jostling in front of the window.

'Two bronzino, a fillet, medium rare and two tuna rare! A dozen oysters! I need runners. Runners. Anytime this week, Juliett. It's hot! It's HOT! You'll need a napkin for that!'

'When are you fucking going to learn to run your own food?!'

I trot behind Steven and a runner to a corner table in the Bishop's Room. The napkin I placed on my forearm has slipped and the plate is burning my wrist.

Side-work is another cartoon. Each station has its side-work.

If you are in Station One your job is to get ice, cut enough bread for 250 people, grind coffee, make iced tea and do the butters. If you're Station Two, you are the cleaner. Being the cleaner involves strapping a vacuum cleaner on your back – you look like an astronaut or something from Ghostbusters – and vacuuming the whole restaurant. Then there are the lavatories to clean …

The dishwashers giggle. They see a woman of a certain age with bracelets on her arms and an important ring on her second finger struggling to carry 18 buckets of ice from the basement (where the ice-machine lives) up the stairs and down the lane to the restaurant. The display counter, the tin tub (in which guests' alcohol is chilled before they are seated) and several assorted ice-chests must be filled.

*

I pray that what people don't see is the inner struggle I am experiencing. I feel like Keats when he wrote to Fanny Brawne: 'I feel as though I have died already and am now living a posthumous existence.'

In this posthumous existence, by some capricious twist of fate, I am no longer the woman for whom Champagne is bought. I am the server who says, 'May I open that Veuve Clicquot for you?' (I make a point of saying *verve* because Americans say *voove*.)

Perhaps Eleanor Roosevelt was right. We are creatures of our fate, not commanding it but being moulded by it.

And yet this can't be so. I did a course on the Names of The Lord. One of his names is El Roi, the God who Sees Everything. Is he seeing my small misery and allowing it? Why? And what about Jeremiah? In Jeremiah it says that the Lord has plans for your life. Plans to make you prosper.

These thoughts occupy me while I am hoovering, cleaning the lavatories and doing the windows. *I do windows now!*

✳

Anthony Bourdain says that the real international language of cuisine – cook talk – is like haiku or kabuki. It's defined by established rules within a traditional framework.

All comments must concern sex. Penis size, who is a homosexual and who is fucking whom. Fuck is used as a comma. A locker-room is like a vicarage tea party by comparison.

The slamming shut of the dishwasher. The belching steam as it is opened. The clatter of crockery as Everardo slings stacks of plates, cups and butter dishes into assorted ziggurats. The shriek of an empty bottle as it is tossed into the recycling bin. The jangle and racket of a rack of glasses being banged on top of two other racks of sweltering glasses that have to be polished. The clash of trays of silverware, broiling hot from the dishwasher, that also have to be polished.

The cursing when someone picks up a scalding hot plate from the line.

The cursing when the bread drawer is yanked open and there is no bread in it.

'Whose side-work was bread, goddamit! Do your goddam side-work, Juliett!'

This is the signal for the kitchen staff and other servers to join in and attack. Like jackals, they turn on the culprit.

'Yes, do your fucking side-work! You're going to have to go to the walk-in freezer and pull out some frozen shit!'

There is more cursing when no one has brewed more coffee and taken the last of the pot or there hasn't been enough iced tea brewed.

The job comes with its own jargon.

'Eighty-six': when there is none left, no *mas*.

'Tell your friends 86 filet mignon.'

'Weeded' means that you are not coping, that you are behind, '*dans la merde*' – in the shit. You are running around like a headless chicken, not knowing what table/service to attend to first. When the restaurant is jamming on a Saturday night, each server will do about 30 covers (a cover being a person served).

You get weeded when you are 'slammed', i.e. you get double-sat or triple-sat. In which case the kitchen will get murdered. Or you can get murdered because some high maintenance person wants you to decant a bottle of wine that really doesn't need decanting because it was bottled last Tuesday but he is trying to show off to his date that he Knows About Wine.

What I have learned as a server is that the restaurant is like the foot of the cross. Everyone is equal at the foot of the cross.

If you can survive a Saturday night shift, you can survive anything. When your last table's order is in the kitchen staff will crack open the Rolling Rocks.

This is the sign that things will come to an end.

Steven and I have established a Champagne sorority. He's hidden a bottle bought from Walkers on the front seat floor of his car in a bucket of ice. It's only Bouvet but when we furtively drink a toast to survival, it tastes like Bollinger.

At the end of a brutal shift, three or four of us pile into Steve's old car, which is jammed with clutter – shirts on hangers, lamps, shoals of CDs and to-go containers – and drive to the shabby Inn of the Hawke.

When our chef Eric calls me 'homes' (aka homie), I find it endearing. It's a term of acceptance. There will be much laughter and joshing and talking about the travails of the night.

No one at the local pub will know that I was once the most famous columnist in South Africa. Frankly, they wouldn't care. And neither do I.

I am learning how to rock with the waves.
I have invented a new way of being in the world.

Index of Names

Some factual information for this book has been derived from Wikipedia.